NEW ORLEANS
THEN AND NOW

Downtown New Orleans, 1944

1964

1994

New Orleans
THEN AND NOW

**RICHARD
AND
MARINA
CAMPANELLA**

Pelican Publishing Company
Gretna 1999

The French Quarter and surrounding areas in 1952. *U.S. Geological Survey*

The word "Pelican" and the depiction of a pelican are trademarks
of Pelican Publishing Company, Inc.,
and are registered in the U.S. Patent and Trademark Office.

Library of Congress Cataloging-in-Publication Data

Campanella, Richard.
    New Orleans then and now / Richard and Marina Campanella.
        p.   cm.
    Includes bibliographical references.
    ISBN: 1-56554-347-5 (alk. paper)
    1. New Orleans (La.)—Pictorial works. 2. New Orleans (La.)—
History—Pictorial works. 3. New Orleans (La.)—Geography.
4. Human geography—Louisiana—New Orleans. I. Campanella,
Marina. II. Title.
F379.N543C36 1999
976.2'35--dc21   98-47016
                                                                CIP

All noncredited "New Orleans now" photographs are by the authors.

Manufactured in the United States of America

Published by Pelican Publishing Company, Inc.
1000 Burmaster Street, Gretna, Louisiana 70053

To our parents:

Mr. and Mrs. Mario and Rose Campanella
Brooklyn, New York

Sr. and Sra. Ernesto López and Porfiria Morán de López
San Juan Trujano, Oaxaca, Mexico

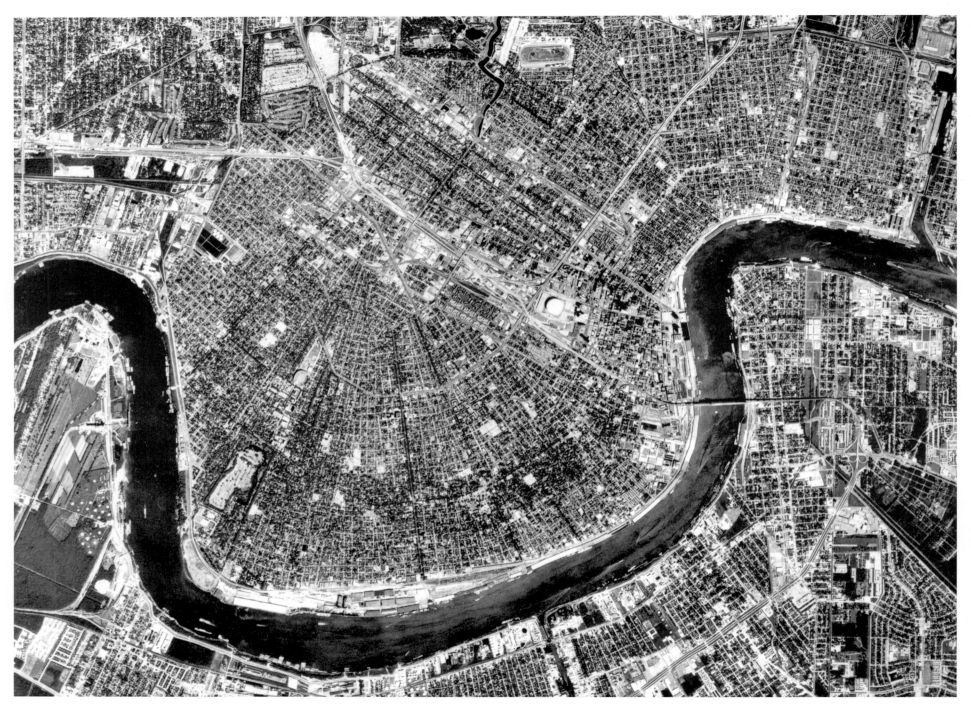

New Orleans in the late 1970s. *U.S. Geological Survey*

Contents

Preface

As history is punctuated with "essential moments"—brief battles that determine the destiny of nations, chance discoveries that commence centuries of colonization—geography is interspersed with "essential places." These crucial locales are keystones in their regions, places through which supply reaches demand, from which officialdom wields power, to which the ambitious arrive to earn riches and the masses come to earn something.

New Orleans is one such essential place. Here, on a once-sleepy yawn of the lower Mississippi, cultural and economic forces from vast geographic regions and scores of societies have synergized for nearly three hundred years to form an urban enclave that exports more memorable signatures of character than any other city in the hemisphere. New Orleans' music, food, festivity, architecture, eccentricities, and even its street names and transportation system are recognized and embraced worldwide as treasured traditions and icons. All are products of this geographic concentration of activity into a single crux.

If New Orleans is the essence of its hinterlands, spiced with an indigenous *lagniappe*, then its neighborhoods, streets, and buildings are elevated to a significance beyond their mortar and brick. This was our suspicion as intrigue brought us to the archives and curiosity took us to the streets to track down those sites in old photographs and witness their evolution. *New Orleans Then and Now* is a freeze frame of the living history and geography of this essential city, our personal effort to understand why we and millions of others are so fascinated by this sweaty old town.

About This Collection: *New Orleans Then and Now* is a historical geography of the Crescent City told through time-sequence photographs from street, roof, and air, spanning 150 years (*circa* 1847 to 1998). Some sequences reflect radical change, others meticulous restoration, others still an interesting inventory of adaptation and evolution. The historical photographs were selected for coverage, content, and availability, not for producing a particular commentary on preservation or modernization. The scenes are arranged geographically, not chronologically, starting with the French Quarter and Faubourg Tremé and then heading downriver toward Chalmette. Next, the scenes return to downtown and head upriver, from Canal Street towards Carrollton, and close by touching upon the West Bank. In "A Bird's-Eye Appendix to New Orleans," spectacular oblique perspectives aid in understanding the urban geography of the Crescent City. Each time-sequence pair throughout the book is referenced to a locator map (lower right corner of the "now" pages), with an arrow indicating the camera station.

A Note on Neighborhood Names: There are a number of ways to identify a neighborhood in New Orleans: by official city name, by ward or district number, by local or historical name, or by National Historic District designation. In this book we generally use a combination of local and historical names (Warehouse District and Faubourg Tremé, for example) and National Historic District names (such as Lower Garden District and Uptown). Refer to the map on p. 27 for locations.

Acknowledgments

We are deeply indebted to The Historic New Orleans Collection and its dedicated staff, especially curators Sally Stassi and John Magill of The Williams Research Center and former director Dr. Jon Kukla, for their expertise, assistance, and generosity in providing access to the historical photographs. This remarkable institution is not only a model archive and research facility but also a monument to the commitment and dedication of New Orleanians to their city. We also are indebted to the following sources for helping us understand New Orleans, then and now: the Library of Congress, Michael Stout of the Army Corps of Engineers (New Orleans District), Capt. Chris E. Mickal of the New Orleans Fire Department Photo Unit, the researchers of the extraordinary Friends of the Cabildo *New Orleans Architecture* series, U.S. Geological Survey, New Orleans Public Library, New Orleans Notarial Archives, Louisiana State Museum, Louisiana State University, Tulane University School of Architecture, Preservation Resource Center, Vieux Carré Commission, Port of New Orleans, City of New Orleans, *The Times-Picayune*, Missouri Historical Society, and the references cited in the bibliography. Gratitude also is extended to those photographers who captured the "then" images in these time sequences.

The Geographical City

A spaceborne perspective serves as a reminder that New Orleans (second crescent from right) is understood only through its geographical context: as the gatekeeper city of the North American interior, perched on the banks of the continent's Father of Waters.

Landsat Thematic Mapper satellite mosaic courtesy Louisiana State University Department of Geography and Anthropology

Writers often grapple with words as they try to explain the distinct character of New Orleans, resorting to adjectives (romantic, sultry, raffish) or nouns (gumbo, jazz, streetcars) rather than reasons. To a geographer, the reasons underlying New Orleans' cultural peculiarity are its strategic location and the consequent impact on human geography. The Crescent City is situated as a nexus between two great "spheres": the open seas beyond the nearby Gulf of Mexico, and the North American interior drained by the Mississippi River. One water body exposed the locale to the explorers, exiles, settlers, and investors of France, Spain, Germany, and the states of the Atlantic seaboard, plus Caribbean islanders, Latin American colonizers, enslaved Africans, and immigrants from the world over. The other water body ushered in frontier explorers, Kaintuck flatboatsmen, Yankee traders, and the barons of the South's plantation economy. These varied groups met and interacted on the remote "isle" of New Orleans; when projected over hundreds of years, it is easy to see how this interaction could have produced a city of unique and fascinating character. What about the other great American ports: Boston, New York, Charleston, San Francisco? All are marvelous cities with especially rich heritages, but none have had the long-term exposure to such a large number of diverse cultural regions as New Orleans. After all, the city sits astride

At 29°58' north latitude and 90°04' west longitude (approximately 30° N, 90° W), New Orleans sh]ares a parallel with Cairo, Egypt, and is exactly a quarter-world west of London, England.

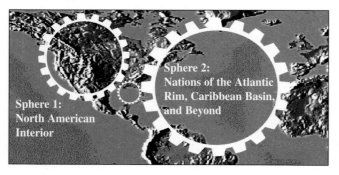

The concentration of cultural and economic activities from vast geographic "spheres" into a single riverbend explains New Orleans' famously unique personality and cityscape.

not just any river, but the Father of Waters, draining 1,350,000 square miles from Alberta to Alabama, New Mexico to New York. And it serves not just one ocean but the Gulf of Mexico, the Caribbean and its islands, and the Atlantic that laps the coasts of the Americas, Europe, Africa, and beyond. These hinterlands and foreign lands have populated the city with a rich diversity of peoples and tongues, and for centuries New Orleans has reciprocated by routing the raw material of

economics from supplier to demander in its round-the-clock business of port business. This concentration of cultural and economic activity from vast and varied geographical regions into a single subtropical riverbend explains New Orleans' famous signatures of character: its architecture, cuisine, accents, customs, place names, and—above all—its atmosphere and personality. New Orleans was and is the gatekeeper city of the North American continent's southern flank, and, as in any place inhabited by humans, things tend to happen around the entrance.

Nexus between the Spheres

The linkage of the lithosphere and the hydrosphere by the Mississippi River is New Orleans' *raison d'être*, but a narrow inlet called Bayou St. John explains the city's exact siting on the famous river crescent. This bayou, part of an old Indian portage and site of the area's first European settlement (1708), eliminated 110 miles of travel on the treacherous meanders of the lower Mississippi by allowing sailors to short-cut from the Gulf of Mexico through Lake Borgne, across the

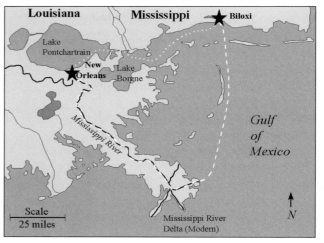

New Orleans was sited as a least-cost/minimum-distance route (short-dash line) between the French settlements along the Gulf Coast and the hinterlands accessed by the Mississippi River. The alternative route through the river's delta (long-dash line) was slow and treacherous.

Rigolets or Chef Menteur Pass, through Lake Pontchartrain, and into the bayou toward the banks of the river. Bayou St. John was accessible to the natural levee of the Mississippi via a corridor of uplands that allowed for passage through the swamps from one sphere to the other. This site—where the uplands accessing Bayou St. John intersected the Mississippi River's natural levee—satisfied the two basic needs of a frontier city in this geographical setting: drainage and accessibility.[1] When Jean Baptiste Le Moyne, Sieur de Bienville, established La

---

[1]A few years after the founding of the city, engineer Pierre Le Blond de la Tour wrote, "In going up the river, I examined the best places to establish New Orleans. I did not find a better situation than the place where it is; not only is the land higher, but it is near a bayou, which is a little river, which falls into Lake Pontchartrain, through which one can at all times communicate with the New Biloxi, Mobile, and other ports, more easily than by the mouth of the river." (Quoted by Alcée Fortier in *A History of Louisiana*, 1904)

Nouvelle Orléans on this riverside upland in 1718, his decision was buttressed by his conviction that the area's alluvial soils would support agriculture (unlike the Biloxi area, which was once favored for settlement by Bienville's brother, Iberville) and that its perch on the Mississippi would make it a good headquarters for developing Louisiana in the business scheme envisioned by John Law's Company of the West. It would also serve as a French military toehold against Spanish expansion from Florida and English probings up the river's mouth.

Precious Topography

In 1721 Pierre Le Blond de la Tour and Adrien de Pauger designed the grid-pattern plan that the world knows as today's Vieux Carré (Old Square), or French Quarter. The few dozen inches of topography that was the natural levee forced this original city and early expansions to cling to the banks of the Mississippi, making nascent New Orleans a virtual island surrounded by water and swamp. An additional spur of relief extending beyond the downriver boundary of the grid (today's Esplanade Avenue) served as a road to Bayou St. John, continuing the ancient role of this corridor as a portage. Piercing the wilderness beyond the engineers' imposition of order in the city, Bayou Road followed its own plan—one based on topography, not neatness—as it lazily violated the rectangular street pattern by leaning to the right and then to the left before finally finding its destination. Properties demarcated along this route were aligned to face the arched road; decades later, when adjacent lands were subdivided into rectangular blocks with orthogonal property lines, the crooked lots of Bayou Road stuck out like stubborn old-timers. To this day, houses following the old orientation may be detected from the street and counted from aerial photographs. The swath between Bayou St. John and the lower flank of the French Quarter is called the "Esplanade Ridge," an indicator of the significance of topography in the early development of the city.

France and Spain on the Mississippi

Development of the frontier city over the next four decades, guided by the French government after the Company of the West and its successors failed (1731), involved the creation of the first man-made levees, erection of government and religious buildings, and construction of hundreds of *briquette entre poteaux* (brick between post) cottages along the narrow streets. From an initial five-block clearing of the forest in 1721, the struggling city grew by the 1760s to fill the majority of its sixty-six-block grid with a population of more than four thousand. In 1762 Louis XV of France, anticipating defeat in the French and Indian War, secretly ceded the vast expanse of Louisiana west of the river to his Bourbon cousin, Carlos III of Spain. This maneuver allowed France to unload an unpromising colony, hasten the end of the war, and keep the booty out of English hands. Spain benefited in accepting the offer by acquiring a geographic toehold against the encroaching British presence in the eastern Gulf Coast and

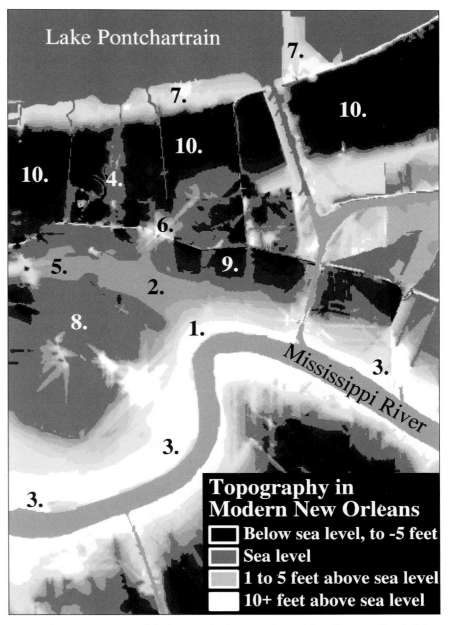

New Orleans' topography: (1) the French Quarter, about 5 feet above sea level; (2) Bayou Road/Esplanade Ridge; (3) Mississippi River natural levee, with man-made levees abutting river, about 10 feet above sea level; (4) Bayou St. John corridor; (5) Metairie Ridge; (6) Gentilly Ridge; (7) lakefront uplands created in 1920s; (8) and (9) lowlands in Mid-City and New Marigny/St. Roch, 2 feet below sea level; (10) lowlands in modern residential areas along lake. *Derived from U.S. Geological Survey*

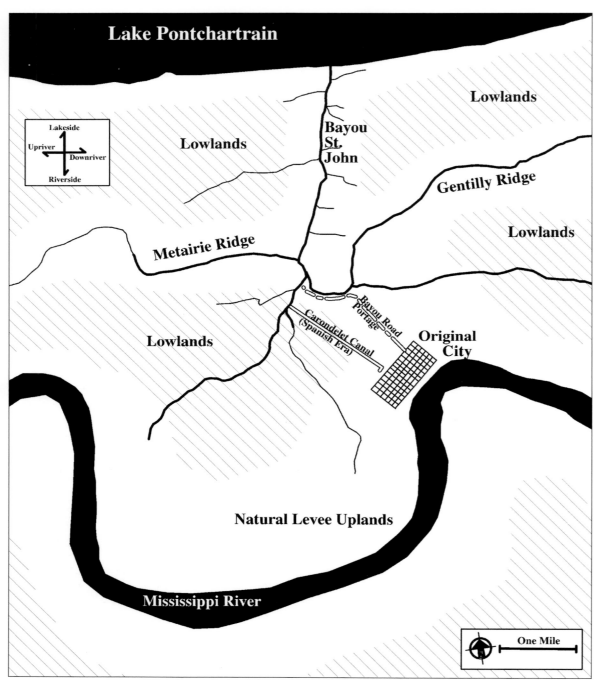

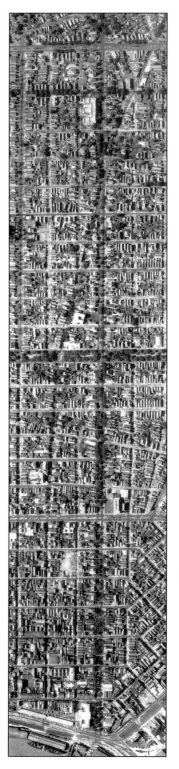

Geography of eighteenth-century New Orleans. Bayou Road was the original route between the spheres, superseded by Carondelet Canal in the late 1790s.

Bayou Road's gentle curve and crooked property orientations are still evident today. *U.S. Geological Survey*

the Caribbean. After the war ended in 1763, Spain controlled Louisiana west of the river plus parts of the Gulf Coast, and England ruled the interior lands to the east of the river. Because New Orleans was thought to be an island, it was not considered part of the eastern bank of the river; hence its future lay not with the English to the east but with the Spanish to the west. News of the political turmoil, which reached "French" New Orleans two years after Spain's 1762 acquisition, stunned residents of the city, but one can only imagine how different New Orleans history—and American history—would be had the English gained power. Although reluctant and unwelcome at first, Spanish rule finally took hold after Gen. Don Alejandro O'Reilly and twenty-six hundred Spanish soldiers repressed a brief insurrection in 1769, sometimes cited as the first revolt against a European colonial power in North America. Despite the initial acrimony, the new regime proved to be relatively benign, and New Orleans remained French in culture and language during the entire Spanish colonial era. In the three decades of Spanish rule, the city restored its fortifications, installed the first street lamps, built a new cathedral and Cabildo on the Plaza de Armas, and excavated a canal to connect Bayou St. John to the rear of the city. Carondelet Canal, named after the Belgian governor in the service of Spain who mobilized the effort, drained the swamps north of the city and later was widened to accommodate commercial traffic using the Bayou St. John-Lake Pontchartrain route to the Gulf of Mexico. The bed of old Carondelet Canal, filled in during the 1930s, is evident in modern maps as a conspicuously open swath following Lafitte Street through otherwise densely populated neighborhoods.

A disastrous fire on Good Friday 1788 destroyed 856 buildings and eliminated most of the French colonial structures in the city. "What lay in the ashes was, at best, but an irregular, ill-built, French town. What arose from them was a stately Spanish city, proportioned with grace and built with solidity, practically the city as we see it to-day," wrote Grace King of the Good Friday fire in her 1895 book, *New Orleans: The Place and the People*. Prompted by a necessity made more urgent by the conflagration, New Orleans commenced its growth beyond de la Tour's sixty-seven-year-old grid-pattern plan for the city. By the late eighteenth century, most of the natural levee outside the city was utilized for plantations, demarcated as long wedges perpendicular to the river (French long lots) and terminating at a point in the back swamp.[2] As the city expand-

ed, the Gravier plantation upriver from the original city became New Orleans' first *faubourg* ("false town," or suburb), Faubourg Ste. Marie (1788), later known as Faubourg St. Mary, the American Sector, and now the Central Business District. In time, these long-lot plantations would cede their croplands to the city, creating the scallop-shell street network immediately apparent in maps of the modern city.

As the new century dawned, New Orleans passed through another period of geopolitical tumult. Unbeknownst to the populace, Spain retroceded the colony to France in 1800 after more than three decades of rule. Three years later, a treaty between Napoleon and representatives of the United States arranged the sale of New Orleans and the western drainage of the Mississippi to the new republic for sixty million francs plus the assumption of a twenty million franc French debt, totaling to about fifteen million dollars. On November 30, 1803, France regained formal possession of Louisiana from Spain for the last twenty days of its storied presence in the region, for on December 20, 1803, the Louisiana Purchase became official, and the gatekeeper city, plus 827,000 square miles of its hinterlands, became American.

A New American City Takes Shape

Now capital of the American Territory of Orleans, the city annexed and subdivided a number of nearby plantations as new faubourgs in the early American years. In 1806 Faubourg Marigny was platted in the former plantation of the famous Creole aristocrat Bernard Xavier Philippe de Marigny de Mandeville, and soon became home to so many German immigrants that it was nicknamed "Little Saxony." This faubourg, downriver from the Quarter across Esplanade Avenue, was laid out to conform with both the grid pattern of the original city and the bend of the river. Also in 1806, the Delord-Sarpy plantation was subdivided and annexed to the upriver flank of Faubourg Ste. Marie. Now known as the Lower Garden District, this community was designed in a grand and classical manner for larger properties in quasi-rural settings, in contrast to the dense urban landscape of the old city. In 1807 the commons (present-day

---

[2] The French government in the New World divided its lands according to the *arpent* system, whereby parallel lines were drawn 40 arpents (roughly 1.5 miles, an arpent measuring about 192 feet) from both sides of the banks of the river. This was the "40-arpent line," sometimes expanded to 80 or 120 arpents in better-drained areas. In most cases in southern Louisiana, the line marked the interface of useful agricultural land and useless backswamp. This swath of land was then divided perpendicularly into "long lots," designed to provide each concession with valuable river frontage. Those lots fronting straight rivers formed elongated rectangles, but when the river meandered, the lots diverged on the outside of the meander and converged on the inside of the meander, like the skeleton of a snake. In New Orleans, the 40-arpent line roughly followed present-day Broad Avenue, and because the city is located on the inside of a river meander, the long lots converged in the center of town, about where Carrollton Avenue intersects Tulane Avenue. Thus we have the foundation for New Orleans' radial street pattern, often compared to a scallop shell, a fan, a pie, or a pinched accordion. It is important to note that the river did not "cause" the pattern—rather, the arpent system, and the economic and political reasons behind maximizing the distribution of river frontage to plantation owners, caused it. Decades of sectionalized growth and the lack of a central planning authority allowed the patterns of the old concessions to persist throughout the development of the city and survive to this day. Note also that within each "blade" of the fan of city streets is a fairly orthogonal grid pattern, occasionally stretched open with a wedge-shaped intersection. See pp. 104, 132, 318, 324, 332, and 356 for examples of these acute-angle intersections.

Canal, Rampart, and Esplanade, plus adjoining lands) surrounding the Vieux Carré were granted to the city by the federal government and eventually developed into their modern roles as axes and interfaces between neighborhoods. Plans to connect Carondelet Canal with the Mississippi via a canal excavated between Faubourg Ste. Marie and the Vieux Carré, part of the continuing effort to improve the connection between the spheres, were abandoned but not forgotten: the misnomer *Canal Street* has survived nearly two centuries. In 1810 the Tremé plantation was subdivided for development across the old fortifications of Rampart Street, exploiting the farther reaches of the natural levee behind the French Quarter. Above-ground cemeteries abutted the residential areas, echoing the living city's characteristics through ornate tombs, wrought-iron gates, vaults, and alleys. New Orleans' earliest cemetery, on St. Peter Street at the city's edge, was subterranean, but by the late 1700s, physical and cultural factors brought forth the custom of above-ground burial: the region's high water table (now drained away) made subterranean interment difficult and unsanitary, and the Spanish tradition of above-ground entombment provided a logical solution. The custom was adopted by immigrants from a variety of backgrounds and persists to this day as a reminder of New Orleans' Latin heritage. In southern Europe and Latin America, above-ground cemeteries are the rule, even in arid mountain valleys.

New Orleans' geographic accessibility, economic opportunity, and cultural diversity attracted (and still attracts) various waves of immigration, each of which contributed to the city's legendary character. Among the early waves were Germans, Canary Islanders, Americans who came after the Louisiana Purchase, and the whites and *gens de couleur libres* (free people of color) exiled from Saint-Domingue, now Haiti, by rebellious slaves between 1803 and 1809. The Saint-Domingue exiles infused the young American city with a fresh dose of Francophone culture that would survive for decades. *Gens de couleur libres* formed a distinct society in New Orleans and contributed to the city's material culture through their craftsmanship in wrought iron, brickwork, tomb sculpture, and other trades. (A notable part of New Orleans' spiritual heritage, voodoo, was brought to the city by slaves imported from Saint-Domingue.) *Gens de couleur libres* settled primarily in faubourgs Tremé and Marigny and prospered as artisans and businessmen. In later decades German, Irish, and Italian immigrants would form new elements of the city's cultural geography. On the subject of early immigration, it should be noted that although the Cajuns (French Acadians exiled from Nova Scotia by the English in 1763 who found their way to the bayou country) were drawn to Louisiana because of its French heritage, they settled in rural areas well west of New Orleans and contributed to the city's economy primarily through their agricultural production. New Orleans is not and never was a Cajun city; its Creole populace is as distinct from its rural Cajun neighbors as Parisians are from their compatriots in the provinces.

Between 1812 and 1815, two events served to pry New Orleans away from its European heritage and to assimilate it into the United States. First, Louisiana was granted statehood in 1812, drawing to a close the unstable aftermath of the area's colonial era. Second, the War of 1812 reached the region in late 1814 as the English approached New Orleans from Lake Borgne and the river, frightening the vulnerable city and uniting its disparate Creole, American, and immigrant populations against a common enemy. On January 8, 1815, Maj. Gen. Andrew Jackson and a hastily assembled army of militiamen and local volunteers routed 5,400 professional British soldiers on the Chalmette plantation downriver from the city, saving New Orleans from possible destruction and forever ending English antagonism of the young United States. The resounding victory elevated General Jackson to the status of national hero and ensured his commemoration in numerous New Orleans place names and monuments.

Old World and New, Glaring across Canal Street

The famous cultural dichotomy of New Orleans, the Creoles versus the Americans, was well established by the early nineteenth century and had a strong geographical signature. Volumes have been written on the definition of the word *Creole*, but in those times the word generally implied one of French or Spanish lineage, Catholic in faith, Latin by culture, and native to the region.[3] Americans were those of northern European (primarily Anglo-Saxon) ancestry, Protestant in faith and recently arrived from points north. The two groups sneered at each other, ridiculing the other's idiosyncrasies and resenting each other's position in New Orleans society. Creoles lived in the older, downriver half of the city: the Vieux Carré, Faubourg Tremé, and Faubourg Marigny. In Creole New Orleans, Esplanade Avenue served as the affluent thoroughfare, Carondelet Canal as the waterway to the lake, St. Louis Hotel and Maspero's

---

[3] These were the white Creoles. Black Creoles were those of mixed African and French or Spanish ancestry, including the *gens de couleur libres*. However, there is no pat definition for *Creole*; its various (and sometimes contradictory) meanings better reflect New Orleans history in their ambiguity than in their formalization. Confusion about the word's meaning may stem from its use as both a noun and an adjective: as an unmodified noun, it referred to a specific white ethnic group descended from the French and Spanish, but as an adjective, it described a wide range of peoples and things *associated* with that group. The word's meaning evolved over the course of the twentieth century, and today *Creole* as an unmodified noun mainly refers to Catholic blacks of mixed ancestry in the New Orleans area, generally no longer implying white New Orleanians of French or Spanish descent. As an adjective, it currently describes a plethora of things associated with Louisiana's melting-pot heritage, from cooking styles to architecture to tomatoes. *Creole* is a Gallicized version of the Spanish *criollo* (meaning "native" or "born here" and probably derived from the verb *criar*, to create), implying New World-born offspring of Old World-born parents. See Virginia Domínguez's *White by Definition: Social Classification in Creole Louisiana* (1986) for an analysis of the evolution of *Creole*.

Exchange as the rendezvous of the upper class, St. Louis Cathedral as the religious focal point, the St. Louis cemeteries as burial grounds, and the *Place d'Armes* as the cultural hearth. The Americans generally lived in Faubourg St. Mary and upriver neighborhoods, built mansions on St. Charles and Jackson Avenues, transported on the New Basin Canal, recreated in Lafayette Square, convened at the St. Charles Hotel and Banks' Arcade, worshiped at First Presbyterian Church, and were laid to rest in the Girod Street Cemetery. Architecture in the Creole city meant stucco walls, tiled roofs, French doors, center chimneys, entresols, and courtyards; architecture in the American city

Remnant imprints of the turning basins of the Creoles' Carondelet Canal (left, *circa* 1795) and the Americans' New Basin Canal (*circa* 1835) in 1952. According to the City Planning and Zoning Commission (1927), "For many years community activities subsisted entirely upon these waterways." *U.S. Geological Survey*

at first resembled Creole styles but soon reverted to the red brick walls, slate roofs, hallways, single doors, columns, and Greek Revival styles familiar to the displaced Northerners. Separating the rival Creole and American cultures was 171-foot-wide Canal Street and its symbolic "neutral ground," a term now used for traffic medians throughout the city. Canal Street plays an equivalent role in modern New Orleans, where the French Quarter on one side paints a mental picture of Old World charm, and the American Sector on the other side (now known as the Central Business District) projects an image of modernity and bustle.[4] Even their names reiterate the chasm: the melodious Vieux Carré and

the hurried *CBD*. In a way, the two sides of Canal Street at the dawn of the twenty-first century represent the Creoles' and Americans' nineteenth century images of each other, projected over two hundred years.

The first third of the nineteenth century witnessed new components of New Orleans' urban geography fall into place. Carrollton City developed on the former Macarty plantation at the opposite end of the river crescent, a likely place for a town because its location fulfilled the same geographic criteria—accessibility and topographic relief—used to site its downriver mother. Powerful steamboats replaced keelboats and flatboats on the Mississippi, providing faster upstream travel and eliminating the need for traders to sell their boats and trek over land routes such as the Natchez Trace to return home. A shift in the course of the river in the early 1800s allowed sediments to build up beside the natural levee in downtown New Orleans, forming a valuable *batture* that was exploited as a port and warehouse district. New Orleans' first railroad penetrated the swamps between Faubourg Marigny and Lake Pontchartrain via Elysian Fields Avenue in 1831. Old roads paralleling the bayous of the backswamps developed into transportation corridors: Metairie Road to the west, Gentilly Road to the east, the Bayou St. John road to the north, and the Bayou Barataria road to the south. Following the Mississippi River's natural levee, the River Road connected New Orleans with Baton Rouge and numerous towns and plantations in between. Long-lot plantations between New Orleans and Carrollton began to be interlaced with the graceful arcs and spokes that define the Crescent City's unique street network. The primary arc between the two cities, St. Charles Avenue (evolved from Barthelemy Lafon's *Cours des Nayades*—Route of the River Nymphs—in his 1806 plan of the area), transected the middle of the forty-arpent plantations, and the primary spokes (Jackson, Louisiana, Napoleon, and other avenues) of the street network marked the property lines between plantations. In 1835 the New Orleans and Carrollton Railroad, forerunner of today's streetcars, was laid out on St. Charles to couple rural uptown with bustling downtown. Immigration boosted the city's 1830 population to more than forty-five thousand and prompted settlement along riverside Tchoupitoulas Street in Faubourg St. Mary and Lafayette, a rough neighborhood that would come to be known as the Irish Channel. Culturally, the Americans began to gain the upper hand over the Creoles,[5] a trend that had repercussions in political geography, for in 1836, the state legislature divided New Orleans into three self-governing municipalities. A. Oakey Hall's *The*

---

[4]Wrote Ernst von Hesse-Wartegg of "the magnificent Canal Street" in *Travels on the Lower Mississippi, 1879-1880*: "This Mississippi of streets opens onto the Mississippi itself, the street the perfect counterpart to the river. . . . Here the South lies at one end of an international thoroughfare, the tropical West Indies at the other. The contrasts collide in one city, it seems, and in *this* street. Situation, prospect, traffic, the splendor of shops, all of life as lived in a street—in a word, *everything*—says we stand on the boundary between two great but distinct cultures. Anglo-Saxon and Latin meet *here*. Everything says we tread the

contiguous edges of geographical zones. Tropical and temperate intersect *here*."

[5]In his 1845 book *New Orleans and Environs*, Benjamin Moore Norman caricatured a French Creole who never ventured "three squares beyond [his] favorite cabaret" in the French Quarter, upon hearing of the Americans' progress in Faubourg St. Mary: "Ah Monsieur B. dat is too much! You von varry funny fellow—I no believe vat you say—it's only von grand—vot you call it—vere de mud, de alligator, and de bull frog live?—von grand—grand—mud swamp, vere you say is von grand city, I no believe it!"

The French Quarter, or Vieux Carré (Old Square), in 1989. *U.S. Geological Survey*

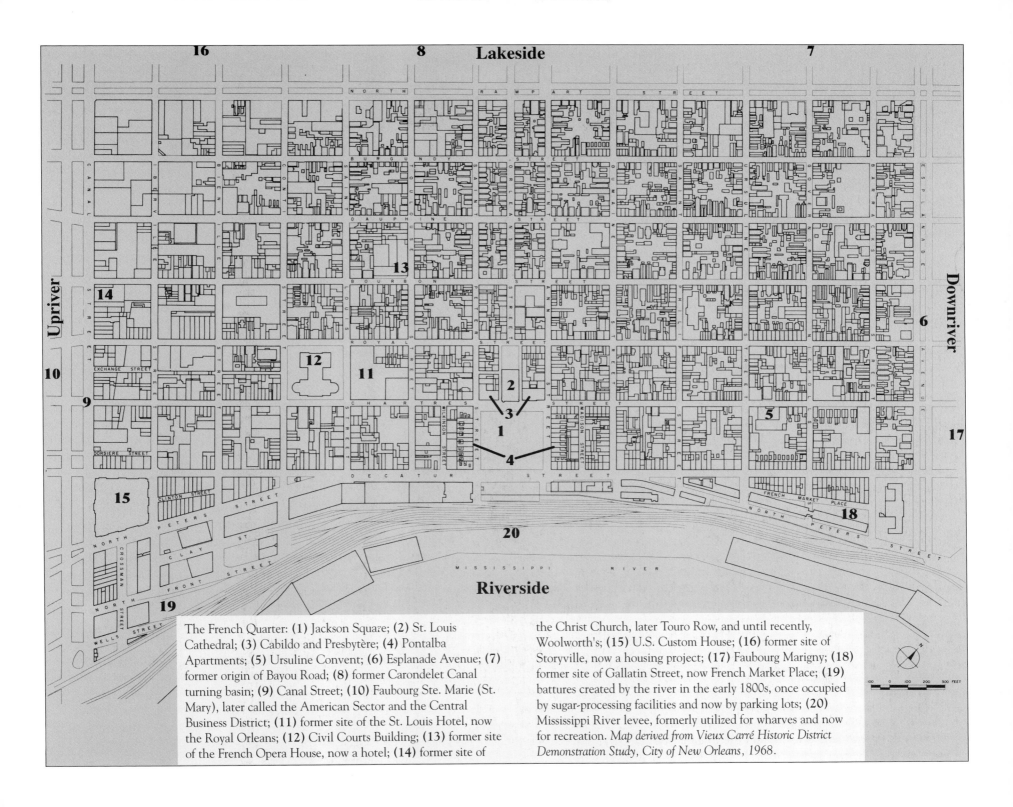

The French Quarter: **(1)** Jackson Square; **(2)** St. Louis Cathedral; **(3)** Cabildo and Presbytère; **(4)** Pontalba Apartments; **(5)** Ursuline Convent; **(6)** Esplanade Avenue; **(7)** former origin of Bayou Road; **(8)** former Carondelet Canal turning basin; **(9)** Canal Street; **(10)** Faubourg Ste. Marie (St. Mary), later called the American Sector and the Central Business District; **(11)** former site of the St. Louis Hotel, now the Royal Orleans; **(12)** Civil Courts Building; **(13)** former site of the French Opera House, now a hotel; **(14)** former site of the Christ Church, later Touro Row, and until recently, Woolworth's; **(15)** U.S. Custom House; **(16)** former site of Storyville, now a housing project; **(17)** Faubourg Marigny; **(18)** former site of Gallatin Street, now French Market Place; **(19)** battures created by the river in the early 1800s, once occupied by sugar-processing facilities and now by parking lots; **(20)** Mississippi River levee, formerly utilized for wharves and now for recreation. *Map derived from Vieux Carré Historic District Demonstration Study, City of New Orleans, 1968.*

Manhattaner in New Orleans, written in the late 1840s, describes these three separate entities with all the cultural biases of the time:

> One section of New Orleans, the First Municipality, is the old city, left to the tender mercies of the French and Creole population; narrow, dark, and dirty (meaning either their city or the people). One, in the Second Municipality, the new city; with here a little of Boston, there a trifle of New York, and some of Philadelphia. . . . The third section a species of half village, half city, (unmistakable in its French Faubourg look) is given over to the tender mercies of the Dutch and Irish, and the usual accompaniments of flaxen-polled babies and flaxen-tailed pigs.

The division of the city proved impractical and was dissolved in 1852, when a new charter consolidated the city into four districts under one government—a government based, for the first time, on the American side of town.

The institution of slavery in New Orleans was complex and unusual compared with the conventional image of plantation slavery in the antebellum South. First, bondsmen arrived to New Orleans not just from the Atlantic Coast and Mississippi Valley states but also directly from West Africa (prior to 1808) and from European colonies throughout the Caribbean. Like the city's immigration waves, each group brought with it unique perspectives and customs. Second, laws governing the institution in urban New Orleans were generally more tolerant toward bondsmen's cultural expressions than regulations in the rural interior South. Third, slavery was not as hopelessly permanent a condition in New Orleans as it was in other areas; freedom was sometimes obtained through redemption (many slaves were skilled craftsmen) or upon the death of the master. Fourth, *gens de couleur libres*, comprising 45 percent of the total African-American population in New Orleans in 1860, prospered in their freedom to the extent that many actually owned slaves themselves—a situation unthinkable in other parts of the South. Finally, the residential patterns of whites, free people of color, and enslaved blacks in New Orleans were more heterogeneous and integrated than other Southern cities and towns. As the South's premier port, New Orleans also was the largest slave-trading marketplace in the region, with three hundred slave dealers operating in some twenty-five downtown markets by 1850. Some remnants of New Orleans' brand of the "peculiar institution" survive today, namely Congo Square (roughly the slaves' equivalent of the Creoles' *Place d'Armes* and the Anglos' Lafayette Square), Banks Arcade on Magazine Street, and the slant-roof servant (slave) quarters appended to hundreds of old townhouses. Long gone are the slave yards in downtown and Algiers, and the elegant hotels in which surreal slave auctions were held.

The Crescent City Emerges in the Golden Age

The middle years of the nineteenth century are often referred to as the city's golden age. Population exploded to more than 102,000 by 1840, a 122 percent increase in just ten years, making New Orleans the South's premier city and the nation's fourth largest. Over the next two decades, most of the crescent's remaining plantations were transformed from croplands to communities, Algiers and Gretna were platted on the west bank of the Mississippi, and urban development expanded downriver to the neighborhood now known as Bywater. Spiky transportation routes (roads, railroads, and canals) converged in the pivot of the crescent, an area that was otherwise still a cypress swamp known as "the woods" or "back of town." Swirling tangentially to the city was a riotous nonstop parade of steamboats, sailing ships, towboats, and other craft depositing and loading cotton, sugar, rice, and other cargo along the newly developed riverside batture. Like a swift current churning a giant waterwheel, this stream of incoming goods fresh from voyages across the spheres fueled the very existence of the city and drew ambitious newcomers to its bustling port business. The most influential port-business professional was the "factor," or commission merchant, who served as the big-city agent for wealthy rural plantation owners. By the end of the antebellum era, 450 factor firms in New Orleans represented 9,300 planters in Louisiana, Mississippi, Arkansas, and Texas, a tremendous concentration of wealth from the hinterlands into the city. New Orleans' *nouveaux riches*, often recently arrived Americans from the North, formed much of the city's professional class and brought American styles of wealthy residential living to the portion of Lafayette (annexed into the city in 1852) now known as the Garden District. In contrast to the muddy slums of the neighboring Irish Channel, the Anglo-dominated Garden District was graced with immense mansions of Greek Revival, Italianate, and other nonnative architectural styles. Homes in this spacious district were set back from the streets, distanced from their neighbors, and obscured by shady gardens, precisely the opposite of the Vieux Carré cityscape. It is tempting to say that, in the Garden District, New Orleans finally becomes *Southern*, in the traditional image of pearl-white mansions among magnolias and moss. But it is more accurate to view the Garden District, in the words of scholar S. Frederick Starr, as the *Americanization* of New Orleans: many residents of the tony neighborhood were Northerners who imported a suite of tastes and lifestyles from a variety of geographic areas and who chose to live in the city primarily for its port-business opportunities. Once again, New Orleans' physical geography instills the elements of its character.

Grand and culturally significant structures arose during the midcentury years, many of which are still active and vibrant components in the modern cityscape. The Thirteen Sisters of Julia Street, a good example of Greek Revival American row houses popular in the Mid-Atlantic states, went up in

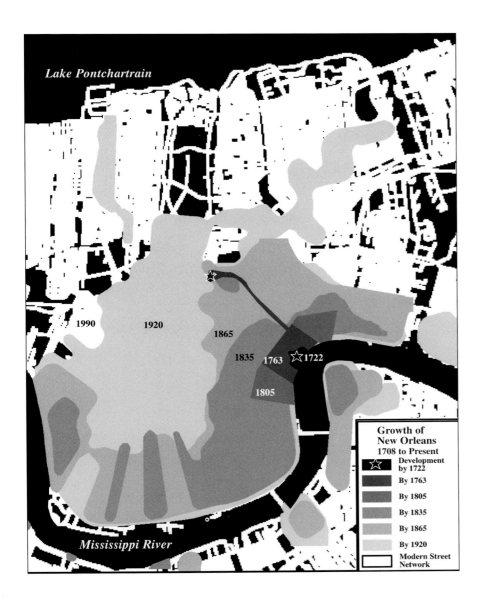

Lake Pontchartrain

1990   1920

1865

1835 1763 1722

1805

Mississippi River

**Growth of
New Orleans
1708 to Present**

Development
by 1722

By 1763

By 1805

By 1835

By 1865

By 1920

Modern Street
Network

promptly rebuilt. On Canal Street, work commenced on the United States Custom House (1848), the second-largest government building in the nation at that time; and Touro Row (1856), a landmark block of galleried commercial buildings between Royal and Bourbon streets. In the Vieux Carré, the Place d'Armes underwent a transitional period from 1846 to 1856, led by the great lady Micaela Almonester, Baroness de Pontalba. In this era the Pontalba Buildings were constructed on both sides of the square, the Cabildo and Presbytère were topped with new roofs and cupolas, the St. Louis Cathedral was rebuilt to its present appearance, a statue commemorating Andrew Jackson was unveiled at the center of the beautifully landscaped park, and the plaza's name was Americanized to Jackson Square. At the end of the 1850s, the French Opera House, a landmark that would take on cultural significance in the increasingly besieged Creole society, was constructed on Bourbon Street. West of Bayou St. John, the Allard plantation was purchased by miser-turned-philanthropist John McDonogh, who upon his death in 1850 donated it and the rest of his estate to the cause of public education in New Orleans and his hometown of Baltimore. Allard plantation eventually became City Park, and McDonogh's gift helped establish the infrastructure for the city's public schools that lasted, at least in name, into the 1990s. In sum, architects and builders of this golden age produced many of the important structures that to this day anchor rows of humble shops and cottages, instilling a sense of greatness and purpose in the gatekeeper city.

The Creoles' Andrew Jackson statue in Jackson Square and the Americans' Henry Clay statue on Canal Street—salutes to the Democrats and the Whigs, respectively—were symbols of the increased political partisanship in New Orleans during the late antebellum years. The decade following the 1852 consolidation of the city was marked by a renewed cultural competition between the American-dominated First and Fourth Districts (Faubourg St. Mary and newly annexed Lafayette) and the Creole- and immigrant-dominated Second and Third Districts (the Vieux Carré and adjacent faubourgs). By the late 1850s, the anti-Catholic and anti-foreigner "Know Nothing" party, an outgrowth of the Whig party that drew its support from the American element, emerged victorious over the Creole- and immigrant-supported Democrats. This was a surprising circumstance for a city of Catholics and immigrants and indicates the depth of the American resistance to the Creoles and the strength of their new numbers.

One interesting cultural development of this era was the commencement of public Mardi Gras parades by secret "krewes" cast in tongue-in-cheek mythology. Long celebrated by upper-class Creoles in private balls and by the masses in generalized street mayhem, Carnival was embellished in 1857 by spirited Americans who imported the idea of ritualized festivities for the pre-Lenten feast from similar traditions in Mobile, Alabama. For once, the prudish

1833, as did Banks' Arcade on Magazine Street, a meeting hall and exchange that hosted large political and business conventions. The respective hotels of the Creoles and the Americans, the St. Louis and the St. Charles, were constructed between 1835 and 1840 and soon became community nuclei. The St. Charles, an enormous domed Greek Revival structure that was the highest point in the city (185 feet including the cupola), burned in 1851 and was

Americans outdid the Creoles at their own game of society rituals and *joie de vivre*. A century and a half later, the words "Mardi Gras" come to mind only moments after the words "New Orleans" are spoken, a product of Creole religious custom and American mischievousness.

Geography as a Burden: The Civil War and Reconstruction

The American Civil War pitted New Orleans against its economics and geography, placing the city first in a position of reluctance, then vulnerability, and finally occupation. With so many successful merchants and bankers (many of whom were Yankees) who had no quarrel with the status quo, and so many immigrants (46 percent of the white population in 1860) who had no great interest in faraway political abstractions, New Orleans was understandably hesitant to secede from the Union. Still, dependency on the plantation economy and the issue of states' rights caused the city to vote heavily against Lincoln in 1860. Soon after, a volatile secessionist convention tilted public opinion toward rebellion, and on January 26, 1861, Louisiana left the Union. By early spring Louisiana was a member of the Confederate States of America, and in the predawn hours of April 12, 1861, the Creole "Napoleon in Gray," Gen. Pierre Gustave Toutant Beauregard, fired upon Fort Sumter in South Carolina and commenced the Civil War.

The same geographical factors that forged New Orleans made it a strategic prize in the Union's so-called Anaconda Plan to strangle the Confederacy. By controlling the Mississippi, the North would divide the South and deprive it of its principal artery; federal gunboats would start at each end of the river and conquer their way to the middle, like an anaconda encircling its prey. The gatekeeper city was in the cross hairs, a fact that the Confederacy neglected to act upon, for the city was left largely to its own defenses. The downriver forts of Jackson and St. Phillip and a small Confederate fleet failed to stop Flag Officer David Farragut's forty warships and additional troop transports, and by May 1862 New Orleans was an occupied city. Had New Orleans not surrendered, much of downtown might have been leveled. Union Gen. Benjamin ("Beast") Butler ruthlessly ruled the city for the rest of the year, insulting the city's women, religious establishment, and alien population while countering Confederate loyalty with immediate and severe suppression. (He also set the unemployed to cleaning the city, a novel endeavor that drastically reduced the death rate from the city's summertime scourge, yellow fever.) Despised throughout the South, his vindictiveness can be seen today in the inscription he added to the pedestal of the Andrew Jackson statue in Jackson Square: "The Union Must and Shall Be Preserved."

Union occupation deprived New Orleans of its ability to serve the spheres: the river and lake were blockaded, trade evaporated, banks failed, and businesses folded. At the same time, wartime industrial growth in the North accelerated the development of railroads that would compete with New Orleans'

monopoly on transportation. Louisiana, once the richest state in the South, was now one of the poorest in the nation, a rank that it maintains to this day. For twelve more years after the war, the occupied city struggled under the political intrigue and racial strife of the Reconstruction era, culminating in a bloody fifteen-minute battle on Canal Street in 1874 between the Democratic White League and the Republican Metropolitan Police, a predominantly black unit supported by the federal presence. The defeat of the Metropolitans empowered the White League to seek to regain control of the city, and after a bizarre period when Louisiana had two separate governments mutually rejecting the other's legitimacy, a deal was reached in which the Democrats would recognize Republican Rutherford B. Hayes' presidency if he withdrew all federal troops from the state and accepted Francis T. Nicholls as governor. Thus ended New Orleans' most turbulent era, 1861 to 1877.

Despite the economic deprivations of war, Reconstruction, and Northern competition for Mississippi Valley trade, the city grew to fill the crescent and expand across the river as Jefferson City (upriver from the Garden District) and Algiers (on the West Bank) were annexed in 1870. A year later, the last undeveloped plantation within the crescent was purchased and designated Upper City Park, later Audubon Park. The once-distant Carrollton City was absorbed into New Orleans in 1874, and the community now known as Holy Cross developed as the city's farthest downriver neighborhood. The postwar era saw an influx of Northerners into New Orleans, paralleled by thousands of freedmen migrating from the poverty-stricken countryside to the hope of the city. Ensuing racial polarization ended the relatively privileged status of the *gens de couleur*, and after the departure of the Federals in 1877, the mechanisms of segregation gradually fell into place and would remain until the 1960s.

From 1875 to 1879, Capt. James Eads contributed immeasurably to the New Orleans economy by constructing parallel jetties at the Mississippi River delta, one hundred miles southeast, forcing the water to increase speed, carry away more sediment, and deepen the river's channel. Now oceangoing vessels could enter the river without waiting for the proper water conditions. Coupled with the development of barges, the growth of a local railroad network, and improving economic conditions, the Eads jetties helped New Orleans rebound.

A Cosmopolitan City at the Turn of the Century

The final years of the nineteenth century were an exciting and hectic time for New Orleans. Recuperating from the occupied era and economic stagnation caused by Northern railroad competition, the city boomed in the 1880s with a pent-up energy. Numerous ornate business buildings, early skyscrapers at five to eight stories, arose in the American Sector, among them the Cotton Exchange, the Mercier Building, and the Gravier Building. Gone were the days of the Creole townhouse and corner store—these new postwar buildings exhibited national and international styles such as Victorian, Romanesque, and Italian Renaissance. A monument to Gen. Robert E. Lee was dedicated at Place du Tivoli (renamed Lee Circle), symbolizing the continued departure of New Orleans away from its European past and toward its American—its *Southern American*—future. Highlighting the decade was the 1884 World's Industrial and Cotton Centennial Exposition, an event that drew world attention (if little else) to New Orleans. The exposition was sited at the fairgrounds of present-day Audubon Park, the only place that fulfilled the requirements of size, drainage, accessibility, and location between the old part of the city and newly annexed Carrollton. Amid the five exhibit halls was the Main Building, then the largest structure in the world at a quarter-mile long by a fifth-mile wide, housing twenty-two miles of walkways and twenty elevators. Aside from the urban development spurred by the event, the sole remnants of the exposition today are a chunk of Alabama iron ore in Audubon Park (suspected locally to be a meteorite) and a terra-cotta pedestal at Gayarré Place on Bayou Road.

After the exposition, uptown New Orleans took shape as Audubon Park was landscaped, the sites for Tulane and Loyola University were acquired, and the land between the former cities of Jefferson and Carrollton was developed for affluent residential neighborhoods. Telephone and electrical service reached the city in the 1880s, and electric streetcars rolled on the St. Charles line by 1893, strengthening the connection of uptown with downtown. In the American Sector, ambitious new commercial structures designed by Thomas Sully, Albert Toledano, and others grew to dominate the streets, among them the third and last St. Charles Hotel (its two predecessors succumbed to fire). Meanwhile, the Creoles had begun to desert the crowded and decaying French Quarter, eventually relegating it to the status of an inner-city slum. Although pockets of wealth still existed in the Vieux Carré, an increasing percentage of the population comprised poor immigrants attracted by the low rents, availability of rooms, and familiar Mediterranean atmosphere of the old city.

In 1897 an interesting exercise in political geography was transpiring in City Hall, with memorable results. Like any port city, New Orleans had its share of notorious sin districts, including Gallatin Street, now site of the French Market flea market, and "the Swamp" on Girod Street near the docks. By the late 1800s prostitution had abandoned its tendency to concentrate into districts, instead dispersing throughout the city to the point that nearly every neighborhood had brothels. Enter Alderman Sidney Story, a respected businessman and avowed enemy of vice, who banned prostitution in all parts of the city *except* a fifteen-block ghetto adjacent to the Vieux Carré. By default, the hemisphere's first legal red-light district was born and inevitably dubbed "Storyville." For twenty years, Storyville pulsated with gaudy "sporting houses," filthy cribs, memorable characters, and vice that makes today's Bourbon Street scene look prudish by comparison. Storyville became a tourist attraction (travelers arriving at Terminal Station

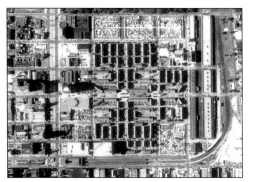

The former Storyville red-light district was replaced in the early 1940s by the Iberville housing project. Note the four above-ground cemeteries surrounding the site. *U.S. Geological Survey*

exited right into rollicking Basin Street), even for those not intending to partake of its commodities, and it may be said that New Orleans secured its reputation for rowdiness and licentiousness from whispered stories of the "Tenderloin District." Jazz, too, launched to greater audiences through Storyville. Evolved over decades from a musical gumbo of African rhythms, old spirituals, ragtime, and parade tunes seasoned with improvisation, jazz blossomed among the cottages and fraternities of Tremé, Marigny, and neighborhoods throughout the city. Later, Storyville provided employment for jazz musicians (primarily pianists, not bands) and an opportunity to associate the memory of their music with the impressions of the festive city exported by visitors from all over the world. After Storyville was closed in 1917 by order of the Navy Department, the post-World War I emigration of Southern blacks to the North carried off some of New Orleans' best jazz musicians, among them Louis Armstrong, to Chicago and New York. Sidney Story's idea of geographic containment of vice actually worked in controlling prostitution, though its cultural spin-offs were, to say the least, unforeseen. The turreted mansions and decadent hovels of Storyville were demolished in the early 1940s for the Iberville federal housing project; only five old "District" structures remain today.

Important progress in the city's eternal battle against water marked the turn-of-the-century period. In 1893 the city hired a team of leading engineers to design an extensive sewerage and drainage system. Their plan, approved in 1895, proposed pumping excess rain and groundwater into Bayou Bienvenue and Lake Pontchartrain through an extensive network of pumps and canals. Between 1897 and 1903, seven pumping stations and a central power station were constructed to lift water out of New Orleans' lowlands and into neighboring water bodies, the first step toward opening up the entire swath between the river and the lake for development. By 1915 revolutionary "screw pumps," invented by New Orleanian Albert Baldwin Wood and later utilized in Holland, China, and India, greatly increased the capacity of the pumping stations to draw excess water out of the streets and bottomlands. Potable water, sewerage systems, and the control of standing water ended the city's summertime bouts with yellow fever and moved the subtropical city into the twentieth century. Today, New Orleans' world-class drainage system, with many turn-of-the-century pumping stations still in use, defies the city's bowl-shaped topography and literally bails out the city after every heavy rain.

Old Creole society was disappearing by the early 1900s as a result of internal economic and professional inflexibility and external pressure to assimilate into the greater Americanized society. The French Quarter, too, seemed to be going the way of its founders, as it decayed into a slum of laundry strung from galleries and pigs wandering in courtyards. A number of events in this era aroused the city to the realization that it was about to lose something unique. Between 1907 and 1909, an entire block of classic Vieux Carré structures was demolished for the Civil Courts Building, a marble Beaux Arts behemoth that violates the *tout ensemble* of the French Quarter in just about every way imaginable. In 1915 a severe hurricane buffeted the city, causing extensive damage and toppling the steeples of many old churches. Among the historic structures affected was the nucleus of Creole society in the last century, the St. Louis Hotel and City Exchange, most of which was torn down the following year. In 1919 the French

From *Map of New Orleans Showing Street Railway System of the N.O. Railways Co., 1904.* Only the theater district remains in the location described in 1904:

Approximate Centers of Districts.
Canal Street is New Orleans' principal Street, and is the Broadway of the Crescent City. All cars pass along or terminate on this street, at or about Carondelet and Bourbon Streets.
PRINCIPAL SHOPPING DISTRICT. Canal Street, at Bourbon and Dauphine Streets.
GENERAL OFFICE DISTRICT. Carondelet and Common Streets.
SHIPPING DISTRICT. Canal Street, at Canal Street Ferry Landing.
WHOLESALE COTTON DISTRICT. Carondelet and Gravier Streets.
WHOLESALE GROCERY DISTRICT. Poydras and Tchoupitoulas Streets.
WHOLESALE SUGAR AND RICE DISTRICT. North Peters and Customhouse Streets.
NEWSPAPER DISTRICT. Camp Street, between Gravier and Poydras Streets.
HOTEL DISTRICT St. Charles and Common Streets
THEATRE DISTRICT. Canal and Baronne Streets and St. Charles Street.
FRENCH SECTION OF CITY. Between Canal Street and Esplanade Avenue, and from Rampart Street to the River.
AMERICAN SECTION OF THE CITY. That portion of City above or South of Canal Street

Opera House, another landmark of Creole high society, burned on the corner of Bourbon and Toulouse. Department stores, industrial buildings, and hotels such as the Monteleone on Royal Street transformed the upper Quarter into practically an extension of the Central Business District. Ironically, the indigent Sicilians who lived in other parts of the Vieux Carré economically justified the maintenance of many old buildings and unknowingly saved them from alteration and demolition. Out of this precarious era emerged New Orleans' preservationist movement, and initial efforts of restoration and regulation ensued. During the 1920s artists and writers discovered the low rents and Old World atmosphere of

the Vieux Carré and founded what was to be a significant component of the district's twentieth-century cultural landscape, its intellectual community.

Engineering toward Modernity

Still at the heart of the city's business was its port business, and its obligation to serve the spheres was attended through a number of initiatives from 1901 to the 1920s, when the newly formed Dock Board constructed riverside warehouses, grain elevators, and other port facilities. The Inner Harbor Navigation Canal (1923), connecting the river with the lake and later with the gulf, was and is the ultimate answer to the old Bayou Road portage, the Carondelet Canal, and the New Basin Canal. Known locally as the Industrial Canal, the waterway provided swifter access between New Orleans and the Gulf of Mexico and created extensive deepwater dock space to which many old riverfront wharves would eventually relocate. Across the river, the Harvey Canal was expanded and eventually joined with the Gulf Intracoastal Waterway, providing ships with alternatives to the meandering Mississippi.

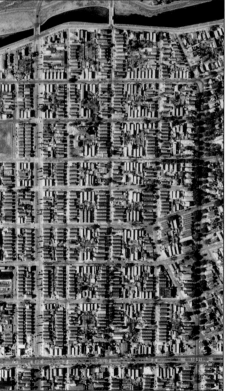

Shotgun houses and bungalows in the densely populated Mid-City neighborhoods near Bayou St. John, 1952. *U.S. Geological Survey*

The reclamation of the backswamps released thousands of uninhabited acres to satisfy the housing needs of the city's ever-growing population (339,000 by 1910). Many new neighborhoods, plus older areas that were adapting to a growing middle class, were developed with ubiquitous and imaginative "shotgun houses." So named for its ability to host a shotgun blast that would enter the front door and exit the rear without touching a wall, the shotgun house is the simplest of house designs (associated with poverty throughout the South), and only in New Orleans would it take on so many styles and embellishments. The city boasts thousands of single shotguns, double shotguns, L-shaped shotguns, camelbacks, galleried and double-galleried shotguns, and even Greek Revival shotguns. Roofs are hip, gable, or both, and as many as three or four well-crafted chimneys punctuate the roofline. Shotguns probably date from the early 1800s, but the turn-of-the-century varieties are especially notable for their "jigsaw Victorian" brackets, balustrades, and friezes, which were mass-produced and distributed through catalogs. At once festive and dignified, the simplicity of the shotgun house allowed the middle class to invest in its civic space, transforming plain residential blocks into colorful neighborhoods with a strong sense of place. No sight exudes the spirit of New Orleans more than a half-dozen consecutive double-shotgun houses brimming with jigsaw ornamentation and painted every pastel shade of the rainbow.

The modern city of New Orleans emerged from the decade of the 1920s. By the dawn of the decade, automobiles and electric streetcars were swiftly replacing horse-drawn transportation, Storyville was closed, first-generation jazz artists were migrating north, Creole society and its French language were nearly extinct, and signs of gentrification and tourism appeared in the Vieux Carré. Urban development progressed in the drained (but sinking) soils of the former backswamps, pulling the city away from its two-hundred-year cling to the natural levees of the Mississippi and the bayous. In 1927 the City Planning and Zoning Commission proposed the widening of Dryades, Saratoga, Poydras, and other streets, the elimination of markets, canals, quirky intersections, and other "traffic obstacles," and the creation of connector streets such as McShane Place to adapt the city's nineteenth-century street network to twentieth-century transportation needs. Many of these recommendations were executed over the next four decades. In the late 1920s the Orleans Levee District strengthened the lakeside levee to protect the city from hurricane-induced storm surges and in the process created nearly two thousand acres of uplands along the shore of Lake Pontchartrain, land that was rapidly developed for beachfront recreational facilities, residential neighborhoods, and a new airport. The grand project, conducted by the Levee Board and later the Works Progress Administration, prompted a planned and managed building boom in the northern half of the city, in contrast to the erratic sectional growth patterns along the Mississippi in the previous century. As a result, the old riverside half of New Orleans is a heterogeneous quilt of micro-scale grids arranged in the long lots of the early arpent-system land concessions, while the new lakeside half of the city follows a macro-scale grid pattern indicative of a centralized planning authority. By the end of the decade, New Orleans spanned (but did not fill) the entire swath between the river and the lake. California bungalows and Spanish Revival residences characterized the architecture of the new neighborhoods (typified by Gentilly), in contrast with the more indigenous styles found in the old faubourgs. In the Central Business District, a series of high-rise banks redefined the city's skyline in the booming 1920s, led by the 355-foot Hibernia Bank Building (1921) on Carondelet Street, the highest point in the city for the next forty years. In port activity, Latin American imports (primarily coffee and bananas) increased as traditional Southern exports (namely cotton) decreased, another indicator of changing times.

The stock market crash of 1929 and the ensuing Great Depression ended this era of growth and transferred construction activity from the private sector and the city to the Works Progress Administration. The WPA was a fixture in the streets of Depression-era New Orleans, taking over levee construction, street maintenance, drainage work, and restoration (albeit heavy-handed by today's standards) of historic buildings in the French Quarter. Despite the protests of the Vieux Carré Commission, empowered in 1936 to regulate development in the Quarter, the WPA replaced many decaying remnants of the old French Market with sturdy replications.

War shook New Orleans out of the Depression with a vigor. The gatekeeper city had a vital and heroic role to play in transporting troops and matériel in and out of the spheres, and its location spawned major war industries such as the Delta and Higgins Shipyards, builders of the landing craft that stormed Normandy on D-Day. The reclaimed lakefront land was largely dedicated to the war effort, providing space for hospitals, airfields, and even a German prisoner-of-war camp. One lasting impact of the thousands of troops in transit through wartime New Orleans was the transformation of Bourbon Street from a bohemian nightspot to the world-famous strip that it is today. By V-J Day in 1945, New Orleans had regained its position as the country's second-busiest port, and a prosperity missing since the Civil War returned to the Crescent City at this optimistic moment in American history. Modernization of the city, perceived by many to be a subtropical backwater, became the byword of the postwar era. Efforts to correct the sporadic growth of the past ensued, including standardization of road and rail infrastructure, construction of modern port facilities, and creation of thoroughfares such as Loyola Avenue to connect downtown with residential areas. Loyola Avenue also became the new home of City Hall, which had been based for a century at Jackson Square and another century at Lafayette Square. The nearby New Basin Canal, dug in the 1830s to connect the American Sector with the lake, was filled in by 1950 to provide a corridor for the upcoming interstate highway system. International-style office buildings replaced galleried row structures in the Central Business District, and suburban ranch houses appeared everywhere, from St. Charles Avenue to the new lakeside neighborhoods. Downriver from the city, the Kaiser aluminum plant opened in the early 1950s and spurred urban development in St. Bernard Parish. Later in the decade, two remarkable bridges punctuated the expansion of the metropolitan area with concentrated accelerations of growth: the Greater New Orleans Mississippi River Bridge finally connected downtown with the West Bank, and the twenty-four-mile Lake Pontchartrain Causeway provided residential access to rural St. Tammany Parish, a development that would have strong socioeconomic implications in the near future.

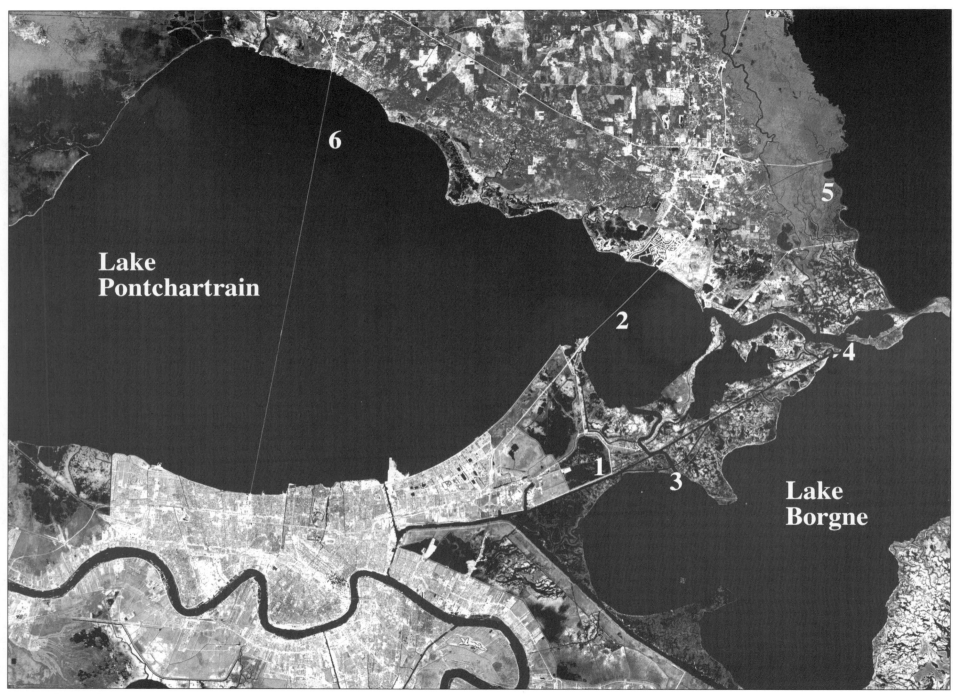

Satellite image of New Orleans and environs: **(1)** Eastern New Orleans and the Rigolets land bridge; **(2)** Interstate 10 connecting Orleans Parish with St. Tammany Parish; **(3)** Chef Menteur Pass and **(4)** the Rigolets, historic routes for maritime traffic between the Gulf of Mexico and New Orleans; **(5)** Pearl River Basin, separating Louisiana from Mississippi; **(6)** Lake Pontchartrain Causeway, connecting New Orleans with the north shore. *Landsat Thematic Mapper satellite imagery courtesy Louisiana State University Department of Geography and Anthropology*

Satellite image of Greater New Orleans: (1) Audubon Park and Zoological Gardens; (2) Harvey Canal; (3) Irish Channel neighborhood; (4) Greater New Orleans Bridge/Crescent City Connection; (5) French Quarter; (6) Inner Harbor Navigation Canal (Industrial Canal); (7) Chalmette Battlefield; (8) Algiers Canal; (9) turning basin between the Industrial Canal and Mississippi River-Gulf Outlet (MR-GO) canal; (10) Lake Pontchartrain Causeway; (11) reclaimed land forming new lakefront, *circa* 1920s; (12) New Orleans Lakefront Airport, also based on reclaimed land, *circa* 1930s. *Landsat Thematic Mapper satellite imagery courtesy Louisiana State University Department of Geography and Anthropology*

Construction of the river bridge through areas known today as the Warehouse District and the Lower Garden District eliminated scores of historical and architecturally significant homes, churches, and stores, reminding New Orleanians that progress, though great and necessary, has a price.

Departure from Geography in the Late Twentieth Century

Three rudimentary developments sculpted present-day New Orleans out of the emerging city of the 1950s: the forging of a modern infrastructure, the exodus of the middle class, and a newfound appreciation for the city's celebrated character. Infrastructural developments from the 1960s to the present were manifested primarily in modernized office districts, transportation networks, and shipping facilities. From the mid-1960s to the 1980s, Poydras Street evolved from a functional commercial corridor into the gleaming Sixth Avenue it is today, lined with chiseled glass towers and basking in importance. True skyscrapers first rose in the mid-1960s, dwarfing Hibernia Bank and eventually transforming the 1920s-era skyline with summits higher than any natural point in the state and footings in the hard Pleistocene clays a hundred feet below the streets. Commercial jets landed at the new New Orleans International Airport in 1962, while downtown, buses replaced streetcars as the primary mode of public transportation (only the St. Charles line remained after 1964). Interstate 10 bisected the city by the early 1970s, darkening portions of Claiborne Avenue, skimming the chimneyed rooftops of Faubourg Tremé, and straddling the former corridor of the New Basin Canal. The Superdome, a stunning marvel completed in 1975, landed in the old railroad yards near Poydras Street that, together with the snarl of highways that runs tangentially to it, constitute the single most-altered section of New Orleans. (Construction of the Superdome was controversial on a number of levels, but the stadium and the Poydras skyscraper corridor that it helped spawn have played important roles in revitalizing downtown and keeping the "business" in the Central Business District.) In the eternal effort to improve the port, the Dock Board decided to relocate wharves from the crowded banks of the Mississippi River to the spacious docks of the Industrial Canal and its adjoining waterways in the eastern part of the city. Although the eastward movement of port activity— potentially "the most drastic change in New Orleans economic geography since the city's founding," as geographer Peirce Lewis predicted in the 1970s— did not fully come to fruition, new wharf development along the Industrial Canal did foster growth in eastern New Orleans and helped give the metropolitan area a new "spread-eagle" shape. Additionally, the opening of the Algiers Canal in 1956, the excavation of the Mississippi River-Gulf Outlet (MR-GO) canal between 1958 and 1968, and the development of the Intracoastal Waterway provided barge traffic with myriad routes through the Port of New Orleans to and from the 14,500 miles of inland waterways that drain into the Mississippi River. Each year, 2,400 ocean carriers and 100,000 barges utilize the 22 miles of wharves and terminals that constitute the Port of New Orleans. Although the Industrial Canal and the MR-GO are important components of the port, most wharves remain on the Mississippi River, especially along the east bank from Audubon Park to Bywater. Infrastructure confronted hydrology on a second front in this era: the world's largest urban drainage system currently can draw as many as 29 billion gallons of rain water daily through 22 pumping stations, 180 miles of canal, 1,200 miles of pipe, and out into Lake Pontchartrain, reclaiming the nation's only below-sea-level metropolis after every heavy rain. On another level of infrastructural change, national and regional chains began to replace local restaurants and mom-and-pop stores on the corners of New Orleans' neighborhoods. The sum effect of these infrastructural advancements was to diminish, for better and for worse, the effects of physical and cultural geography on the experience of the city. In years past, experiencing New Orleans meant partaking of its geographical attributes: its isolation, its port activity, its well-adapted cottages and townhouses, the subtropical aura, the indigenous cuisine. The modernized infrastructure of recent decades divorced the experience of New Orleans from the geography of New Orleans, so that now one may visit or reside in the city and rarely have to negotiate the factors that formed it. Now, New Orleans is *New Orleans* if you so choose, or any other southeastern U.S. city if you do not.

A second trend of recent decades was the exodus of blue-collar and middle-class whites from the city. For a variety of "push" reasons (crime, urban decay, cost of living, and—for some—integration) and "pull" reasons (mobility, better schools, suburban lifestyle, oil jobs), thousands of New Orleanians departed for Jefferson Parish, the north shore, and other outlying areas, from the late 1960s to the 1980s. It was the largest racially correlated demographic shift in New Orleans since the migration of rural blacks into the city during Reconstruction. Between 1960 and 1990, the population of the city proper decreased by 21 percent (628,000 to 497,000), while the metropolitan area increased by 37 percent (907,000 to 1,239,000). Concurrent with the alarming demographic trends was the economic depression triggered by plunging oil prices in the latter half of the 1980s. In this period, the crime rate soared to tragic proportions and, though currently decreasing, is unquestionably the worst and most destructive aspect of modern New Orleans. The fleeing New Orleanians brought elements of their port heritage to the suburbs, including Mardi Gras traditions, cooking styles, and the Brooklynesque accent of blue-collar "New Awlins," which now seems more likely to be heard in Covington or Slidell than on Tchoupitoulas or Melpomene. A predictable result of this exodus was the loss of the city's tax base and the economic polarization of those who remained—a contrast readily apparent in the city today, where wealthy neighborhoods and slums are distributed more heterogeneously than in most

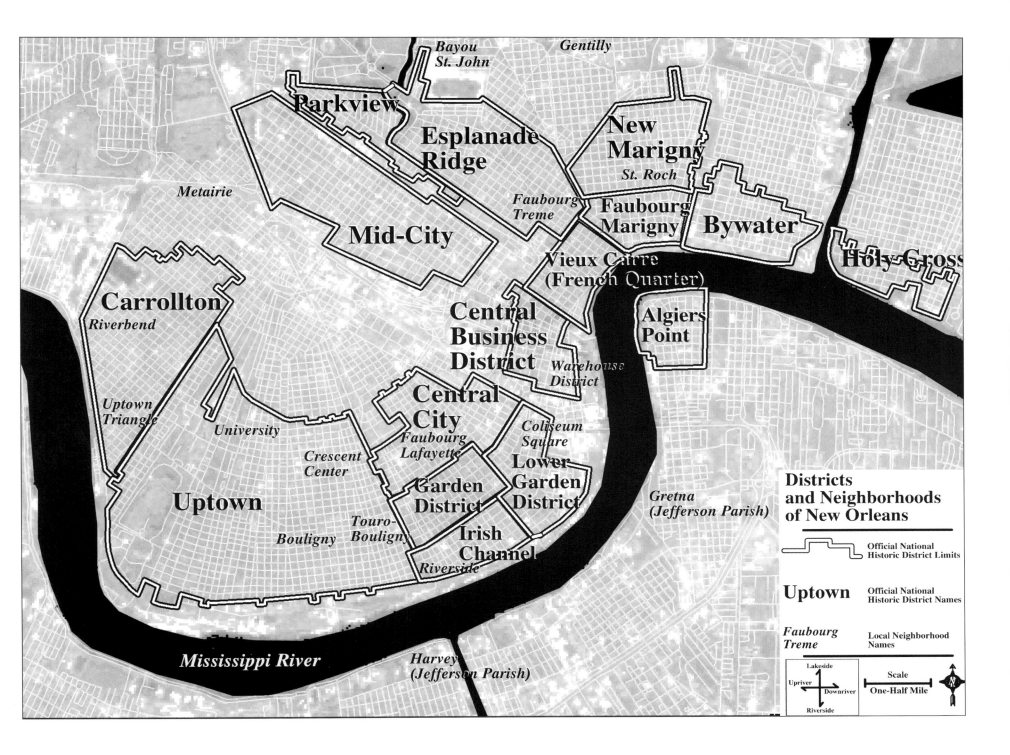

Districts and Neighborhoods of New Orleans

American cities. (Since the 1970s, affluent professionals have been restoring and gentrifying portions of decaying old neighborhoods, contributing to the surprising proximity of wealth and poverty in New Orleans.) Paralleling these changing demographics, political power and social influence in the city swayed away from the white middle class and the uptown "blue blood" aristocracy and toward the majority-black downtown community, a shift that was dramatized in the Mardi Gras krewe desegregation battles of the early 1990s. In recent decades, it seems that New Orleans' extraordinary cultural diversity has dichotomized into two categories, "black" or "white," despite the complexity of each group's true heritage. On a subtler level, however, diversity within these two groups is still recognized, as many blacks proudly identify themselves as Creoles and many whites point with pride to their French, Spanish, and other ancestries.[6] Using the broader categories, black people constitute 62 percent of present-day New Orleans and 39 percent of the metropolitan area; white people (including Hispanics) make up 35 percent and 58 percent respectively, with Asians and other groups accounting for the remainder.

As a counterpoint to the infrastructural progress and middle-class exodus, a third trend—the newfound appreciation for New Orleans' unique character—has affected the city in a variety of interesting ways. To the business community, the appreciation is manifested in the convention and tourism industry, which ranks with the shipping and oil industries in terms of economic importance to the city. The geographical signature of tourism is seen in the skyscraper hotels on or near Canal Street; the sprawling convention facilities along the river; the hundreds of shops, bars, and restaurants in the French Quarter; and countless other attractions and gimmicks. *Charm* has been institutionalized through the tourism industry, and although much of its material is superficial and ersatz, it may be said that the characteristics of New Orleans depicted in postcards and T-shirt slogans are the ones that millions of visitors take home and spread, just as visitors to turn-of-the-century New Orleans took home tales of Storyville.

To preservationists, newfound appreciation of the city was manifested first and foremost in the defeat of the proposed Riverfront Expressway in 1969—"The Second Battle of New Orleans," according to attorneys Richard Baumbach and William Borah. First visualized by Robert Moses in a post-World War II study on modernization, the elevated superhighway would have devastated the ambiance of the French Quarter by barricading it from its river-side geography with a wall of noise and fumes.[7] Beyond this issue, the preservationist community fought and continues to fight countless civic battles to maintain the architectural character of the city and the human scale of its neighborhoods. Victories include the designation of new National Historic Districts (some among the largest in the nation), restorative efforts on hundreds of structures ranging from tiny cottages to notable public buildings, and the founding of dedicated grass-roots neighborhood associations. Defeats include the loss of many St. Charles Avenue mansions in the early 1970s, demolition of scores of old American Sector buildings during the oil boom, and the obliteration of nearly ten square blocks of nineteenth-century Creole houses in Tremé for the creation of a cultural center and a landscaped park later dedicated to Louis Armstrong. It is ironic that the city saluted its most famous son by destroying a portion of the old neighborhood in which jazz evolved and replacing it with unseemly berms and bridged lagoons. Nevertheless, preservationists have come a long way since the 1950s, and the days of unanswered destruction of the city's physical heritage are largely, though not entirely, over. The threats of fire, Formosan termites, and deterioration, however, still loom, reminding us that the wisteria-veiled ruins and sagging galleries that make New Orleans so mysterious and endearing also make it a city out of equilibrium, under siege, living on borrowed time. Or perhaps it is this sense of impending doom that mystifies and endears the city to so many.

The Enduring Geographical City

Today, more than half of greater New Orleans' economy is dedicated to three endeavors: port business, in which it serves the two spheres in its traditional role as a gatekeeper city; the oil and gas industry, where the geological coincidences that form petroleum are exploited for processing and exportation; and the convention and tourism trade, in which the city hosts millions of visitors seeking its allure and festivity. Despite the forces of homogenization that have subdued the city in recent decades, few American cities still economically depend on their geography and history to the extent that New Orleans does. The Crescent City, rebounding with a renaissance in art, industry, and spirit, remains unique among American cities today, south of the American South, apogee of the Caribbean cultural region, keeper of one of the world's great ports. What instills New Orleans with such a strong sense of place is the fact that the city's allure—its romantic, sultry, raffish character, in all its manifestations—is a direct product of its physical geography. Nearly three centuries of guarding the gate between the North American interior and the rest of the world have created a complex and peculiar enclave in the swamps, one of the world's few truly beloved cities, a city that can never be known entirely.

---

[6] The shifting definition of the word *Creole* over the centuries sometimes causes interesting confusion today. The 1997 *Louisiana Tour Guide* (p. 69) listed chess champion Paul Morphy (1837-84), a white Creole from an aristocratic family, and writer George Washington Cable (1844-1925), an Anglo-Saxon who wrote of Creole culture, as famous African-American Louisianans.

[7] To "cool tempers on both sides of the controversy," the pro-expressway Chamber of Commerce of the New Orleans Area (1966) floated the idea of constructing a "third Pontalba" building on Decatur Street to shield Jackson Square from the expressway. Thumbnail sketches of the edifice more closely resembled a "second Cabildo," stretched to span from the French Market to Jax Brewery. Mercifully, it never had to be built.

Then and Now

A downriver perspective of New Orleans (crescent at top). After the hairpin meander known as English Turn, the Mississippi River straightens out as it heads for the Gulf of Mexico. *Landsat Thematic Mapper satellite imagery courtesy Louisiana State University Department of Geography and Anthropology*

1952 The French Quarter, or *Vieux Carré* (Old Square)

The original plat for La Nouvelle Orléans was designed by Pierre Le Blond de la Tour and Adrien de Pauger in a series of iterations from 1721 to 1723, after a few years of unplanned settlement. The city remained within the six-by-eleven-block grid during the French colonial era (1718-62) and spread into Faubourg *Ste. Marie* (left) in 1788, Faubourg Marigny (right) in 1806, and Faubourg Tremé (top) in 1810. See pp. 378 and 387 for oblique perspectives of the French Quarter. *U.S. Geological Survey*

1994 Same area

Note the extensive alteration in the upriver flank of the Quarter (left) and in the Central Business District. The land in the lower left is a riverside batture built up by the shifting Mississippi during the early 1800s; at the opposite end of the Quarter, the river cuts into the bank and has eliminated a few acres. The Vieux Carré today contains more than three thousand structures, of which 75 percent are one to two-and-a-half stories and 80 percent are masonry (the remainder are wood). Few buildings, perhaps 2 percent, are recognized as nationally significant; what makes the Quarter so treasured is the *tout ensemble* (total impression) of thousands of old structures, most of which are unusual by American standards, assembled in a dense and contiguous distribution. The historic layout, street names, and architecture of the old city endure in today's Vieux Carré. *U.S. Geological Survey*

French Quarter

circa 1906 **View of the French Quarter, from above the corner of North Front and Bienville**

A splendid view of the French Quarter just before the construction of the Civil Courts Building and the demolition of the former St. Louis Hotel and City Exchange, the domed building at left. The St. Louis Hotel (1838; rebuilt after a fire in 1840) hosted local history like few other places, as nucleus of the Creole social and business world, scene of lively auctions and elegant balls, seat of Reconstruction-era government, and finally as the epitome of ruin. Its original timber-supported dome (destroyed in the fire) was replaced by this light-weight fireproof dome, constructed of a honeycomb of clay pots. Damage inflicted by the 1915 hurricane led to its demolition the next year. At right, St. Louis Cathedral overlooks Jackson Square. The Quarter's residential and commercial cityscape contrasts with the American Sugar Refinery industrial facilities in the foreground. This photograph was probably taken from the refinery's ten-story Old Filter House. *Detroit Publishing Company, Library of Congress, no. LC-D4-10988 L DLC*

1998 Same view

The Civil Courts Building, upper left, was completed in 1909 in an effort to improve the decaying neighborhood. To its immediate right is the Royal Orleans Hotel (1960), designed by Koch and Wilson on the site of the old St. Louis Hotel and maintaining the tradition of grand hotels at this location. In front of the Royal Orleans is the cupola of the Girod House (1814), a distinctive component of the French Quarter roofscape. The foreground acreage reflects the shift of land use in this area from industrial infrastructure to the infrastructure of the tourism and convention trade: hotels and parking lots. The last major *circa* 1900 warehouses in this batture area burned down in the 1970s; only the restored Louisiana Sugar Refining Company Building (1884) at 111 Iberville and a few other remnants survive today. This photograph was taken from the Canal Place complex.

French Quarter

circa 1906 Adjacent view of the French Quarter riverfront, from above the corner of North Front and Bienville

Aside from a small colony along Bayou St. John in 1708, this riverside arc hosted the initial settlements (where present-day Conti meets the river, roughly at center) that formed La Nouvelle Orléans in 1718. St. Louis Cathedral is at far left; to its right are the long lines of the Pontalba Apartments bordering Jackson Square. The downriver community of Faubourg Marigny appears in the distance by the river. The sugar and rice district, dominated by the saw-tooth storehouses and facilities of the American Sugar Refinery, occupied the foreground area in the early 1900s, about a century after the river gratuitously created the valuable batture by depositing sediments along the levee. This photograph was probably taken from the American Sugar Refinery's ten-story Old Filter House. *Detroit Publishing Company, Library of Congress, no. LC-D4-10988 LC DLC*

1998 Same view

Although the sugar and rice district is gone, the railroad tracks reference the modern scene to its *circa* 1906 appearance. The French Quarter's batture is akin to the Warehouse District in its historic development, and it is only by geographical accident that these young lands are "in" the Vieux Carré. The Moonwalk (1976) and Woldenberg Park (1989), two riverfront landscaping projects visible at right, have reconnected the Vieux Carré with the river in the postindustrial era, making the Mississippi an integral memory of a trip to the French Quarter and symbolizing the area's transition from the port to the tourist economy. It was along this riverside corridor that planners proposed to route the Riverfront Expressway (Interstate Route 310) to connect the bridge with the main Interstate 10 trunk at Elysian Fields. The proposal, which polarized the city in the 1960s and helped launch the modern preservationist movement in America, was finally scrapped in 1969. Jax Brewery (1891, center) was modified in the mid-1980s from a local brewery to a theme mall.

French Quarter

35

circa 1913 **View of Maison Blanche, Canal Street, and the French Quarter, looking toward the river from the Hotel Grunewald**

The Maison Blanche Building, designed by the Stone Bros. and completed in 1909, overlooks Canal Street and the Vieux Carré. In the distance beyond Maison Blanche's cornice (upper center) is the domed St. Louis Hotel and City Exchange, three years before its demolition. To its right is the Civil Courts Building, the infamously out-of-place Beaux Arts edifice that replaced an entire block of classic Creole structures in 1906-09. The steeples of St. Louis Cathedral are visible at upper center; the cupola of the Chess, Checkers, and Whist Club (p. 204) appears in the foreground; a streetcar plies Canal at lower right; and the Mississippi rolls away in the upper right. *Detroit Publishing Company, Library of Congress, no. LC D401-15657 L DLC*

1996 Same view

Maison Blanche, operating in the lower three floors of this thirteen-story building, was the last of New Orleans' great downtown department stores. It closed it 1982 but reopened under new ownership in 1984, to the cheers of even its competitors. Then in May 1998, the 101-year-old retailer was bought by Dillard's—the same company that purchased and closed the 147-year-old D. H. Holmes department store on Canal in 1989. Little Rock-based Dillard's decided to close this flagship Maison Blanche branch in the summer of 1998. The Whitehouse Hotel Limited Partnership, which owns the structure, is converting the unoccupied upper floors (once professional offices) into a Ritz Carlton Hotel and the Iberville Street annex into living space, while the former retail area is slated for a shopping gallery, possibly under the Maison Blanche name. The large courtyard patios at center right, once the second floor of the D. H. Holmes warehouse, mark the new Chateau Sonesta Hotel, a partnership between the city and the private sector designed to bring new investment to Canal Street through adaptive reuse of historical structures. Businesses on this part of Canal are rapidly orienting away from a local clientele and toward the tourist dollar. The French Quarter's picturesque roofscape is still intact in the central and lower portions of the district, but it no longer exists here in the upper Quarter.

French Quarter

circa 1913 **Adjacent view of Canal Street and the French Quarter, looking toward the river from the Hotel Grunewald**

The French Quarter appears on the left; the Central Business District (formerly known as the American Sector and originally as Faubourg Ste. Marie) is on the right, and Canal Street separates the two distinct districts. The high-rise at left is the Beaux Arts-style Hotel Monteleone (1908), with its pearl-white terra-cotta ornamentation; directly below it is the Bourbon Street entrance of the Cosmopolitan Hotel, built upon the ashes of the 1892 Bourbon/Canal fire. The D. H. Holmes department store, a New Orleans institution since 1842, is visible on Canal Street; the chimneys at upper right mark the sugar refineries below Decatur Street. This scene captures the Vieux Carré in the midst of a precarious era, when important elements of the historic city were lost or threatened. *Detroit Publishing Company, Library of Congress, no. LC D401-15657 LC DLC*

1996 Same view

This photograph captures the degree to which the upper French Quarter and Canal Street have been dedicated to the modern tourism industry: nearly every high-rise in sight is a hotel, two of which sandwich the original Hotel Monteleone. Tourism and convention business ranks behind only port business and (sometimes) the oil industry in terms of economic importance to the city. D. H. Holmes closed in 1989, but its building was refurbished in the mid-1990s as the Chateau Sonesta Hotel. Aside from the massive interior restoration to create 243 unique high-ceiling rooms, the effort returned the structure's Canal Street façade to its traditional appearance and even reinstalled the famous clock that served as a rendezvous for New Orleanians since 1913 (immortalized in John Kennedy Toole's novel *A Confederacy of Dunces*). Note the modifications made to the side of the Godchaux Building, at center foreground. Refer to pp. 178-79 for perspectives of Canal Street viewed from the opposite direction.

French Quarter

circa 1903 Restaurant de la Louisiane, 717 Iberville Street, in the French Quarter

George François Mugnier captured this cart delivering milk and Creole cream cheese to the Restaurant de la Louisiane (founded 1881) on Iberville Street. The cart is owned by a German, Adam Schoendorf; perhaps this is his son we see here. Iberville Street was known as Customhouse Street (for its proximity to the old Spanish Custom House and the later U.S. Custom House) until 1901, when it was renamed to honor the French founder of Louisiana. The Hotel de la Louisiane operated in the galleried structure to the left. *Photograph by George François Mugnier, Leonard V. Huber Collection, The Historic New Orleans Collection, accession no. 1974.25.20.179*

circa 1915 Same site

circa 1996 Same site

Top scene, *circa* 1915: Mugnier's scene was adapted into a nostalgic postcard in which the somber boy is replaced by a bonneted girl, an early example of the "institutionalization of charm" apparent in modern tourist-oriented depictions of New Orleans. The girl is turned away either to pour milk into a customer's pitcher or to relieve the artist of having to draw a face! **Bottom scene, 1996:** The much-altered front of the old restaurant was razed during the 1961 demolition of the adjoining Solari's building (p. 48); visitors now drive through the site and climb into the parking garage that replaced Solari's. A Vieux Carré Survey photograph shows Moran's Bar and Restaurant ("Since 1835") operating in the galleried building in 1964; a latter-day La Louisiane ("Since 1881") occupied the same building until recently. *Postcard from The Historic New Orleans Collection, accession no. 1958.85.184*

French Quarter

circa 1910 Wallace Magazines & Periodicals, 103 Royal Street, in the
French Quarter

This magazine stand operated on the Royal Street side of the first unit (1852) of Touro Row, a series of twelve identical structures that spanned Canal Street from Royal to Bourbon (pp. 196-97). Surrounding the stand is the familiar sight of a postcard rack, with some famous New Orleans scenes discernible on the cards. *Detroit Publishing Company, Library of Congress, no. LC-D4-43503 DLC*

1996 Same site

A similar newsstand, attended by a similarly vested gentleman, now operates at 107 Royal, just to the right of the former site. Seven of the original twelve components of Touro Row still stand; five maintain their original hip roofs, but only the three closest to Royal, including this one, retain their historical upper-story façade. The units at the Bourbon Street end of the row were redeveloped in the 1880s and burned in 1892. All ground-floor interiors in the entire block are completely modernized.

French Quarter

43

circa 1950 Cosmopolitan Hotel and Gem Coffee-house, 121 to 129 Royal Street, in the French Quarter

The Astor Hotel (left), reminiscent of a townhouse in Brooklyn or Manhattan, was designed by Thomas Sully and built in 1892 as the Cosmopolitan Hotel. The hotel occupied two buildings (see pp. 38, 122, and 124), this one on Royal and the other at 124-128 Bourbon, which had a very different stone façade. (The connection was not straight across the block but offset by a parcel.) Note the treacherously long ladders serving as fire escapes. The former Gem Coffeehouse (center) boasts a rich history as a rendezvous for aristocrats, as birthplace of the Pickwick Club (whose members founded the Mardi Gras Mistick Krewe of Comus here in 1857), as an anti-Union gathering place during the Civil War and Reconstruction, and allegedly as an illicit slave depot in its early years. *Charles Franck Collection, The Historic New Orleans Collection, accession no. 1979.325.2139*

1997 Same site

The first block of Royal Street is a gritty place, in contrast to the sophistication of the antique and art district just a block away. Businesses here, at least on the lakeside half of the block, cater more to locals than tourists. On a typical night, the crowd is a mix of local service-industry employees heading to and from work, Quarter residents heading home, tourists, loiterers, and the homeless; the street is a snarl of impatient taxi cabs and delivery trucks. While Bourbon Street makes its living feigning honky-tonk authenticity, the first block of Royal Street lives the real thing. The past glory of the Gem Coffeehouse and the now-rusting Cosmopolitan Hotel, like an old tenement on the Lower East Side, looms gloomily above this intensely urban scene. Note the "new" fire escapes.

French Quarter

circa 1945 Union Bank and Merchants' Exchange, Royal Street at the Iberville intersection, in the French Quarter

The Union Bank (1838) served as an influential money-lending institution during the city's antebellum golden age. Its four-columned Greek Revival entrance was later enclosed to produce the storefronts seen here on Royal Street, while its Iberville side remained in its original state. The Merchants' Exchange (1835, right), designed by the famed Gallier-Dakin partnership and noted for its surprisingly modernistic façade, classical interior, and unlikely dome (p. 124), served as a post office, exchange, and district court for many years. By the end of the century, the former Union Bank building housed Citizens' Bank (1874), the New Tivoli Concert Saloon (1885), and the Bijou Variety Theater (1896), while the Merchants' Exchange was used as a restaurant. *Charles Franck Collection, The Historic New Orleans Collection, accession no. 1979.325.2141*

1996 Same site

The Union Bank was demolished in the late 1940s and replaced by this corner drugstore; the neighboring Merchants' Exchange—the last surviving building of the Gallier-Dakin partnership in New Orleans—was stolen from the efforts of preservationists by an arsonist in 1960. The Vieux Carré Commission, a regulatory group constitutionally empowered in 1936 to guard the historic ambiance of the French Quarter, never had jurisdiction of the block between Canal and Iberville, which explains the drastic alteration of the riverside half of Royal Street's first block. The corner building just out of view on the extreme right was falling into dilapidation until 1996, when a local bank restored it as a branch office, a historically appropriate business for this former financial district. This block is now in the Central Business District National Historic District.

French Quarter

circa 1950 Solari's, 201 to 207 Royal Street at the Iberville intersection, in the French Quarter

Solari's, founded in 1864 at St. Louis and Royal, was a popular grocery store and lunch spot specializing in gourmet foods and wines. It moved to this location in 1873 and into this structure, designed by Thomas Sully and constructed in 1887, to become a New Orleans institution for the next eight decades. *Charles Franck Collection, The Historic New Orleans Collection, accession no. 1979.325.2142*

1997 Same site

The building housing Solari's since 1887 was demolished in 1961 and replaced by a parking garage disguised with rudimentary French Quarter accouterments. Solari's returned to the ground floor of the new structure but closed down permanently a few years later. From a utilitarian perspective, there is something logical about converting unoccupied upper floors to satisfy a particular economic demand (parking, in this case) while maintaining the traditional street-level use for pedestrian access. From an architectural and historical perspective, the demolition and eventual demise of Solari's was a sad loss for New Orleans. The popular Mr. B's Bistro now does a brisk business at the corner site.

French Quarter

circa 1920 Hotel Monteleone, 200 block of Royal Street looking toward Canal, in the French Quarter

The Hotel Monteleone (left, 1908), with its terra-cotta façade, was the first high-rise hotel in the Quarter. Since then, a line of similar structures (though much less ornate) have arisen around the Monteleone so that the first two riverside blocks of Royal Street now form a concrete canyon. The Monteleone, designed by Toledano and Wogan, was one of three great Beaux Arts-style buildings to punctuate the nineteenth-century roofscape of the French Quarter in the early twentieth century, along with the Civil Courts Building (1909) and Maison Blanche (1909). Behind the Monteleone in this scene is the Commercial Hotel, the Union Bank, and the Merchants' Exchange, in the distance to the left of the Camel banner. See p. 38 for a *circa* 1913 view of the Monteleone taken from a rooftop near Canal Street. *Detroit Publishing Company, Library of Congress, no. LC-D4-71830 DLC*

50

1996 Same site

The left side of this block was gerrymandered out of Vieux Carré Commission jurisdiction by city ordinance during the administration of Mayor Robert Maestri (1946) and remained in this unprotected state for eighteen years. Thus by the 1960s, the second block of Royal (not to mention the first block, which was never under commission protection) was dominated by modern hotels. Although four times taller than a typical French Quarter structure and a lot less interesting architecturally, upper Royal's high-rises abut the street in a manner that maintains the pedestrian scale of the district. The Monteleone annex on the corner (with the vertical sign), built on the site of the old Commercial Hotel, is topped with a penthouse designed as a Quarter townhouse, a curiosity of the skyline when viewed from afar (p. 39). The historic Union Bank and Merchants' Exchange are both gone.

French Quarter

51

circa 1925 **LaBranche Buildings, 700 Royal Street at the St. Peter intersection, in the French Quarter**

The LaBranche Buildings, a series of eleven townhouses erected 1835-40, occupy most of the tiny block surrounded by Royal, St. Peter, Exchange (Cabildo) Alley, and Pirate's Alley. Despite their centralized location in the Vieux Carré and the splendid iron-lace galleries (added in 1850), the structures are Greek Revival in style and more akin to the architectural heritage of the American Sector. Unusual Gothic-arch doorways are found on the Cabildo Alley side of the LaBranche complex. *Charles Franck Collection, The Historic New Orleans Collection, accession no. 1979.325.2168*

1996 Same site

The corner LaBranche Building is probably the most photographed galleried structure in the city, as it conforms perfectly to visitors' expectations of old New Orleans. Iron-lace galleries came into vogue in the 1840s and are found in the historic downtowns of many Mississippi Valley and Gulf Coast cities, but only in New Orleans do they form entire streetscapes. They are now among the premier symbols of the city. This LaBranche Building operates today as a restaurant overlooking one of the most festive street corners in the French Quarter, a favorite locale for street musicians. Doreen's New Orleans Jazz Band is seen here setting up for a Saturday afternoon performance.

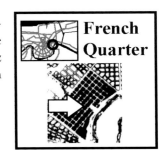

French Quarter

circa 1915 Civil Courts Building, looking up Royal Street from the St. Louis intersection, in the French Quarter

The Civil Courts Building (left, 1909) replaced a portion of Exchange Alley and more than fifty nineteenth-century Creole structures similar to those on the right of this scene. The Beaux Arts-style courthouse was originally planned in 1902 as the new home of the Supreme Court, then functioning in the aging Cabildo, and was sited in the decaying French Quarter in an effort to revive the slum. The completed courthouse was at first well received by the city and put to use for courts and agency offices. As appreciation for the French Quarter increased over the years, the Civil Courts Building came to be seen as an ill-conceived, out-of-scale, and stylistically inappropriate intrusion—a view held even by the Vieux Carré Commission, which considered its demolition. Up one block on the left of this photograph is the Bank of Louisiana (1826); behind it in the distance is the Hotel Monteleone (1908), another large-scale Beaux Arts project of the early twentieth century. *Detroit Publishing Company, Library of Congress, no. LC-D4-71851 DLC*

1997 Same site

Today, magnolias soften the hulking marble of the Civil Courts Building, until 1981 the unlikely home of the Wildlife and Fisheries Commission and possibly the future home of its original occupants, the Louisiana Supreme Court, if restoration funds continue to flow. The trees were planted at the suggestion of architect Richard Koch, who also proposed enclosing the block with an iron fence, like Jackson Square, to reduce the impact of the building's excessive scale and setback. Criticism of the edifice has softened in recent years as people have simply grown accustomed to it or have come to see it for what it is (rather than *where* it is): an ambitious and rather spectacular example of an early-twentieth-century public building, constructed with as much good intention as disregard for environs. Ironically, after decades of criticism as an intrusion, the revived courthouse may emerge as one of the few refuges from the tourist venue that has truly intruded upon the French Quarter. Interior restoration work commenced on March 2, 1998.

French Quarter

circa 1890 Looking down Royal Street toward the St. Philip intersection, in the French Quarter

Balconies and galleries draw the private space of these French Quarter residences into the public space of Royal Street. In New Orleans, balconies are unsupported platforms that extend to about half the width of the *banquette* (sidewalk), and are enclosed by a simple railing that in older specimens may be of wrought iron. Balconies originate from the architectural heritage of the Spanish colonial era. Galleries cover the entire sidewalk, are supported by columns, and are usually entwined with an extravagant wisteria of cast-iron designs. Iron-lace galleries came into fashion in the 1840s and forever changed the streetscape of the city. Balconies and galleries are front porches adapted to the confines of a crowded and steamy city; they work very well in the Vieux Carré, providing residents with fresh air, garden space, and an observational perch while sheltering pedestrians from the elements and beautifying the vista in the streets. *Photograph by William Henry Jackson, Detroit Publishing Company, Library of Congress, no. LC-D418-8110 DLC*

1998 Same site

"The cry to abolish by city ordinance the galleries and balconies which shelter the sidewalks in the business section is raised in the name of progress by those who would rob New Orleans of a distinctive charm and reconstruct her according to the stereotyped pattern of some cities in the Middle West." (*The New Orleans Book*, Orleans Parish School Board, 1919) That distinctive charm is indeed gone from most of the Central Business District but lives on under constant vigilance in the Vieux Carré.

French Quarter

circa 1900 **Looking down Royal Street at the Ursulines intersection, in the French Quarter**

The Vieux Carré of the public imagination: narrow streets; galleries with iron lace; granite-block paving; a flag saluting Rex, King of Carnival; and a streetcar. Tennessee Williams immortalized this route, which accessed Desire Street from 1920 to 1948, in his 1947 classic, *A Streetcar Named Desire*. *Detroit Publishing Company, Library of Congress, no. LC-D4-5738 DLC*

1996 Same site

Aside from its architecture, the French Quarter's physical appeal derives from its narrow streets and lack of setback distance from *banquette* to building. Things that crowd the streets—balconies, galleries, hanging ferns, awnings, flags—enhance this appeal, while open spaces and front gardens detract from the charm. This block roughly marks the point in the modern French Quarter where the bars and shops peter out and a quiet, residential neighborhood emerges. During the 1980s the Quarter's residential population decreased by 30 percent, while the annual number of visitors doubled. All streetcars are gone from the Quarter streets, and one now gets to Bywater on a bus named Desire.

French Quarter

1943 741 Iberville Street at the Bourbon intersection, in the French Quarter

This American-style townhouse forms a picturesque scene on World War II-era Bourbon Street (left). At this time businesses on Bourbon catered to locals and their needs as well as to visitors (mostly servicemen) seeking *bon temps*. According to the Vieux Carré Survey, this three-story Greek Revival-style dwelling was extant as early as 1831; notarial records prior to that year have been lost. *Charles Franck Collection, The Historic New Orleans Collection, accession no. 1979.325.2001*

1996 Same site

The sturdy townhouse guards the "first" corner of Bourbon Street, offering frozen daiquiris to tourists but no shoe repair, hemstitching, or pleating. Upper Bourbon is now 100 percent dedicated to the tourist trade. The actual first block of Bourbon, between Canal and Iberville, lost most of its older structures and is bypassed by visitors as they beeline for the rollicking strip. Note the new box balconies on the third floor.

French Quarter

circa 1905 Old Absinthe House, 240 Bourbon Street at the Bienville intersection, in the French Quarter

The Old Absinthe House (1806) exemplifies Vieux Carré architecture in the late Spanish colonial and early American years: commercial use on the ground floor, residential use on the top floor, an entresol in between, French doors with fanlight transoms, and a narrow balcony (wider iron-lace galleries came into fashion in the 1840s). An undocumented local legend holds that Maj. Gen. Andrew Jackson planned the defense of New Orleans here in 1814-15 over glasses of absinthe, an alcohol derived from licorice. On the extreme right, the profile of the Cosmopolitan Hotel is visible. *Detroit Publishing Company, Library of Congress, no. LC-D4-33065 DLC*

circa 1935 Same site

circa 1996 Same site

Top scene, *circa* 1935: The sheer wall to the left of the Old Absinthe House is the American Brewing Company bottling facility, built in the early 1900s on the site of a colonial-era structure with a double-pitch roof. **Bottom scene, 1996:** The American (Regal) Brewing Company building was replaced by a hotel around 1970. Always earning a pause from tourists on Bourbon Street, the Old Absinthe House is still a popular bar today. Its entresol was removed in the late 1950s, creating a high ceiling supported by walls encrusted with patrons' business cards, a tradition practiced by a number of famous bars in the French Quarter. Circa *1935 photograph: Charles Franck Collection, The Historic New Orleans Collection, accession no. 1979.325.1986*

French Quarter

circa 1910 **French Opera House, 541 Bourbon Street at the Toulouse intersection, in the French Quarter**

The French Opera House (1859) was an internationally famous landmark on Bourbon Street for sixty years. Operas, concerts, and carnival balls held in the Greek Revival hall, designed by James Gallier Jr., served as important events in Creole high society at a time when the Creoles were losing their cultural identity and economic power in the city. In the wee hours of December 4, 1919, after a rehearsal of *Carmen*, a fire broke out and enveloped the grand hall while threatening its neighbors. The ruins that morning reminded a journalist for the *New Orleans Item* of a scene from the recent war in Europe: "The high-piled debris, the shattered remnants of the wall still standing, the wreathing smoke, all made the historic site resemble a bombarded cathedral town." *Detroit Publishing Company, Library of Congress, no. LC-D4-39617 DLC*

1996 Same site

The loss of the French Opera House is often cited as a milestone in the demise of the French Quarter and Creole society in the early twentieth century. The site was used as a lumberyard for the Samuel House Wrecking Company and remained empty until this hotel (1965), called "Le Downtowner Du Vieux Carre" in the early 1970s, was built to accommodate the increasing numbers of Bourbon Street visitors. The only remaining trace of the opera house is the indented sidewalk, which allowed patrons to disembark from their carriages without blocking the street.

French Quarter

1952 Bourbon Street at Bienville looking upriver (top) and downriver (bottom), in the French Quarter

Top scene: Tanking up on Bourbon Street. Once an elegant residential street, home to such notables as Confederate statesman Judah Benjamin, writer Lafcadio Hearn, and historian Charles Gayarré, Bourbon Street evolved into a bohemian nightspot in the early 1900s and gained worldwide fame as a night-club strip during World War II, when servicemen sought and found the street's opportunities for escapism. "What's Happened to Bourbon Street?" asked an exasperated writer in the title of a 1948 *Times-Picayune* article. "Look what they've done to one of the Vieux Carre's quiet residential thoroughfares!" On the left is the Old Absinthe House (1806); straight up into the Central Business District are the American Bank Building (1929), the Hibernia Bank Building (1921), and the angularly oriented Hennen Building (1895). **Bottom scene:** Looking downriver toward the interior of the Quarter. On the left is Brennan's Restaurant (before it moved to Royal Street); the white buildings on the right were associated with the Regal Brewery, which operated in an era when local beer makers served local markets. *Charles Franck Collection, The Historic New Orleans Collection, accession nos. 1979.325.4873 and 1979.325.4874*

1997 Same sites

Upper Bourbon Street is now institutionalized as the city's (and the nation's) premier night strip, perhaps the best-known party spot in the world. Merchants associations maintain its "scene" as rangers manage resources in a national park. Local disdain for the strip is almost obligatory. Lower Bourbon, starting from around the Dumaine intersection, retains its residential character. **Top scene:** Looking toward Canal, with the Old Absinthe House (1806) at left. **Bottom scene:** The nostalgic DESIRE sign on the galleried structure at right earns itself a place in postcards and movies, but the establishment (Royal Sonesta Hotel), which occupies half the block bound by Bourbon, Bienville, Royal, and Conti, was built only three decades ago, on the site of the Regal Brewery. Excavation of its underground garage in 1966 caused neighboring structures to crack as their underlying soils leaned toward the enormous hole (solifluction). The weight of the new hotel eventually stopped the movement, and a number of lawsuits financed repairs to the nearby structures. The trees at left shade Edison Place, site of an electrical distribution substation (1908) that was donated to the city by New Orleans Public Service Inc. (NOPSI) in 1973. It is the only green space on Bourbon Street.

French Quarter

circa 1950 **Famous Door Bar, 339 to 341 Bourbon Street at the Conti intersection, in the French Quarter**

The Famous Door Bar in the heart of the Bourbon Street strip. Founded by Hypolite Guinle in 1935, this nightclub has presented numerous jazz musicians, some rising to national prominence, to a long list of notable guests (posted next to the entrance). Although technically facing Conti Street, its wraparound canopy and "famous" corner door give the establishment a valuable Bourbon Street address. The townhouse at 327 Bourbon (left, with dormers) was home to Confederate Secretary of State Judah P. Benjamin and briefly housed former Confederate President Jefferson Davis in 1876. *Charles Franck Collection, The Historic New Orleans Collection, accession no. 1979.325.2014*

1996 Same site

The scene depicts as little change as can be expected over a forty-five-year period. The same cannot be said for the other side of the 300 block of Bourbon (to the left; see p. 66), which was leveled in the mid-1960s for the construction of the Royal Sonesta Hotel. The gaping hole ("Lake Vieux Carré") excavated in 1966 for the underground garage caused earthquake-like cracking to some neighboring buildings, including the Judah Benjamin house, seen here on the left. While workers raced to fill in the ditch to prevent further settling, observers were provided rare elevational views of this 300 block of Bourbon and the 700 blocks of Bienville and Conti. Bourbon Street has since recovered from that near-disaster, and there have been no major structural changes on the street in recent decades. Every morning just about 365 days a year, Bourbon Street wakes up to littered gutters reeking of stale beer; by 9 A.M. the sidewalks are washed, beer trucks fuel up the bars, and many of the establishments are open and pouring music into the streets.

French Quarter

324-26-BIENVILLE St
JUNE-5-1953
A.Pelle

circa 1950 and 1953 924 Bienville Street between Dauphine and Burgundy, in the French Quarter

Left scene, *circa* 1950: A boardinghouse in the upriver/lakeside quadrant of the Vieux Carré. The sign reads: "For White Only." Its neighbor on the left is a solid Greek Revival townhouse that, together with other old structures on Bienville, would soon be considered for removal. The demolition permit, filed in 1952 by the nearby Maison Blanche department store to build a warehouse, was initially refused by the Vieux Carré Commission. The president of the store then appealed to the City Council and recruited the support of some heavy hitters of the day, his counterparts at the Chamber of Commerce, the International House, Krauss Company, and Greater New Orleans, Inc. The City Council voted unanimously to reverse the commission's ruling. **Right scene, 1953:** The boardinghouse's neighbor is peeled away, revealing the rears of the larger commercial buildings along Canal Street. *Charles Franck Collection, The Historic New Orleans Collection, accession nos. 1979.325.1995 and 1979.325.1995*

70

1997 Same site

The old segregated boardinghouse has a new set of neighbors, each built to belie their relatively young ages. The structure on the left, the Maison Blanche warehouse (1954), is now a parking garage, a highly demanded and easy-to-manage business that exerts constant economic pressure on owners of old buildings in the city.

French Quarter

1887 and *circa* 1935 The Three Sisters, 228 to 238 North Rampart at the Bienville intersection, in the French Quarter

Left scene, 1887: James Gallier Sr. built three identical Greek Revival mansions on residential Rampart Street, about three blocks from Canal, in 1834. The relatively small lot was owned by three men who requested that three houses be constructed; the satisfied customers named their new homes the Three Sisters. The mansions were noted for their impressive columns, porticoes, courtyards, and terraces. Service units were appended to the right of each

structure. **Right scene, *circa* 1935:** The middle and right units of the Three Sisters in their mundane twilight years, a century after construction. The "sister" on the corner of Bienville had been replaced by a parking lot. *Engraving by Eldridge Kingsley, photograph by Richard Koch, The Historic New Orleans Collection, accession nos. 1957.04 and 1985.120.100*

1996 Same site

The Three Sisters, all demolished by the 1960s when the Rampart flank of the French Quarter was removed from Vieux Carré Commission jurisdiction, are irreplaceable elements of the interesting commercial-residential composition of North Rampart. In the distance, the Marriott marks the hotel district of lower Canal, and Place St. Charles (now the First NBC Center) in the distant center of the left photograph points to the heart of the Central Business District.

French Quarter

circa 1890 Citizens' Bank, 620 Toulouse Street between Royal and Chartres, in the French Quarter

The Citizens' Bank (1838) was designed by J. N. B. de Pouilly and financed by the New Orleans Improvement Company, the same two parties responsible for the St. Louis Hotel and City Exchange, to which the bank was connected in the rear. One could access Canal Street directly from this point on Toulouse by entering the Citizens' Bank, passing into the St. Louis Hotel, exiting the front of that building, and strolling up Exchange Alley for four blocks right to the edge of the grand avenue. Two alleys separated the bank from its neighbors on Toulouse Street (note gate in foreground). As the neighborhood decayed, the structure was used as a steam laundry (1885) and as a storage shed (1896). The words "Old Bank" scrawled on the column of the ruins may have been for the benefit of curious first-generation tourists exploring the decadent old city. In terms of style, scale, and setback, the Greek Revival-style Citizens' Bank was somewhat out of place in the Vieux Carré. *The Historic New Orleans Collection, accession no. 1981.247.12.82*

1996 Same site

Portions of Exchange Alley were obliterated in 1906; Citizens' Bank was razed by 1910; and the St. Louis Hotel and City Exchange, last operated as the Hotel Royal, followed in 1916. This façade, masking a parking garage, marks the site of the old bank. Portions of the alley on the right still exist.

French Quarter

1906 Looking down Chartres Street between St. Louis and Toulouse, in the French Quarter

A classic view of the St. Louis Cathedral (reconstructed 1849-51; see pp. 82-87) and the cupola of the Cabildo (1799), framed by the buildings of Chartres Street. The doorway at far left is one of a series of stores in the former St. Louis Hotel and City Exchange (1840), later the State House and the Hotel Royal. According to the 1885 and 1896 Sanborn insurance maps, the Burgess Hotel occupied the upper floors of the galleried structure on the left, the Strangers (Orleans) Hotel used the building with the dormers, and a Chinese laundry—a common business in the French Quarter in these years—operated near the Toulouse Street corner. Feldman's furniture store utilized the ground floor of both hotels. By 1908 an ice manufacturer occupied the buildings at the Chartres/Toulouse corner. *Detroit Publishing Company, Library of Congress, no. LC-D4-19296 DLC*

1997 Same site

Chartres Street was once the city's most fashionable commercial thoroughfare, described as "the Broadway of New Orleans" by Joseph Holt Ingraham (1835), until Canal Street surpassed it in the 1850s. (In 1879 Ernst von Hesse-Wartegg used the same metaphor to describe Canal.) Chartres is now on par with Royal Street in terms of elegance and sophistication. The former St. Louis Hotel has been gone for eighty years, but its stores on Chartres survived for a few decades and a fragment of their wall (far left) was incorporated into the Royal Orleans Hotel in 1960. (This photograph was taken about twenty feet upriver from the 1906 site.) The firm of Koch and Wilson, the first name in restoration architecture in New Orleans, dismantled the old granite arches and reassembled them on the foundation of the Royal Orleans. Adjoining parking garages occupy the sites of the other old hotels from the turn-of-the-century years. The early-morning sun projects a dramatic shadow of the Girod House's cupola upon the wall of the Royal Orleans.

French Quarter

circa 1930 **Girod House (Napoleon House), 500 Chartres Street at the St. Louis intersection, in the French Quarter**

Among the city's most cherished buildings is the French and Spanish Colonial-style Girod House, designed by Jean Hyacinthe Laclotte and Arsène Lacarrière Latour and built in 1814, with some components from the 1790s. It was constructed for Mayor Nicholas Girod and is forever entwined in the legend that Girod offered it as a refuge for Napoleon Bonaparte after the former emperor's departure from Elba Isle and later in a plot to rescue him from his St. Helena Isle exile, probably the world's only grocery store to claim such a heritage. Historian Simone de la Souchère Deléry observed that despite the lack of evidence for the rescue plan, New Orleans (not to mention the Girod House) has gained prestige and glamour from its Napoleonic association. The emperor's physician on St. Helena, Francisco Antommarchi, might have been exploiting this association when he set up office in the Girod House in 1834, thirteen years after Napoleon's death. The structure at right dates from 1797; at lower left is the empty lot where the St. Louis Hotel stood until 1916. *Charles Franck Collection, The Historic New Orleans Collection, accession no. 1979.325.2044*

1996 Same site

Like the legend, the Girod House's steep hip roof, original flat tiles, and octagonal cupola enrich the ambiance of the Vieux Carré. Inside is a favorite bar and restaurant, rich in atmosphere and filled with classical music. Owners Joe and Rosie Impastato, who purchased the historic structure in 1920 for $14,000, sold groceries on the ground floor and lived "above the store," in the tradition of generations of American immigrants. They added the now-famous Napoleon House bar prior to World War II, and after "Mr. Joe" died in 1985 at the age of

one hundred, the family renovated the upper floors into an elegant reception hall. The Impastato family has succeeded in maintaining the Girod House's aged authenticity while keeping its structure and utility sound. Across the street, the Royal Orleans (1960, left) now occupies the site of the St. Louis Hotel.

French Quarter

8107. STREET IN NEW ORLEANS NEAR CATHEDRAL. DETROIT PHOTOGRAPHIC CO.

circa 1890 **Looking down Orleans Street toward the Bourbon intersection, in the French Quarter**

Noontime in the neighborhood behind St. Louis Cathedral (rebuilt 1851). As the axis of the original grid-pattern city, Orleans Street is 7 feet wider than the standard 22-foot width of French Quarter streets. (Measured between property lines, including sidewalks, Quarter streets are about 38 feet wide and were originally measured as 36 French feet; Orleans is about 45 feet wide, or 42 French feet.) This photograph was taken near the Gardette-Le Prêtre House (p. 96), corner of Orleans and Dauphine. *Photograph by William Henry Jackson, Detroit Publishing Company, Library of Congress, no. LC-D418-8107 DLC*

1996 Same site

The turn-of-the-century era saw some new construction in the French Quarter, most often in the form of charming, bucolic wooden cottages that soften the intensely urban aura of the district's older masonry architecture. Each evening, the Sacred Heart of Jesus statue in St. Anthony's Garden, behind the cathedral in the distance, is illuminated to cast a dramatic shadow upon the wall, causing Bourbon Street carousers to do a double take as they pass the Orleans/Bourbon intersection.

French Quarter

circa 1905 **The Cabildo, St. Louis Cathedral, Presbytère, and Jackson Square, in the French Quarter**

Structures of church and state, in the form of the Cabildo, St. Louis Cathedral, and the Presbytère, staked out New Orleans on the banks of the Mississippi River. The French Place d'Armes (now Jackson Square) was a rudimentary element of Le Blond de la Tour's 1721 plan of the original city; it became the Plaza de Armas when Spain gained formal control in 1769 and was especially busy in 1803, when flags were raised to France as the mother country regained control from Spain on November 30, and to the United States when Napoleon's deal with the young republic made Louisiana American on December 20. From 1846 to 1856, the architectural components that currently define the square fell into place as the Pontalba Apartments were constructed, the cathedral was rebuilt, the square was landscaped and fenced, the Andrew Jackson statue was erected, and the name was Americanized to Jackson Square. Union Gen. Benjamin F. Butler left his mark in 1862 by inscribing "The Union Must and Shall Be Preserved" in the pedestal of the statue. *Detroit Publishing Company, Library of Congress, no. LC-D4-33062 DLC*

1997 Same site

Jackson Square today is an energetic and essential urban place, the truest heart of the city, and one of the busiest pedestrian sites in the nation. The square and its architectural ensemble lever the time of day and the weather of the moment to form a fleeting character: mysterious in the dawn fog, friendly in the morning sun, festive in the afternoon heat, awesome in the twilight thunderstorm, and intimidating in the dark of night. The Jackson Monument (left) is one of two replicas of Clark Mills's original statue, which stands today in Lafayette Square, directly in front of the White House in Washington, D.C. The original statue is mounted on a pedestal inscribed with the somewhat less stirring quotation "Our Federal Union: It Must Be Preserved."

French Quarter

circa 1910 St. Louis Cathedral and the Cabildo, looking up Chartres Street, in the French Quarter

The Cabildo, left of the cathedral, was the political focal point of colonial New Orleans and of Creole culture in the nineteenth-century American city. The site has had official significance since the planning of the city in 1721: a *corps de garde* and prison stood here throughout the French era, followed by the first Spanish Cabildo (1769), which burned in the 1788 fire that destroyed most of the city. The present structure was designed by Gilberto Guillemard and erected 1795-99 for the Spanish governing body, *Cabildo*. In late 1803 its *Sala Capitular* saw the transfer of Louisiana from Spain to France and, twenty days later, from France to the United States. For the next half-century, the Cabildo served as City Hall until the honor transferred to Gallier's Greek Revival hall at Lafayette Square (p. 270), and the power shifted from the Creoles to the Anglos in the newly consolidated city. The Louisiana Supreme Court operated here until 1910, when the building's governmental life ended and its curatorial life began. At far left is the Orue-Pontalba House (1790s), probably designed by Guillemard. This photograph was taken on Good Friday. *Detroit Publishing Company, Library of Congress, no. LC-D4-39641 DLC*

1996 Same site

The Cabildo, perhaps the most historic building in the lower Mississippi Valley, is in service today as a component of the Louisiana State Museum. The structural history of the Cabildo is nearly as engrossing as its political history, as the edifice has been rescued numerous times from decay, gravity, fire, water, wind, and heavy-handed remodeling. (See Abbye Gorin's *Conversations with Samuel Wilson, Jr.* for an account of the Cabildo's restoration history.) To its left is Le Petit Théâtre du Vieux Carré, operating in the 1962 reconstruction of the *circa* 1790s Orue-Pontalba House, which was demolished—amid controversy—in the early 1960s because of structural decay. The skyscraper at left marks the site of the old St. Charles Hotel (p. 212), a popular rendezvous in the American Sector and a landmark in the Anglo/Creole rivalry of nineteenth-century New Orleans. The Creole equivalent, the St. Louis Hotel and City Exchange, was located two blocks up Chartres Street. Note the room added in the nook behind the tower at right.

French Quarter

circa 1910 St. Louis Cathedral and the Presbytère, looking down Chartres Street, in the French Quarter

St. Louis Cathedral and the Presbytère are integral parts of one of America's great architectural ensembles, Jackson Square. The original St. Louis Cathedral, designed in 1724 by Adrien de Pauger, burned in the Good Friday fire that leveled New Orleans in 1788. (Bells to warn of the fire were apparently silenced in deference to the holy day.) The second cathedral, completed in 1794 by Cabildo architect Gilberto Guillemard, had twin hexagonal towers and bell-shaped domes, similar to that of St. Augustine's (p. 148). A third tower was added in 1820 by the eminent American architect Benjamin Latrobe, designer of the Capitol in Washington. This church of distinct Spanish Colonial flavor was all but demolished in 1850 for the construction of the present-day cathedral, designed by J. N. B. de Pouilly and blessed in 1851. Only the lower thirty feet of the front wall date from the 1794 structure. The neighboring Presbytère was built over a twenty-year period spanning the Spanish and American regimes and was originally intended to be a rectory. It was instead rented and eventually sold to the city as a courthouse. This photograph was taken on Good Friday. *Detroit Publishing Company, Library of Congress, no. LC-D4-71844 DLC*

1996 Same site

St. Louis Cathedral was elevated to the status of "minor basilica" by Pope Paul VI in 1964 and for a while was officially called Basilica of St. Louis, King of France. As one of only a handful of minor basilicas in the United States, St. Louis Cathedral has certain ceremonial privileges and rites and must forever remain a place of worship. Its papal association was reinforced in 1987 during the visit of Pope John Paul II, for whom a stretch of Chartres Street was renamed. The Presbytère, like the Cabildo, is now a component of the Louisiana State Museum.

French Quarter

May 11, 1988 The Cabildo, Chartres Street at the St. Peter intersection, in the French Quarter

Two centuries after the Good Friday fire of 1788, New Orleans was once again reminded of the vulnerability of its historic treasures. Workmen renovating the Cabildo's gutters apparently left behind some embers that ignited a fire that severely damaged the mansard roof and cupola. Streams of water needed to extinguish the blaze caused additional damage, as did the rain that fell on the roofless building in the weeks after the conflagration. The building's sprinkler system, installed by the WPA in the 1930s, had been removed because it was thought to be more of a threat to the museum than fire. The disaster had the odd effect of returning the Cabildo to its original Spanish Colonial appearance, in that it eliminated the unlikely mansard roof that had been added to the flat-roofed structure about fifty years after the Cabildo's 1799 construction. *Photographs by Capt. Chris E. Mickal, New Orleans Fire Department Photo Unit.*

1996 Same site

Restoration of the mansard roof, dormers, and cupola of the old Spanish government building was contracted to Koch and Wilson, led by architect Robert J. Cangelosi Jr., and carried out by Grimaldi Construction, Inc. The restoration took three times longer than expected, but the job provided an opportunity to correct a number of persistent problems, including termite damage, rewiring, drainage, and sprinkler installation. Reconstruction of the rafters commenced in August 1991, followed by the raising of the cupola a year later and the completion of the excellent restoration in September 1993. New exhibits were installed in late 1993 in time for the Cabildo's gala reopening on February 27, 1994. Sadly, Samuel Wilson Jr. (1911-93), premier expert on the structure and dean of architectural history and preservation in New Orleans, died four months before the reopening.

French Quarter

circa 1925 Vignié townhouses, 715 to 719 Royal Street at the Orleans intersection, in the French Quarter

The Vignié townhouses (1833) bring to mind a scene in a Mediterranean village or a Caribbean city, with French doors thrown open, laundry drying on the balconies, and items for sale on the sidewalk. This parcel, located behind the St. Louis Cathedral, was once owned by Cabildo architect Gilberto Guillemard in the 1790s and was used by a "Mr. Latourneau, Professor of Natural Philosophy" in 1812 for performances of electrical experiments and other curiosities, according to the Vieux Carré Survey. The last utilization of this parcel prior to the current structures was for a circus and animal menagerie (1829-

31), which, combined with a nearby theater, ballrooms, and cafés, formed a sort of entertainment district. The Vignié townhouses were contracted by Jean Baptiste Benjamin Vignié with architects Claude Gurlie and Joseph Guillot in August 1833 for $21,000 and remained in the Vignié family until 1873. At the time of this photograph, the French Market Homestead Association, a lending institution, operated at 715 Royal, while the American Furniture Store occupied the corner (and apparently the sidewalks). *Charles Franck Collection, The Historic New Orleans Collection, accession no. 1979.325.2084*

1996 Same site

In Joseph Holt Ingraham's account of his 1834 visit to New Orleans, he comments on the atmosphere of this particular intersection of Royal and Orleans: "We were in the French part of the city. There was no apparent indication that we were not really in France. Not an American building was to be seen, in the vicinity, nor scarcely an American face. A numerous, loud-talking, chattering crowd of every grade and color, congregated before the doors of the ballroom and cafe adjoining." Today the ground floor of the Vignié townhouses is occupied by the Chinese-American Company and shops, while the upper floors are in residential use. Note the fire escapes accessing the attic. The trees in the foreground shade artwork displayed for sale on the fence of St. Anthony's Garden, behind St. Louis Cathedral.

French Quarter

1952 The Upper French Quarter, adjacent to Canal Street and the Mississippi River

Canal Street appears along the bottom of this aerial photograph; Rampart Street borders the left edge, and the Mississippi River flows toward the upper right. In colonial times the river would have occupied the industrial district visible on the right edge of this scene to about one block away from the U.S. Custom House (the large building with the skylight at bottom right). A windmill was located near this site, now Canal and North Peters, in the 1720s. Note Jackson Square at top right. *U.S. Geological Survey*

1989 Same area

Note the two new hotels in the blocks surrounding the Civil Courts Building (the large T-shaped edifice at center): the Royal Orleans above it and the Royal Sonesta to its lower left. Note also the Canal Place development (lower right corner) that swallowed up Crossman Street and a group of nineteenth-century commercial buildings in the late 1970s. Skyscraper hotels shade portions of Canal Street structures, and parking lots are the rule by the riverside. *Army Corps of Engineers, New Orleans District*

French Quarter

1903 Le Carpentier-Beauregard-Keyes House, 1113 Chartres Street near the Ursulines intersection, in the French Quarter

The Le Carpentier House (1826), designed by François Correjolles and constructed by James Lambert, is an elegant blend of French and Greek Revival styles. It was originally built for Joseph Le Carpentier (grandfather of chess champion Paul Morphy, a New Orleans Creole) and briefly housed Confederate Gen. P. G. T Beauregard after the Civil War. By the early 1900s it gradually fell toward ruin, housing at one time the C. Giacona & Co. wholesale liquor dealership. The mansion was rescued by local citizens from threats of demolition in 1925 and was eventually restored by novelist Frances Parkinson Keyes (*The Chess Players, Dinner at Antoine's*), who resided here from 1944 until her death in 1970. *Detroit Publishing Company, Library of Congress, no. LC-D4-16333 DLC*

1996 Same site

After the building on the far left of the 1903 photograph was removed, Mrs. Keyes hired Koch and Wilson in 1954 to restore the elegant garden that once adjoined the house from the 1830s to 1865. To the right of the mansion, a sturdy townhouse has replaced the old dormered Creole cottages of the 1903 scene. Across the street at the extreme right is St. Mary's Catholic Church (1845), connected to the Ursuline Convent (1750), one of the very few surviving French colonial structures in the city and probably the oldest building in the Mississippi Valley. The Ursuline nuns, agents of religion and education to the isolated colonial outpost of New Orleans, controlled the four blocks surrounding this site until the early American years, when they moved to a convent near today's Industrial Canal.

French Quarter

circa 1890 715 Dauphine Street at the Orleans intersection, in the French Quarter

An 1864 notarial record of the 715 Dauphine home (right) describes it as "a two story brick dwelling house, slate roofed, having one room on the ground floor used as a store and hall, and on the second floor three rooms with fire places, hall, closet and iron veranda in front, one large room in the attic, a two story brick kitchen, slate roofed, having two rooms on the ground floor, and three rooms upstairs, all with fire places, yard paved with brick, privies built of brick, water works, etc." The building briefly housed the German Evangelical Lutheran Bethlehem Orphan Asylum Association from 1900-1902. On the left is the Gardette-Le Prêtre House (1836), outstanding for its unusual arrangement of floors and cast-iron lace galleries supported by eighteen-foot columns. The Victorian dome of the Mercier Building (p. 187) on Canal Street is visible in the distance. *Photograph by William Henry Jackson, Detroit Publishing Company, Library of Congress, no. LC-D418-8109 DLC*

96

1996 Same site

Note the changes to the corner structure's roof and to its neighbors on Dauphine. Streets such as this one in the Vieux Carré and other historic districts in New Orleans are among the last significant pedestrian-scale urban settings in the South, places where corner stores, analog bank clocks, alleys, and sidewalks (occasionally still called *banquettes* here) are the rule, not the exception. About 50 percent of the urbanized area within the New Orleans city limits and perhaps 25 percent of the greater metropolitan area comprise these historically and architecturally interesting human-scale neighborhoods.

French Quarter

circa 1906 "Italian Headquarters," Madison Street at the Decatur intersection, in the French Quarter

This scene of Madison Street, near the French Market, has a diorama-like effect to it. The two-story structure at left is a replacement (or possibly a modification) of a three-story Creole townhouse that housed the J. Tassin clothing store in previous decades; at right is Madame Bégué's Restaurant, a famed local eatery catering to the market crowd. In the turn-of-the-century years, this part of the French Quarter was New Orleans' Little Italy. The cast-iron cones marking the corners were designed to prevent horse-drawn carts from cutting across the curb and were a common sight in the pre-automobile age. *Detroit Publishing Company, Library of Congress, no. LC-D4-19309 DLC*

1996 Same site

The Creole townhouse (1830) at right, now Tujague's Restaurant, retains its original design, but the structure at left has passed through a series of alterations. Its cornice was replaced by this parapet sometime before 1920, and by about 1940 the gallery was removed for a Spanish Revival-style tiled awning, leaving only a box balcony, and a corner entrance was created. In 1948 the second-floor French doors and their heavy moldings were simplified into plain windows when the lower half of the building was modernized and the awning removed. Sometime during these changes, the hip roof barely visible in the *circa* 1906 scene was flattened into a terrace roof, though the chimney remains. Use of the structure also varied with the times: the Glose Bargain Store catered to sailors and marketers in the 1910s, Buck's sold its "famous fried chicken" in the 1950s and 1960s, and today a more upscale Greek restaurant operates here. The stylistic changes reduced the once-picturesque storehouse to a rather plain building. Corner cones have been removed throughout the city, though some old ones remain and others have been reinstalled as interesting "street furniture."

French Quarter

circa 1906 823 Decatur Street at the Madison intersection, in the French Quarter

A closer look at the Creole corner building (1830) in which Bégué's Restaurant operated, across from the French Market. Madame Bégué (Elizabeth Kettenring) was a German immigrant woman who, through her Creole cooking and famous six-course, four-hour Bohemian breakfasts (cost: one dollar, including wine), made this site famous from 1856 to the early 1900s. Guillaume Tujague, a Frenchman who worked as a butcher in the market, opened another restaurant next door in the 1880s. *Detroit Publishing Company, Library of Congress, no. LC-D4-16337 DLC*

1996 Same site

The two old market restaurants that occupied this corner share their heritage today as Tujague's Restaurant. Its neon sign, dormers, and chimneys contribute to the picturesque roofscape of the French Market area. Note the corner entrance, a very common and logical feature of ground-floor commercial establishments in the old city, designed to maximize the store's exposure and accessibility to pedestrian traffic.

French Quarter

1952 French Market district of the French Quarter

Between Jackson Square (left) and the U.S. Mint (lower right) are the elongated structures comprising the French Market. This swath of the Mississippi River's natural levee has been used continuously as a market since 1791; though some components date back to 1813, most of the current market buildings were remodeled or rebuilt by the Works Progress Administration during the Depression. The cars parked in front of the U.S. Mint (1835; bottom right) occupy former Gallatin Street, a violent nineteenth-century red-light district that evolved into a slum (p. 110) until the WPA eliminated half its buildings.

At right center is the Ursuline Convent (1750); just below it, casting a shadow on the lot behind the convent, is St. Mary's Italian School (*circa* 1870), a two-story addition to a 1787 chapel built for the Ursulines by Don Andres Almonester y Roxas. The school complemented St. Mary's Church (1845), on the other side of the convent. Note the degree to which the Quarter is separated from the river by a barrier of industrial infrastructure. *U.S. Geological Survey*

1989 Same area

Since the 1970s, the Vieux Carré riverfront has shifted from the port to the tourist industry, with wharves and warehouses largely replaced by parking lots and landscaped parks, such as the Moonwalk (1976, lower left). In a 1992 article on the riverfront, writer Frank Gagnard of the *Times-Picayune* noted the gentrification of adjacent Decatur Street—"once a gamy preserve of boisterous foreign seamen's bars"—and observed that "gains in civility sometimes mean a loss of defining character." Today only the Governor Nicholls Street Wharf (lower right) maintains the French Quarter's historic association with the shipping industry. Note the cleared lot behind the Ursuline Convent (right center): St. Mary's Italian School closed in 1963 and was partially demolished in the early 1970s; its remaining ground floor, the 1787 Almonester Chapel, deteriorated away in the 1980s. In the residential areas along Chartres and Royal (upper half of photograph), note the intricate cityscape formed by dormers, chimneys, hip roofs, servants' quarters, and courtyards. This is a rare sight in modern America. *Army Corps of Engineers, New Orleans District*

French Quarter

circa 1906 Looking down Decatur (left) and North Peters Streets near the Dumaine intersection, in the French Market district of the French Quarter

A busy French Market scene in turn-of-the-century New Orleans. Note the tropical fruits for sale in the stall, and the price of bananas: ten cents a dozen. New Orleans has played an important role in the development of the tropical-fruit industry in Central and South America and—not unrelatedly—has been embroiled in a number of political intrigues in Latin American countries. The river rolls a few hundred feet to the right. *Detroit Publishing Company, The Historic New Orleans Collection, accession no. 1974.25.20.16*

circa 1940 Same site

1996 Same site

Top scene, *circa* **1940:** The Morning Call Coffee Stand, shown in this postcard after the WPA renovations of the 1930s, was founded by an immigrant from Yugoslavia, Joseph Jurasich, and operated near this end of the French Market from 1870 until its move to suburban Metairie in 1974. **Bottom scene, 1996:** The intersection as it appears today. Once the sun rises a bit higher, this section of the French Quarter will come to life as thousands of visitors peruse the many shops and restaurants of the French Market and adjacent areas. Note both the removal of the "Market Store" pediment and the dormers and chimneys of the buildings along Decatur Street and the continued use of canvas awnings along the galleries of the buildings on the left. *Postcard from The Historic New Orleans Collection, accession no. 1981.350.126*

French Quarter

circa 1905 North Peters Street at the Decatur intersection, in the French Market district of the French Quarter

This is a side view of the stall shown in the previous photograph. Here the grid pattern of the original city bends to adjust to the river; the resultant wedge-shaped blocks have been home to a series of markets for more than two centuries. This stall marks the first tip of those triangular blocks, between angular North Peters in the foreground and orthogonal Decatur in the background.

Stalls in city markets were often family-owned and passed down from generation to generation. The children of immigrants in this Sicilian neighborhood worked alongside their parents in the French Market. *Detroit Publishing Company, Library of Congress, no. LC-D4-39639 DLC*

1996 Same site

The stall is long gone, eliminated during the WPA renovations of the 1930s. The ensemble of commercial structures lining Decatur Street persists, and although the clientele consists mostly of out-of-town tourists, these businesses still depend on their proximity to the French Market for a steady stream of customers.

French Quarter

8113. THE OLD FRENCH MARKET, NEW ORLEANS,   DETROIT PHOTOGRAPHIC CO.

circa 1890 Looking up North Peters and Decatur Street toward the Dumaine intersection, in the French Market district of the French Quarter

William Henry Jackson captured this unposed moment of history at the French Market, where North Peters bends away from Decatur and follows the river.

Photograph by William Henry Jackson, Detroit Publishing Company, Library of Congress, no. LC-D418-8113 DLC

1997 Same site

North Peter's bend and the dormered storehouses, two of which had been demolished since the 1890s, anchor the modern scene to its former moment. Municipal markets are gone from New Orleans and the nation (except for those oriented toward tourist or upscale specialty items) but are alive and well in nearly every Caribbean and Latin American city.

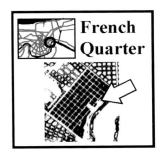

French Quarter

circa 1930 Gallatin Street looking toward Ursulines (top) and toward Barracks (bottom), in the French Quarter

Gallatin Street, "the most dangerous place on Earth," was a violent and seedy strip at the downriver corner of the Vieux Carré. It had quieted down by the time these photographs were taken but was still considered an eyesore whose time had come. Note the U.S. Mint (1835) in the distance of the bottom photograph. A 1922 oblique perspective of Gallatin Street appears on p. 379. *Photograph by C. Gill, Koch and Wilson, The Historic New Orleans Collection, Sq. 12-13, Vieux Carré Survey.*

110

1996 Same sites

The street and its riverside buildings were wiped off the French Quarter map by the Works Progress Administration during the Depression. Gallatin Street is now French Market Place, and its buildings have been replaced by the fruit and vegetable market and the flea market. Vendors set up booths every morning to sell produce, crafts, and souvenirs. The dismantling of Gallatin Street robbed the area of the impressive vista formed by the cluttered, narrow street scene in the foreground terminating at the great Greek Revival U.S. Mint in the background. A very similar vista survives today at the exact opposite end of the Quarter, where Clinton Street frames a dramatic view of the U.S. Custom House. Coincidentally, Clinton Street today is almost as quiet and forgotten as Gallatin Street appeared in the 1930s.

French Quarter

111

circa 1950 93 to 97 French Market Place at the Barracks intersection, in the French Quarter

Construction of this Creole-style structure (1838) was initiated by John Boyd Gilchrist and completed by John de Young on Barracks between former Gallatin Street (now French Market Place) and Levee Street (now Decatur). The complex is well balanced across the span of Barracks Street, with identical two-bay, two-and-a-half-story elevations at each end. Across the street to the right is the U.S. Mint. Throughout the late 1800s and first half of the 1900s, this downriver section of the French Quarter, adjacent to the French Market, was populated largely by Sicilians engaged in the fruit and vegetable trade. The Monteleone Bros. owned a wholesale produce business here in the 1950s. *Charles Franck Collection, The Historic New Orleans Collection, accession no. 1979.325.1983*

112

1996 Same site

As the area evolved from a working-class market district to a tourist destination, the Monteleone Bros. produce business was eventually replaced by a gourmet-pizza restaurant. Some traces of the old Sicilian population, in the form of fading advertisements painted on walls, are still visible on the structures paralleling the French Market, and some of the buildings are still dedicated to the storage and movement of produce to the fruit and vegetable market. In December 1996 this corner was the site of a spontaneous public memorial to the victims of the terrible triple murder that occurred in the restaurant kitchen.

French Quarter

circa 1890 United States Mint, 400 Esplanade Avenue at the North Peters intersection, in the French Quarter

Ships heading toward colonial New Orleans passed this corner of the original city first, hence lower Esplanade was fortified throughout the colonial era (Fort San Carlos) and early American era (Fort St. Charles) until 1821. For the next fifteen years, a landscaped commons called Jackson Place occupied the site. The United States Mint, shown here, was designed by William Strickland and erected in 1835-38 to stamp gold and silver coinage for the growing republic. The Greek Revival edifice was seized for Confederate use in 1861; during the 1862 capitulation, a man named William B. Mumford desecrated the newly raised Union flag at the mint, an act of defiance that prompted the federals to threaten New Orleans with destruction. After the formal surrender, occupying Gen. Benjamin F. Butler earned the hatred of the city when he hanged Mumford at the scene of his defiance. The building was back in operation as a federal mint when this photograph was taken. Note the large chimneys used in the minting operation, now removed. *Detroit Publishing Company, Library of Congress, no. LC-D4-4885 DLC*

1997 Same site

After the mint closed in 1909, the building was used as a prison, veterans office, and Coast Guard station before it was surplussed by the Government Services Administration in 1966 and eventually transferred to the state of Louisiana. Political apathy at the state level allowed the old mint to slide toward ruin in the 1970s, until local activists and the Louisiana State Museum acquired money to restore it as part of the state museum system. Today the structure lives on as the first major mint established outside the Northeast, the only mint where Confederate coins were struck, and the oldest surviving mint in the nation. The museum, reopened in 1983, contains a research library and exhibits on jazz, Mardi Gras, and the building itself. Sturdy and massive, it anchors Esplanade Avenue as the U.S. Custom House anchors Canal Street at the opposite end of the French Quarter.

1952 Upper Chartres, Decatur, North Peters, and the riverfront, in the French Quarter

A closer look at the cityscape by the river, with the U.S. Custom House on the left, Jackson Square on the right, and the Civil Courts Building at top center. To the right of the T-shaped courthouse is the empty lot that once was the St. Louis Hotel. Only four of its Chartres Street stores, visible at the bottom of the empty lot, remained after the hotel's 1916 demolition. This photograph covers the area that burned in the great fire of December 8, 1794. The blaze, which consumed 212 structures and resulted in stricter building codes, started at 534 Royal Street, about one block to the upper right of the Civil Courts Building. For oblique perspectives of this area, refer to pp. 32-35. *U.S. Geological Survey*

1989 Same area

The land at lower left was built up by sediments deposited by the shifting Mississippi during the early nineteenth century. The resulting batture was well utilized by port businesses for a century and a half, giving this district a gritty, industrial atmosphere. From 1946 to 1964, the area bounded by Iberville, Decatur, St. Peter, and the river was removed from Vieux Carré Commission jurisdiction; consequently, many old industrial structures were gradually replaced by parking lots. By the late 1960s, the French Quarter riverfront came to be seen as a great land-development opportunity, as evidenced by the ambi-

tious proposals produced by the Tulane University School of Architecture. The more grandiose plans never materialized; instead, the riverfront was landscaped and named Woldenberg Park, designed to connect French Quarter visitors with the river and place their experience in a geographical context. The remaining acres of parking lots, however, have worked against this connection. *Army Corps of Engineers, New Orleans District*

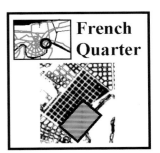

117

1920 Douglas Public Service "Block Y" Warehouse, 118 North Front Street near the Iberville intersection, in the French Quarter

1951 Douglas Public Service "Block Y" Warehouse, 118 North Front Street near the Iberville intersection, in the French Quarter

Left scene, 1920: The Douglas Public Service "Block Y" Warehouse, located in the industrialized young batture of the upper Quarter, offers its services to the port city. Notarial records for this block commence in the 1840s, when the new land was sold by the First Municipality to the private sector. In 1888 Allen Moffett sold the block bounded by North Front, Customhouse (now Iberville), Wells, and Crossman (now gone) to the Louisiana Sugar Refining Company for $40,000, which in 1891 sold it to the American Sugar Company for $111,000. The drastically increased price may reflect the construction of this warehouse. In 1919 the sugar interest sold the block to William H. Douglas who in the same year sold it to the Douglas Public Service Corporation, also for $111,000. The unchanged price after twenty-eight years may reflect decreased land values after the relocation of some sugar facilities to St. Bernard Parish, where Domino currently operates. **Right scene, 1951:** The messages are reworded, and the mules are replaced by dinosaurs. The parking lot at left is a harbinger of future uses of this area. *Charles Franck Collection, The Historic New Orleans Collection, accession nos. 1979.325.679 and 1979.325.682*

118

1997 Same site

Because its former industrial use precluded the development of classic French Quarter streetscapes, this section of the Quarter was altered greatly as the area retooled for the tourism trade. The elimination of old sugar and port facilities was further enabled by the 1946-64 exclusion of the area from Vieux Carré Commission jurisdiction. Later in the 1960s, this land was slated for the construction of the Riverfront Expressway, which would have ascended from its Canal Street tunnel at the site of the Block Y Warehouse. The project was canceled in 1969. Three years later, the Douglas Public Service Corporation sold the warehouse to real-estate tycoon Joseph Canizaro for $500,000, and for a while the fine brick structure seemed to be heading for a career change as a restaurant and nightclub arcade, part of Canizaro's vision for the Canal Place development. On Mardi Gras morning 1975, vagrants with other ideas set the empty warehouse ablaze, thus ending the landmark's interesting history. Today parking lots cover much of the batture, and the site of the old warehouse is now occupied by a garage topped with an upscale hotel. This is the rear of Canizaro's ambitious Canal Place complex, which wiped Crossman Street off the map.

French Quarter

1895 Sugar and Rice Exchange, 301 North Front Street at Bienville, in the French Quarter

The Louisiana Sugar Exchange was organized in 1883 and moved into this new building, designed by James Freret and located near the riverside sugar facilities, the following year. Responsible for the buying, selling, grading, regulation, and promotion of sugar and molasses, the organization expanded to include the rice industry in 1889 and changed its name to the Louisiana Sugar and Rice Exchange. For decades, the economics of these vital Louisiana crops were played out under the sixty-five-foot dome and timber columns of this graceful building. *The Historic New Orleans Collection, accession no. 1974.25.3.210*

1997 Same view

The scene today presents an equally intriguing roofscape, ranging from nineteenth-century church spires to satellite dishes. In recent decades, the first block of Bourbon Street was bleak and featureless, a surprising lost opportunity at the intersection of the city's two most famous streets, Bourbon and Canal.

Since 1995, some new businesses have been carved out of the brick walls. See pp. 192-93 for perspectives of this area taken from the opposite direction. *Special thanks to Latter & Blum for access to this view.*

French Quarter

circa 1905 **Adjacent view of Bourbon Street, Canal Street, and the French Quarter, looking from the Central Business District**

The domed St. Louis Hotel and City Exchange (1840) appears at center, aligned with the spires of the St. Louis Cathedral. At right is the dome of James Gallier's Merchants' Exchange on Royal Street, built in 1835-38 in what was once an important financial district. The Cosmopolitan Hotel's Bourbon Street unit is the large six-story structure just beneath the brewery smokestack; its Royal Street branch (p. 44) is well marked near the domed Merchants' Exchange. The galleried stores (lower right center) on Canal Street are the remnants of Touro Row, which once spanned Canal from Royal to Bourbon (p. 196). *Detroit Publishing Company, Library of Congress, no. LC-D4-37050 LC DLC*

1997 Same view

An island of high-rise hotels (one of which, the original Monteleone, dates from 1908) emerges from the upper French Quarter. While economic pressure has encouraged downtown hotel development to expand upwards by dozens of stories, retail space has shrunk down to street level. Note how the Woolworth building (now closed) indents the once-contiguous line of multistory commer-

cial buildings. Along Canal Street and adjacent areas, upper stories that were once occupied by shops and offices are now largely empty. See pp. 36-39 for other oblique perspectives of the upper French Quarter. *Special thanks to Latter & Blum for access to this view.*

French Quarter

circa 1858 Esplanade Avenue at the Royal Street intersection, looking toward Lake Pontchartrain

Esplanade Avenue was a corridor of Creole affluence in the nineteenth century, countered by the Anglos' St. Charles and Jackson Avenues. The grand avenue follows a slight ridge from the natural levee of the Mississippi inland toward Bayou St. John. The leeches advertised here were probably used for bloodletting, a common treatment for yellow fever and other illnesses. (Architect

James Gallier Sr. described in his autobiography such a therapy for his 1835 bout with "yellow jack," in which he lost ninety-six ounces of blood. Today leeches are used to circulate blood in severed digits during operations.) *Photograph by Jay Dearborn Edwards, The Historic New Orleans Collection, accession no. 1982.167.11*

126

1996 Same site

Nearly the entire span of Esplanade Avenue, from the Mississippi River to Bayou St. John, retains its indigenous, historical character. Live oaks shade most of the avenue, and although many nineteenth-century Creole mansions have been replaced by early-twentieth-century Spanish Revival-style homes, the *tout ensemble* of the avenue survives.

Esplanade Avenue

circa 1858 **Esplanade Avenue at Royal Street, looking toward Lake Pontchartrain**

A broader view of Esplanade Avenue and its neutral ground of sycamore trees. Esplanade between the French Quarter and Faubourg Marigny roughly follows the oblique path of the colonial palisades and moat that connected Fort San Carlos (near the site of the U.S. Mint) and Fort San Juan (now the Barracks/Rampart intersection). From 1836 to 1852 the avenue served as a political boundary between the First and Third Municipalities, essentially two separate cities. Due in part to this heritage, the properties along lower Esplanade have a complex cadastral history. The twin Greek Revival town-houses at left were built in the 1840s on land once owned by Judah Touro, an influential businessman responsible for numerous commercial, charitable, and religious institutions in the city. *Photograph by Jay Dearborn Edwards, The Historic New Orleans Collection, accession no. 1982.167.5*

1996 Same site

The left unit of the twin Greek Revival townhouses in the *circa* 1858 perspective burned in 1893; the remaining structure was restored to its antebellum appearance in the 1970s. Esplanade's shady neutral ground draws joggers and strollers from the Vieux Carré (left) and Faubourg Marigny (right). See p. 379 for an oblique perspective of historic Esplanade Avenue.

Esplanade Avenue

05737 ESPLANADE STREET, NEW ORLEANS,   COPYRIGHT 1900 - BY DETROIT PHOTOGRAPHIC CO

circa 1900   Esplanade Avenue at Burgundy Street, looking toward Lake Pontchartrain

This view of Esplanade Avenue was taken three blocks up from the previous scenes and about forty years later. Most of these townhouses, near the site of old Fort St. Jean (San Juan to the Spanish, St. John to the Americans) when the city was fortified, were built between 1830 and 1850. The whitewashed tree trunks are a tradition still seen in the region, especially in the bayou country south and west of the city. It is a very common practice in Latin America. *Detroit Publishing Company, Library of Congress, no. LC-D4-5737 DLC*

1996 Same site

Behind the leafy magnolias and oaks, the scene is intact today. Of the city's grand avenues, Esplanade maintains perhaps the most contiguous collection of historical and architecturally significant buildings. The avenue forms the spine of the Esplanade Ridge National Historic District.

Esplanade
Avenue

circa 1910 **Gayarré Place, 2200 block of Esplanade Avenue at Bayou Road, in the Esplanade Ridge**

This gentle intersection, forming a triangular park dedicated to local historian Charles Gayarré, is not the repercussion of a riverbend but the product of an ancient road that connected the original city with Bayou St. John and thence Lake Pontchartrain, the Gulf of Mexico, and the world. As the first road in the area, Bayou Road (left behind statue) ran along a slight ridge, a few feet above sea level but enough to rise above the surrounding swamps, and followed a crooked course from Bayou St. John to the natural levee of the Mississippi River. This statue of Ceres stands on a terra-cotta pedestal that is one of the few remnants of the World's Industrial and Cotton Centennial Exposition, held at present-day Audubon Park in 1884. *Detroit Publishing Company, Library of Congress, no. LC-D4-39613 DLC*

1996 Same site

Bayou Road (left behind statue) veers toward Bayou St. John, about one mile behind the photographer; Esplanade Avenue (right) heads straight down to the river, a mile ahead. Like other old residential districts in New Orleans, Esplanade Avenue's beautiful canopy of trees constitutes the major apparent difference in the modern streetscape. Properties along curved Bayou Road (which joins Governor Nicholls at its lower end and Grand Route St. John at its upper end) face their street perpendicularly but appear crooked when compared (on a map or from the air) with the orthogonal lots abutting rectilinear Esplanade Avenue. See pp. 12, 146, and 380 for aerial views of Bayou Road. To see how New Orleans handles other acute-angle, wedge-shaped intersections such as this one marked by Gayarré Place, see pp. 104, 318, 324, 332, and 356.

Esplanade Avenue

1952 Faubourg Marigny

Faubourg Marigny was subdivided out of the plantation of Bernard de Marigny in 1806 and became New Orleans' second suburb, after Faubourg Ste. Marie in 1788. For years the downriver community was home to a diversity of ethnicities, including French, Spanish, African, German, Dutch, Irish, and *gens de couleur libres* (free people of color), many from Saint-Domingue. In 1836 Faubourg Marigny and adjacent Creole faubourgs were designated as the Third Municipality in the city's sixteen-year experiment with self-governing municipalities. In this scene, the arteries forming the "Marigny Triangle" are shady Esplanade Avenue and sunny Elysian Fields, which converge at the Mississippi River at bottom right, and McShane Place (curved street at upper left), created in 1927 to ease the flow of traffic between North Rampart and St. Claude. Note the shadow of a steeple touching the lower edge of Washington Square, the park at center right: this is cast by the Holy Redeemer Roman Catholic Church (1858, formerly the Third Presbyterian), on Royal between Frenchmen and Elysian Fields. For a 1922 oblique perspective of this area, refer to p. 379. *U.S. Geological Survey*

1989 Same area

Removed from business-district congestion and industrial tourism, Faubourg Marigny has resisted large-scale change and maintains an intimate, village-scale atmosphere, with one exception: the dramatically out-of-place International-style apartment built in the early 1970s on the sites of the Holy Redeemer Church and an old Carnegie library branch at Washington Square. The construction of the Christopher Inn Apartments, visible just below the park at center right, galvanized the formation of the Faubourg Marigny Improvement Association, which has since become a model for grassroots community revitalization. One of its many achievements was the 1976 restoration of Washington Square to its nineteenth-century grandeur after decades as a sloppy baseball field. Note both the shade trees that have grown on Elysian Fields' neutral ground and the cleared lots at the foot of the avenue. *Army Corps of Engineers, New Orleans District*

Faubourg Marigny

1948 Lacroix Building, 501 Esplanade Avenue at the Decatur intersection, in Faubourg Marigny

1950 Lacroix Building, 501 Esplanade Avenue at the Decatur intersection, in Faubourg Marigny

Left scene, 1948: This beautiful mansard-roof structure, located where the old colonial palisade adjoined Fort San Carlos, was built for Julien Adolphe Lacroix in the 1850s. The building was originally Creole in style, with a hip roof and galleries, before the mansard roof was added in the late 1800s. Lacroix and his brother François were wealthy *gens de couleur libres* in antebellum New Orleans, making their fortunes in real estate and groceries. Note the graceful shepherd's crook lamppost. **Right scene, 1950:** A cigarette distributor moves in and—taking no risks—installs exhaust fans and a fire escape. Note also the two new dormers in the mansard roof. Dormers of old structures are more often removed (to improve insulation and minimize leaks) than added. *Charles Franck Collection, The Historic New Orleans Collection, accession nos. 1979.325.670 and 1979.325.671*

1996 Same site

The oak tree in Esplanade's neutral ground practically touches the old Lacroix building, which now houses Checkpoint Charlie, catering to a local crowd as a bar, grill, launderette, game room, and live-music venue. The staff of the shepherd's crook lamppost still stands; this style of lamppost illuminated nearly every street corner in downtown New Orleans during the first half of the twentieth century. A few still exist, and some new ones have been installed.

Faubourg Marigny

1944 and 1951 Lacroix Buildings, 1407 to 1411 Decatur Street and 500 to 506 Frenchmen Street, in Faubourg Marigny

Top scene, 1944: Next to the corner Lacroix Building on the previous page are these townhouses, also built in the 1850s for a successful grocer and businessman, Julien Adolphe Lacroix. The obtuse angle of this intersection reflects the effort to conform the layout of Faubourg Marigny (1806) to the grid pattern of the Vieux Carré, extant land divisions, and the bend of the river. Note the Philippino Community Center, another testimony to the incredible ethnic diversity of this historic neighborhood.
Bottom scene, 1951: The upper floor has been tidied up, and new businesses have moved in below. Note the liquor establishment on the left, tastelessly named "The Lost Week End." *Charles Franck Collection, The Historic New Orleans Collection, accession nos. 1979.325.663 and 1979.325.675*

1996 Same site

Faubourg Marigny is now home to a large gay community, and the Lacroix complex houses the office of an AIDS activist organization. Note the changes on the second floor: masonry posts removed from the gallery railing, air conditioners inserted in some attic windows, and awnings removed from the French doors to reveal the original granite lintels.

Faubourg Marigny

1949 2100 to 2102 Chartres Street at the Frenchmen intersection, in Faubourg Marigny

A commercial-residential corner scene in the neighborhood, at a time when the historic name Faubourg Marigny was not commonly used in reference to this district. The appellation was brought back when citizens revitalized the neighborhood in the 1970s. *Charles Franck Collection, The Historic New Orleans Collection, accession no. 1979.325.676*

1996 Same site

The Home Beverage & Food Service is now the Café Brasil dance club, and within a few years, the funky ambiance of Faubourg Marigny may follow the neighboring French Quarter in terms of gentrification, if not tourism. The pole on the opposite corner bulges with accumulated fliers for live-music gigs, a fair indicator that the neighborhood is no longer a sleepy enclave of "yats" (blue-collar locals known for their distinctive New Orleans accents, epitomized in the salutation "Where y'at?"). Nevertheless, Faubourg Marigny remains a model for neighborhood revitalization, and a spirit of optimism prevails. Note that the manhole covers, like fire hydrants, hold onto their turf in evolving cityscapes.

Faubourg Marigny

circa 1858 Third District Market, Elysian Fields Avenue at the North Peters intersection, in Faubourg Marigny

The Third District Market (Port Market, *circa* 1835) was located along the river near the "vertex" of the Marigny Triangle, formed by Esplanade and Elysian Fields. This scene was captured from the foot of Elysian Fields looking into what is now the 2200 block of North Peters. "Third District" is a post-1852 term for this area, following the consolidation of the city after sixteen years as three self-governing municipalities united by a single mayor. During the municipality era (1836-52), the French Quarter formed the First Municipality, the American Sector was the Second, and this Creole faubourg became the Third. After 1852, the municipalities were renamed "districts" and renumerated as the First District (American Sector), Second (French Quarter), Third (Creole faubourgs), and Fourth (uptown Lafayette). Near this site, New Orleans' first railroad (1831) departed for Lake Pontchartrain via Elysian Fields, the first mechanized connection between the river and the lake. *Photograph by Jay Dearborn Edwards, The Historic New Orleans Collection, accession no. 1982.167.8*

1996 Same site

Riverfront areas such as this one, dedicated to the efficient breaking of bulk, are prone to volatile changes in landscape; today little remains of old riverfront scenes *anywhere* in New Orleans. With the planned relocation of Mississippi River wharves to the Industrial Canal in the 1960s, residential and recreational development of the riverside became an option. A 1974 City Edges Project entitled *New Orleans and the River*, produced by the Tulane University School of Architecture, proposed a grand semicircular residential plaza for this site to exploit the geographical interaction of Esplanade, Elysian Fields, and the river.

The plan never materialized, and the locale is utilized today in an appropriately historical manner—as a series of wharves. After 101 years, rail service on Elysian Fields to Lake Pontchartrain ended in 1932, and the last tracks marking New Orleans' first railroad route were removed in 1954. The railroad explains Elysian Fields' beeline from the river to the lake, the only street in New Orleans to connect those water bodies with a straight line.

Faubourg Marigny

1918 St. Charles Power House, Marigny Street at Decatur, looking toward the river, in Faubourg Marigny

The New Orleans Railway and Light Company's St. Charles Power House and Car Barn operated out of this series of structures near the river in Faubourg Marigny. The shed on the left was the car barn, the two-story corner building served as an office, and the three adjoining units to the right housed repair shops. An engine room anchored the far end of the block. Note the rolling stock in the distance, on the tracks paralleling the river. *Charles Franck Collection, The Historic New Orleans Collection, accession no. 1979.325.664*

1996 Same site

The new building, housing the Standard Coffee Company, has dimensions reminiscent of the former structures. Streetcars are now serviced at the opposite end of the city, in the Carrollton Streetcar Barn (p. 361).

Faubourg Marigny

1952 Faubourg Tremé

Faubourg Tremé was subdivided out of the Claude Tremé plantation in 1810 and, like Faubourg Marigny, was dominated by a Creole populace. North Rampart (double street with neutral ground) runs parallel to the bottom; below it is the French Quarter and above it is Tremé. The rectangular swath at upper left (with the curved railroad tracks that lead to Terminal Station) was the Carondelet Canal (pp. 156 and 381), dug by the Spanish in 1795 to connect the city with the lake and filled in during the 1930s. The large structure to the right of the old basin is the Municipal Auditorium (1929), and among the trees below the auditorium is Congo Square, a slave rendezvous in the early 1800s. Note the above-ground St. Louis cemeteries (upper left) which—together with the nearby Old Mortuary Chapel, original Charity Hospital, and the earliest cemetery (on St. Peters and Rampart)—were all located on the outskirts of town due to fear of contagion. Note also the presubdivision parcel orientations of gently curving Governor Nicholls Street (upper right), which is part of the eighteenth-century Bayou Road portage and bears that historic name lakeside of Claiborne Avenue. *U.S. Geological Survey*

146

1989 Same area

Between 1956 and 1973, ten blocks of old Tremé were leveled and more than one thousand people were relocated to make room for an urban renewal project that eventually became Louis Armstrong Park and the Mahalia Jackson Theatre for the Performing Arts (center). Also in this era, Orleans Avenue and Basin Street were adapted for the traffic exiting Interstate 10 (out of view at top) and heading toward the business district. Despite these drastic alterations and the ongoing scourges of crime and decay, much of historic Tremé endures.

It is often called America's oldest black neighborhood. The landmark tower of St. Augustine (1842, next page) is visible four blocks to the right of the Municipal Auditorium (p. 151); the empty lots next to the church mark the site of Claude Tremé's plantation house, demolished in 1926. See p. 381 for an oblique view of Tremé. *Army Corps of Engineers, New Orleans District*

Faubourg Tremé

147

circa 1910 St. Augustine Church, 1100 block of St. Claude at the Governor Nicholls intersection, in Faubourg Tremé

The city's first institution of higher learning, Collège d'Orléans, operated here from 1811 to 1825. The land near the Claude Tremé plantation house was later donated by the Ursuline nuns for the St. Augustine Roman Catholic Church, designed by J. N. B. de Pouilly and built in 1842 to serve the racially mixed Creole populace of Faubourg Tremé. In 1892 a St. Augustine parishioner named Homer Plessy tested the post-Reconstruction Jim Crow laws by sitting in the whites-only car of a train bound for the north shore of Lake Pontchartrain. The failure of *Plessy v. Ferguson* set the "separate but equal" legal precedent that would entrench segregation in the South for the next half-century. Plessy, who died in 1925, is buried a few blocks from St. Augustine in the integrated St. Louis Cemetery No. 1. John Howard Ferguson, the carpetbagger judge who ruled in the initial case, is buried a world away in the uptown Lafayette Cemetery. In the history books, however, their names are forever linked. *The Historic New Orleans Collection, accession no. 1975.21.44*

1996 Same site

St. Augustine is one of the most picturesque churches in the city, reminiscent of a rural Central American or Caribbean plaza scene. Its bell-shaped patina cupola resembles those that topped the three towers of St. Louis Cathedral prior to its 1851 reconstruction. St. Augustine's pews are arranged in a circular fashion, with the altar in the middle; it is said that the *gens de couleur libres* would sit in the central pews while slaves would occupy the outer benches. Though this section of Tremé is fairly intact, other parts of the historic faubourg have been gradually picked apart by the demolition of Storyville in the 1940s, the rerouting of Orleans and Basin Streets, and the development of Louis Armstrong Park in the 1960s-70s. At about this time, the neighborhood was cut in half and deprived of its "main street," Claiborne Avenue, by the construction of Interstate 10. Surviving sections of old Tremé are included in the Esplanade Ridge National Historic District.

Faubourg Tremé

circa 1890 Parish Prison, Orleans Street at the Tremé intersection, looking toward Lake Pontchartrain, in Faubourg Tremé

This stereogram depicts the ominous and storied Parish Prison (1836), right, on Orleans Street in Faubourg Tremé. In the distance is the Tremé Market, which extended from Marais to North Robertson and straddled the Villere Street intersection (under the tower) to allow streetcars to pass. Like the Poydras Market, the Tremé Market was an elongated public building occupying a neutral ground and marked by a picturesque tower. The Parish Prison served the city for sixty years and was the site of numerous executions and lynchings, most infamously in 1891, when eleven Sicilians recently acquitted of the mob-associated murder of Police Superintendent David C. Hennessy were killed by outraged citizens. At the time of this photograph, Orleans Street ran straight down to St. Louis Cathedral, the spires of which were probably visible from the Tremé Market tower, except perhaps for the trees at Congo Square. See p. 381 for a 1922 oblique perspective of this corridor. *The Historic New Orleans Collection, accession no. 1988.134.8*

150

1996 Same site

The Parish Prison was demolished in 1895 and replaced by a Spanish Revival-style municipal pumping station (1906), blocked from view by this Italian Renaissance-style Municipal Auditorium (1929). Orleans between Congo Square and North Villere has been altered beyond recognition as a result of the construction of the auditorium, the rerouting of the Orleans-Basin connection, the establishment of the Theatre for the Performing Arts, and the construction of Interstate 10. It is amusing to note that the elegant Mardi Gras balls, performances, and other functions held in the Municipal Auditorium over the years have taken place right next to the site of public executions and miserable nineteenth-century dungeons of the Parish Prison. Tremé Market is a distant memory, although commuters pass through its neutral-ground locale as they exit Interstate 10 and head toward the Quarter. In all, this area has played an important role in New Orleans' colorful history: within a few blocks are the sites of the old Storyville red-light district, the Carondelet Canal turning basin, the slaves' park at Congo Square, and the most important historic cemeteries in the city.

Faubourg Tremé

1952 Claiborne Avenue, from Tulane Avenue to St. Bernard Avenue, in Faubourg Tremé

Claiborne Avenue was a principal uptown-downtown corridor, with a bustling business community and a shady neutral ground, connecting a wide spectrum of New Orleans neighborhoods from Carrollton to Bywater. It has been described as the "Main Street of Black New Orleans." The swath of tracks and sheds (center left) running perpendicular to Claiborne marks the former bed of Carondelet Canal (1795). To its left, near the above-ground cemeteries, is the Iberville housing project (1941) that replaced Storyville, the legalized red-light district (1897-1917) that secured New Orleans' reputation for debauchery. This aerial photo covers portions of the Central Business District and Mid-City (left), Faubourg Tremé and the Esplanade Ridge (center and center right), and New Marigny (far right). See pp. 380-81 for oblique views of this area. *U.S. Geological Survey*

1994 Same area

Claiborne Avenue after Interstate 10 was built. Though a damaging intrusion to Tremé and a death knell to this portion of Claiborne, the elevated expressway provides observant drivers with poignant vistas of steep rooftops, ornate chimneys, and sagging servants' quarters in the 150-year-old street scenes of Faubourg Tremé. Many houses are in sad shape, and some are charred, collaps-

ing, or enveloped in wisteria. Claiborne Avenue runs through or near seven National Historic Districts—Carrollton, Uptown, Central City, Mid-City, Esplanade Ridge, New Marigny, and Bywater—more than any other New Orleans avenue. *U.S. Geological Survey*

Claiborne Avenue/ Faubourg Tremé

1947 North Rampart Street at Bienville, looking downriver (top), and at Conti, looking upriver, in Faubourg Tremé

North Rampart Street divides Faubourg Tremé from the Vieux Carré. Top scene: The Mortuary Chapel of St. Anthony (1826), located near St. Louis Cemetery No. 1, was used for funerals for yellow-fever victims during the terrible epidemics that plagued the city throughout the nineteenth century. In 1918 it was renamed Our Lady of Guadalupe and has served New Orleans' Irish, Italian, Philippino, and Hispanic populations, as well as the fire and police departments. Its steeple, similar to those of St. Louis Cathedral, replaced a Spanish-style dome that originally topped the tower. Bottom scene: A streetcar approaches from Canal Street. The last of James Gallier's Three Sisters (p. 72) is visible at center left, partially obscured by a tree and a doughnut sign. *Charles Franck Collection, The Historic New Orleans Collection, accession nos. 1979.325.5478 and 1979.325.5477*

1996 Same sites

Top scene: With automobiles replacing streetcars, North Rampart's neutral ground has shed its flanks to add an extra lane to each direction of traffic, forcing the relocation of the lampposts and the removal of the trees. **Bottom scene:** The skyline of the Central Business District looms in the background. The two blocks bounded by North Rampart, Conti, Burgundy, and Iberville, plus all the French Quarter properties facing North Rampart from Conti all the way to Esplanade Avenue, were excluded from Vieux Carré Commission protection from 1946 to 1964, resulting in the loss of a number of historic structures. Still, North Rampart Street between Faubourg Tremé and the Vieux Carré is an eclectic mix of nineteenth-century cottages, wealthy residences, parks, commercial buildings, and churches, a good sampler of New Orleans streetscapes.

Faubourg Tremé

155

circa 1900 **Carondelet Canal turning basin, Basin Street between Toulouse and St. Peter, in Faubourg Tremé**

New Orleans was strategically sited on the least-cost, minimum-distance route between the Gulf of Mexico and the Mississippi River. Only two terrestrial miles lay in the course from the Gulf, through Lakes Borgne and Pontchartrain, up Bayou St. John, and overland to the banks of the river. From 1792 to 1795, Spanish Governor Carondelet had a canal dug to eliminate most of those two terrestrial miles; this is the turning basin of that canal a century later. The waterway, dug by convicts and slaves, also drained adjacent swamps and was periodically widened to accommodate commerce. Carondelet Canal replaced old Bayou Road as one of the lifelines through which resources and people moved between the hinterlands and the outside world, a geographical concentration that helped form New Orleans' international character. The ballroom behind the tall windows of Globe Hall (Globe Exchange, center) was a famous place in the early days of jazz. The 1885 Sanborn insurance map identified its site as occupied by a two-story Masonic hall; in the map's 1908 revision, the three-story Globe Exchange is identified as a "Negro Dance Hall." *Detroit Publishing Company, Library of Congress, no. LC-D4-39634 DLC*

1996 Same site

Carondelet Canal, called Old Basin Canal to differentiate it from the Americans' New Basin Canal, was filled in from 1927 to 1938. The waterway and its parallel roads and railroads formed one of three important industrial corridors throughout the 1800s until the 1920s, with the New Basin Canal and the Mississippi providing competition. Now an open swath of lots and railroad beds, the configuration of the old canal is still readily apparent in modern maps and aerial photos (see pp. 146 and 381). Also gone are the dozens of lumberyards, mills, charcoal depots, and machinery shops that surrounded the miniature port. The chimney on the right marks the Spanish Revival-style municipal pumping station (1906) that replaced the old Parish Prison (p. 150).

Faubourg Tremé

157

circa 1905 **St. Roch's Chapel and Cemetery, St. Roch Avenue between North Derbigny and North Roman, in New Marigny**

The Gothic chapel (1876) in St. Roch Cemetery was built by the Reverend Peter Leonard Thevis in thanksgiving for the survival of his parishioners during the yellow-fever epidemic of 1868. The quaint Roman Catholic shrine and its Campo Santo cemetery (1874) are located in New Marigny, across St. Claude Avenue from Faubourg Marigny, a few blocks above the community landmark of St. Roch Market. Note the shadow of the entrance gate cast upon the foreground. *Detroit Publishing Company, Library of Congress, no. LC-D4-16331 DLC*

1996 Same site

St. Roch's Chapel was restored in 1949 by the Reverend Magnus Roth. Today the shrine and cemetery are clean, whitewashed, and well maintained. The altar in St. Roch's Chapel is traditionally surrounded with votives left by faithful parishioners and visitors; the mementos are now stored in a room to the side of the sanctuary. Father Thevis is entombed in the chapel.

New Marigny/ St. Roch

circa 1908 **St. Roch's Chapel and Cemetery, St. Roch Avenue between North Derbigny and North Roman, in New Marigny**

A side view of St. Roch's Chapel and Campo Santo. A few years before this photograph was taken, the chapel was enveloped in ivy. Here the Campo Santo brings to mind a place of rest in rural France or Germany; in fact, it was planned after the Campo Santo dei Tedeschi cemetery in Rome. *Detroit Publishing Company, Library of Congress, no. LC-D4-33064 DLC*

1996 Same site

The picket fence is now a wall of vaults, and the scene is decidedly more "New Orleans."

New Marigny/ St. Roch

circa 1910 **St. Michael's Chapel in St. Roch Cemetery No. 2, Music Street between North Derbigny and North Roman, in New Marigny**

Directly behind St. Roch's Chapel is St. Michael's Chapel (Mausoleum of Michael the Archangel, 1893-95) and St. Roch Cemetery No. 2, which served the German Catholic parishioners of the neighborhood. German-American citizens in New Orleans, especially the recently arrived, were less likely to practice the Latin custom of above-ground burial and apparently were not com-pelled by the physical reasons against subterranean interment—a high water table (possibly drained away by this date). Notice, however, the vaults surrounding the chapel. *Detroit Publishing Company, Library of Congress, no. LC-D4-39622 DLC*

1996 Same site

New Orleans eventually caught up with the Germans, and a miniature city of the dead now surrounds the whitewashed chapel. St. Michael's fell into decrepit condition by the 1930s but was eventually restored and is now lined with modernized vaults, inside and outside. Above-ground burial is no longer a necessity in the city since the turn-of-the-century drainage projects lowered the water table in the city to a level below that of a typical burial. The tradition persists: many of the tombs seen here are fairly recent.

New Marigny/ St. Roch

1995 and 1996 Jefferson Davis/Rivers Frederick School, North Johnson Street at the Touro intersection, in New Marigny

Top scene, 1995: For years, drivers on Interstate 10 caught sight of an impressive old brick schoolhouse near the Elysian Fields exit. It was the Jefferson Davis Public School, built in 1896, annexed in 1928, renamed the Rivers Frederick Junior High School after a local civic leader, and used for classes until about 1980. It became a sad dumping ground after it closed permanently in the early 1990s. The complex wooden roof and large windows seemed to invite a fiery end in this rough neighborhood, and in July 1995 the structure burned in a seven-alarm blaze. Shown here is the 1928 annex, viewed from the corner of North Johnson and Touro. **Bottom scene, 1996:** The ruins were cleared away in early 1996. *Photograph by Capt. Chris E. Mickal, New Orleans Fire Department Photo Unit*

164

1997 and 1998 Same site

For more than a year the site was a vacant lot at street level and a volume of air at interstate level, one more element of New Orleans' heritage forever subtracted from the landscape. **Top scene, 1997:** Then in 1997, construction began on twenty-four low-income homes in a development called Rivers Frederick Square. The houses were designed to agree with the scale and form of the cottages in the surrounding neighborhood. **Bottom scene, 1998:** The new community mends the hole in the old neighborhood.

New Marigny/ St. Roch

1952 and *circa* 1954 3301 Chartres Street at the Piety intersection, in Bywater

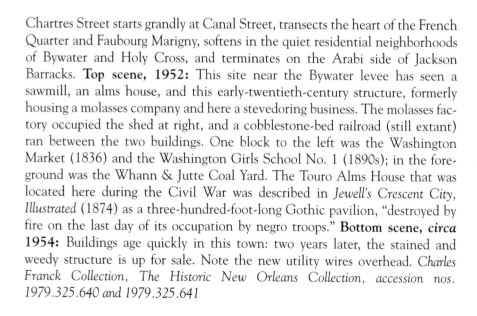

Chartres Street starts grandly at Canal Street, transects the heart of the French Quarter and Faubourg Marigny, softens in the quiet residential neighborhoods of Bywater and Holy Cross, and terminates on the Arabi side of Jackson Barracks. **Top scene, 1952:** This site near the Bywater levee has seen a sawmill, an alms house, and this early-twentieth-century structure, formerly housing a molasses company and here a stevedoring business. The molasses factory occupied the shed at right, and a cobblestone-bed railroad (still extant) ran between the two buildings. One block to the left was the Washington Market (1836) and the Washington Girls School No. 1 (1890s); in the foreground was the Whann & Jutte Coal Yard. The Touro Alms House that was located here during the Civil War was described in *Jewell's Crescent City, Illustrated* (1874) as a three-hundred-foot-long Gothic pavilion, "destroyed by fire on the last day of its occupation by negro troops." **Bottom scene, *circa* 1954:** Buildings age quickly in this town: two years later, the stained and weedy structure is up for sale. Note the new utility wires overhead. *Charles Franck Collection, The Historic New Orleans Collection, accession nos. 1979.325.640 and 1979.325.641*

166

1997 Same site

Little has changed in forty years. Bywater is the former Faubourg Washington, an early-nineteenth-century downriver neighborhood consisting of a number of smaller districts and plantations and dedicated to residential, industrial, and agricultural use. Today, Bywater is mostly residential, with industry lining the river. The neighborhood is a rarity in the 1990s: historic but not gentrified, interesting but not touristy, urban yet quiet and almost bucolic in its atmosphere (though crime and decay are constant concerns). It is one of those increasingly rare places in America, a pedestrian-scale neighborhood where residents may shop and dine at locally owned establishments within walking distance from home. "Bywater," an old telephone exchange and post office branch name, is a recent appellation for this part of the Ninth Ward, the product of a student contest sponsored by local businessmen in 1948.

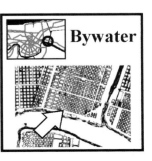

Bywater

1930 Lombard House, 3933 Chartres Street at the Bartholomew intersection, in Bywater

A mile downriver from the French Quarter stands this beautiful French Colonial-style manor house, built in 1826 (possibly earlier) for Joseph Lombard on the former Macarty plantation. The Lombard House embodies many rudimentary elements of early Louisiana architecture: double-pitched roof, center chimneys, dormers, French doors, no hall, gallery with wooden balustrade and colonnettes, and a raised construction. In 1895 a florist's garden and greenhouse adjoined this property, while the St. Mary's Orphan Boys Asylum operated a block away, on Mazant Street. *The Historic New Orleans Collection, accession no. 1979.325.1299*

1996 and 1997 Same sites

Today the Lombard House is beautifully preserved as one of the few remaining plantation houses in New Orleans proper. The Mississippi River, once visible from the gallery of the house before the levees were reinforced, flows about three hundred feet behind the photographer. The distinct roof of the Lombard House is visible from ships on the river.

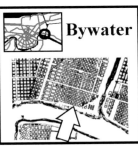

Bywater

circa 1895 Jackson Barracks, Delery Street between St. Claude and the Mississippi River, in Holy Cross

Located in the last downriver corner of New Orleans (the first for traffic coming up the river), Jackson Barracks was built 1825-35 on the former Cotteret-Flood plantation to house the city's federal garrison. Originally called New Orleans Barracks, it served as a jumping-off point for Mexican War operations and was occupied by Confederate troops before the 1862 capitulation and by Union troops for the remainder of the Civil War. Four towers connected by a brick fortress, which passed through the foreground in this photograph, separated the barracks from the Mississippi River. Until its subdivision in the late 1800s, the area now known as Holy Cross (Lower Ninth Ward) consisted of plantations and a few large operations that had outgrown or could not function in downtown New Orleans, including the Crescent City Stockyards, the Jourdan Brickyard, the campus of the Ursuline Academy, and Jackson Barracks. *Detroit Publishing Company, Library of Congress, no. LC-D4-5762 DLC*

1997 Same site

Today Jackson Barracks is one of the best-preserved institutional landscapes in the South, with most of its Greek Revival structures in place and in good condition. The site has served in nearly every conflict since the Mexican War, and after its transfer from federal to state government in 1921, it became the headquarters of the Louisiana National Guard. As Jackson Barracks' connection to the world shifted from the Mississippi River to the adjacent city streets, its main entrance has migrated from the riverside sally port, through which these photos were taken, to a gate on the Delery Street side of the complex. The levee rises a few feet behind the photographer, and the river rolls a few hundred feet beyond. See p. 395 for an oblique perspective of Jackson Barracks and its environs.

Holy Cross/ Chalmette

circa 1900 De La Ronde Plantation Ruins, St. Bernard Highway at the Montesquieu intersection, in Chalmette

Ruins of the De La Ronde plantation house (*circa* 1805, possibly earlier) lie about four miles below downtown New Orleans, on the old Versailles plantation near Chalmette Battlefield. The house served as field headquarters and eventually as hospital for the multitude of wounded and dying British soldiers, among them Maj. Gen. Sir Edward Pakenham, after Maj. Gen. Andrew Jackson and the Americans' resounding victory of January 8, 1815. The graceful French Colonial-style mansion, which bore an external resemblance to the Duverjé House in Algiers (p. 370) and an internal similarity to the Ursuline Convent (1750) on Chartres Street, had a double-pitched hip roof, a wraparound gallery with Doric columns, six dormers, and three chimneys. It was reduced to this shell by a fire in the 1880s and was completely wrecked by the 1915 hurricane. *Photograph by Morgan Whitney, The Historic New Orleans Collection, accession no. 1975.21.30*

1997 Same site

Today the De La Ronde House is a few remnant walls of weathered orange bricks in which an occasional arch or stucco fragment is detectable. It is enough: the effort of local organizations to preserve the ruins is a gift to the city and its visitors, a physical reference to a lost era that piques curiosity and imagination almost more than a sanitized restoration. The ruins, the last standing landmark of the Battle of New Orleans, are sometimes cited as a traffic obstacle to the surrounding St. Bernard Highway, and relocation has been suggested. Across the street, a remnant of the double row of oak trees, planted probably in 1822, forms an alley from the door of the ruins toward the Mississippi River. The area is now a park.

Holy Cross/ Chalmette

circa 1910 **Chalmette Battlefield, between St. Bernard Highway and the Mississippi River, in Chalmette**

Here on the morning of January 8, 1815, Maj. Gen. Andrew Jackson and his militia and volunteers defeated 5,400 professional British soldiers in an important victory both for the new republic and for the disparate populations of post-colonial New Orleans. The Battle of New Orleans, in which British casualties were nearly thirty times greater than American losses, ended the War of 1812 and resolutely ceased English antagonisms of the young United States. To commemorate this spot, the state erected the Egyptian-style obelisk (center) in 1855 but was unable to finish it until federal money arrived in 1907 with the help of the organization U.S. Daughters of 1812. This perspective reflects the former entrance to the park (note the door at the base of the monument) in the days when the battlefield was reached from the riverside road that led to downtown New Orleans. *Detroit Publishing Company, Library of Congress, no. LC-D4-71845 DLC*

1997 Same site

The scene today invites an inspection of the effects of eighty-five years of sub-tropical time on an oak tree. It seems plausible that the tree on the right was a silent witness to the 1815 battle. The Americans fought along this corridor, firing at the British troops to the right over the Rodriguez Canal. Since the River Road was interrupted by the excavation of what is now the Chalmette Slip (1908; see p. 395), access to the park is now gained from the other side of the monument via St. Bernard Highway. Halfway between this point and the Chalmette National Cemetery (next page) was a tiny village called Fazendeville, straddling a single shell road running perpendicular to the river. Determined to unite the Chalmette Monument, battlefield, and cemetery into a single park unit, the National Park Service relocated the thirty families of this rural black hamlet in the early 1960s and bulldozed the town in 1964. Fazendeville is a now a grassy field interspersed with historical markers of the 1815 battle. Perhaps the Park Service would have done better to expand upriver to incorporate the Three Oaks plantation house (1831; see p. 395) into the park. The antebellum mansion was suddenly razed in 1965 for no immediate reason.

Holy Cross/ Chalmette

circa 1910 **Chalmette National Cemetery, between St. Bernard Highway and the Mississippi River, in Chalmette**

In 1864 the occupying Union Army established Chalmette National Cemetery, adjacent to the 1815 battlefield, for interring Union soldiers killed in regional skirmishes. The original entrance was located by the river and accessed by the River Road. The cemetery was expanded inland in 1867, surrounded in 1875 by the brick wall visible here, and expanded again at the time of this photograph. This monument was a gift of the Joseph A. Mower Post No. 1 Grand Army of the Republic (G.A.R.) and was erected by the veterans orga- nization in 1874 at the center of the elongated cemetery. For years it was the scene of annual Decoration Day (now Memorial Day) ceremonies. The pedestal of the monument is surrounded by four cannon and topped by a drum and three unfurled flags; its inscription, which faced the river entrance, reads *Dum Tacent Clamant,* "While They Are Silent, They Cry Aloud." The National Park Service has managed the cemetery since 1933. *Detroit Publishing Company, Library of Congress, no. LC-D4-39626 DLC*

1998 Same site

Chalmette National Cemetery is the final resting place for fifteen thousand individuals, of whom about 45 percent are "known but to God." Veterans from every American conflict since the War of 1812, four of whom fought in that war and one of whom participated in the Battle of New Orleans, rest in the 17.5-acre cemetery, the oldest surviving below-ground burial place in greater New Orleans. An unmarked freedmen's cemetery lies nearby. Like the Chalmette Monument, the cemetery entrance was relocated from the riverside to the St. Bernard Highway when the River Road was severed by the Chalmette Slip (1908). This shift reflects the decreased importance of the river and levees as transportation routes in the twentieth century, replaced by modern inland road networks. In keeping with the reorientation, the G.A.R. monument was relocated in 1956 from the center of the cemetery to its current riverside terminus, about one thousand feet behind the photographer, with the inscription facing away from the river. The telltale arrangement of certain tombstones reveals this site as the former location of the G.A.R. monument.

Holy Cross/Chalmette

circa 1858 **Looking up Canal Street from the roof of the U.S. Custom House**

This spectacular scene captures the principal artery of the South's then-largest city during its antebellum golden age, viewed from the roof of the incomplete U.S. Custom House. Canal Street was created in the early American years when an act of Congress transferred the fortified commons from the federal government to the city, with instructions to excavate a waterway connecting Carondelet Canal (pp. 156 and 381) with the river. Hence Canal Street was laid out in great width (171 feet, among the widest downtown avenues in the nation), but the canal was never dug. Note the degree to which the neutral ground, planned as the canal's right of way, dominated the street. The domed church at upper left is the original Jesuit Church (Immaculate Conception), recently completed in this view. The chimney at extreme lower right marks the Pinson-Piseta store at 507 Canal (p. 188), the oldest surviving structure on Canal. *Photograph by Jay Dearborn Edwards, The Historic New Orleans Collection, accession no. 1982.167.2*

circa 1910 and 1997 Same views

Top scene, *circa* 1910: The grassy neutral ground has given way to a fleet of electric streetcars ferrying passengers up and down the corridor. The location of the corniced high-rise Morris Building at center left (corner of Camp Street) corresponds to the location of the "photographic gallery" in the *circa* 1858 scene. The cupola on the right marks the Godchaux Building (p. 184); the Jesuit Church dome appears in the distance. Buses replaced streetcars on Canal in 1964, except for the one-block run of the St. Charles line. **Bottom scene, 1997:** Note the new streetcar tracks, installed in 1997. The steep roof of the Pinson-Piseta store, visible in the extreme lower right of each perspective, is about the only constant architectural element in all three scenes. This photograph was taken from the Canal Place complex. *Detroit Publishing Company, Library of Congress, no. LC-D4-33060 DLC*

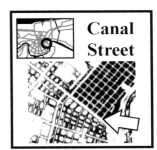

Canal Street

179

circa 1858 Adjacent view, looking into Canal Street between Magazine and Camp, from the roof of the U.S. Custom House

Also taken from the corner of the incomplete U.S. Custom House, this photograph captures a neat vignette of commercial New Orleans in the mid-nineteenth century. Notice the pediment and columns of the second St. Charles Hotel (1853) in the distance; imagine a dome rising halfway into the sky to picture the appearance of the first St. Charles (p. 212), which burned in 1851.

The dome of the Jesuit Church (Church of the Immaculate Conception, *circa* 1850) appears on the extreme right. Judging from the inactivity on Canal Street, this photograph may have been taken on a Sunday. *Photograph by Jay Dearborn Edwards, The Historic New Orleans Collection, accession no. 1982.167.1*

1997 Same view

Government officials restrict access to the roof of the U.S. Custom House, so this view was acquired from the upper stories of the neighboring Canal Place complex. Note the Custom House rooftop (bottom right) that was Jay Dearborn Edwards' perch for the historic photographs. Every building in the *circa* 1858 perspective is gone now, although the twin of the clothing warehouse marked "72" on the extreme left of the *circa* 1858 perspective still stands. The Church of the Immaculate Conception, rebuilt with some original components in 1929, is blocked from view.

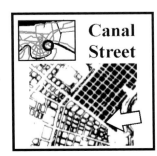

Canal Street

181

circa 1890 and *circa* 1920 Looking up Canal Street from the 400 block

Top scene, *circa* 1890: A horse-drawn wagon loaded with cotton makes it way across electrified Canal Street. Note the 150-foot electrical light and utility tower straddling the neutral ground in the distance at the Bourbon intersection. The dome to the right of the tower marks the Mercier Building (1887), which in 1897 housed the original Maison Blanche. **Bottom scene, *circa* 1920:** A fleet of streetcars, automobiles, and horse-drawn carts services Canal Street in the boom years after World War I. At the Dauphine intersection, the new Maison Blanche Building (1909) replaces the Mercier, while at right center, the Godchaux Building (1899), with its corner cupola and water towers, breaks the even line of structures that defined nineteenth-century Canal Street. *Charles Franck Collection, The Historic New Orleans Collection, accession nos. 1979.325.4920 and 1979.325.4921*

1997 Same site

A number of transformations distinguishes modern-day Canal Street from its early-twentieth-century appearance: the construction of skyscraper hotels, the termination of most streetcar lines, the domination of automotive traffic, the planting of trees, and the removal of utility poles and galleries. Nevertheless, Canal Street today maintains a similar geographical role (but different economic function) in downtown New Orleans that it did 80 years ago—and to some extent even 140 years ago. The ties to the past will be reinforced in the near future as the city installs new streetcar lines and the private sector invests in the neglected upper stories of Canal Street structures. Note the Sanlin Building (1840s) on the extreme left, masked since the 1960s by a garish tin façade.

Canal Street

circa 1945 Godchaux Building, Canal Street at the Chartres intersection

The Godchaux Building (1899) was the last project of Leon Godchaux (1824-99), a French-born Louisianian of Jewish ancestry who rose from childhood poverty to become a successful merchant and major figure in the development of the sugar industry. His enterprise began with a tiny clothing store near the French Market and grew to include sugar plantations, railroads, and stores on Canal Street. Godchaux's clothing store operated here on the ground floor until 1926, when it moved to 828 Canal and thrived into the 1980s. To the right are the triple-unit Virginia Building and antebellum structures, the rooftops of which are visible in the photographs taken from the U.S. Custom House (pp. 178-79). Werlein's for Music, a local retailer founded in 1842, operated in the structure at left for most of the twentieth century. Note the opera advertisement on its front, which depicts the old French Opera House on Bourbon Street that burned in 1919. See also p. 202 for a *circa* 1858 perspective of this area, in which eight of these ten structures are extant. *Charles Franck Collection, The Historic New Orleans Collection, accession no. 1979.325.4934*

184

1996 Same site

The antebellum units adjoining the Virginia Building were razed about 1950; the Godchaux and Virginia followed in 1969. Only three antebellum structures survive in the scene: the corner T-shirt shop, the Pinson-Piseta Building at far right, and the U.S. Custom House behind it. The Marriott Hotel (1972) now occupies the entire block between Chartres and Dorsiere. Lower Canal's skyscraper hotels have brought much-needed investment and attention to downtown New Orleans, but their severe designs and domineering scales have worked against these benefits. A 1972 year-end issue of the *Vieux Carré Courier* pinned its awards for Worst Skyscraper, Quarter's Worst Disaster, and City's Worst Interior Design on the Marriott, calling it a cross between "a 42-story Scarlett O'Hara drag show and a Walt Disney 'Mississippi gambler's' riverboat, a shameless five-star catastrophe of phony historicism, misspelled French, and bald bad taste." The reviewer concluded by recommending that "Willard Marriott needs to learn the difference between atmosphere and odor." Werlein's for Music, the oldest music company in the nation, now operates on Decatur Street, in Metairie, and at other locations, while the Brennan family's Palace Café (1991) occupies the Canal Street landmark at left.

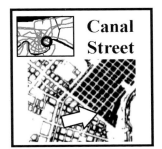

Canal Street

circa 1858 and *circa* 1882 Canal Street looking toward Lake Pontchartrain, from the Bourbon intersection (left) and from the Royal intersection

Top scene, *circa* 1858: By the 1850s Canal Street was transitioning from a stately residential street to the commercial corridor it is today. The angled corner townhouse at left, the Perry House, replaced a part of the block-long Charity Hospital (1815) that served as the Louisiana State House until 1849. The Gothic-style Christ Church (right), designed by James Gallier, was erected in 1847 after two other Episcopalian churches came and went on the Canal/Bourbon corner. It is ironic that three important early Protestant churches were located on the Catholic (Creole) side of Canal Street. Just beyond the church are the classical Union Terrace residences (1837), designed by Dakin and Dakin. **Bottom scene, *circa* 1882:** A completely transformed neutral ground in about twenty-five years. Touro Row (1856), the outstanding block of galleried stores between Bourbon and Royal, appears at right. *Photographs by Jay Dearborn Edwards (top) and George François Mugnier (bottom), The Historic New Orleans Collection, accession nos. 1982.32.15 and 1981.247.12.91*

circa 1890 and 1998 Same sites

Top scene, *circa* 1890: The Christ Church was demolished in the mid-1880s and replaced by the Victorian Mercier Building (dome at center), home of the first Maison Blanche in 1897. The Bourbon Street end of Touro Row (right) has been replaced with taller commercial buildings, and on the distant left, the cupola of Chess, Checkers, and Whist (p. 204) replaces the Perry House. In February 1892 the new buildings on the Touro block burned in a blaze so intense that sparks ignited fires as far away as Tremé Street. Among the businesses affected were Kreeger's Fancy Goods Store, Cluverius' Drugstore, and Werlein's for Music, all visible here. **Bottom scene, 1998:** The site occupied first by the Christ Church and then by the Mercier Building still dominates the area, here as the Maison Blanche store and office building (1909). Touro Row is gone from the scene, though its altered components still underlay the Royal Street half of the block. Canal Street's neutral ground has diminished in size but still provides refuge for pedestrians fleeing the treacherous traffic on the 171-foot-wide avenue. Circa 1890 *photograph by William Henry Jackson, Detroit Publishing Company, Library of Congress, no. LC-D418-8101 DLC*

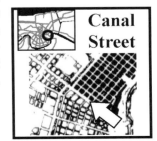

Canal Street

1920 Pinson and Piseta Building, 507 to 509 Canal Street, between Decatur and Dorsiere

This building spans the short Canal Street block between Decatur and Dorsiere. Built in 1821 by Felix Pinson and Maurice Piseta as a five-bay storehouse for Joseph Mary, the original edifice had a more Spanish Colonial design, somewhat like the Girod House (p. 78). New walls, lintels, and a heavy parapet were added to the building in 1899. Glimpses of the original structure can be seen in the *circa* 1858 J. D. Edwards photographs on pp. 178 and 202. The former façade also appears in newspaper illustrations of the 1874 street battle between the White League and the Metropolitan Police, in which the Democrats shook the carpetbaggers' post-Civil War hold on local politics. Thirty-two people were killed within the vicinity of this site. Note the retractable awnings. *Charles Franck Collection, The Historic New Orleans Collection, accession no. 1979.325.546*

1996 Same site

The Pinson-Piseta Building, in the shadows of skyscraper hotels, is now the oldest surviving structure on Canal Street. A brass plaque embedded in the sidewalk identifies it as the Santopadre Building, a reference to John V. Santo Padre, who bought the structure in 1974. The old storehouse leads an ensemble of older buildings that, together with the U.S. Custom House, form the first block of Decatur Street—the only place where a pedestrian can enter the French Quarter right off Canal Street and be completely surrounded by historical structures (or, in the case of 121-123 Decatur, by a historical façade). Note the new gabled dormers and also the fire hydrant—in the same location since 1920.

Canal Street

circa 1917 **Granite Building, 631 to 637 Canal Street, at the Royal intersection**

The Granite Building (Musson Building), built of Massachusetts granite in 1833, overlooks the busy Royal/Canal intersection. The sturdy edifice was constructed by the same builders, Felix Pinson and Maurice Piseta, responsible for the storehouse on the previous page. The circular window on the top floor once held a clock as a promotion for E. A. Tyler's Watches & Jewelry in the 1870s; the company's advertisements are still visible here nearly fifty years later. Note the diversity of businesses, the presence of galleries, and the utilization of every floor of these commercial buildings. *Charles Franck Collection, The Historic New Orleans Collection, accession no. 1979.325.421*

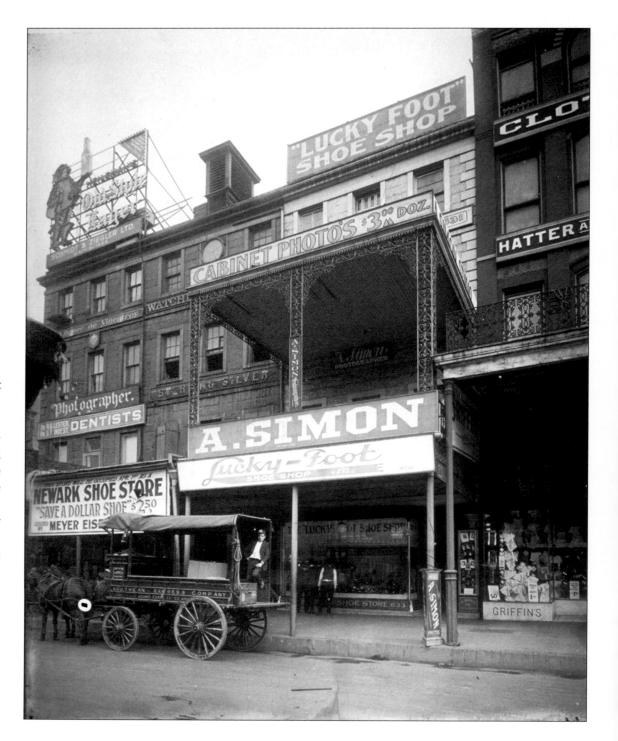

1996 Same site

The Granite Building is now among the oldest surviving structures on Canal Street and probably *the* oldest that maintains its original design. The removal of iron-lace galleries and verandas from Canal buildings in the 1930s marks a major change in the streetscape; here they have been replaced by fire escapes, which also are becoming a thing of the past. Another change on Canal is the commercial abandonment of the upper stories, here covered by billboards. This is probably the result of a number of factors: the greatly decreased dependency of the city on Canal Street for its retail and professional needs, the departure of the city's middle class, the automobile, the orientation of many Canal Street shops toward tourists, and the prevalence of national retail chains, which have little interest in setting up shop on a second or third floor. Recent plans to develop apartments and condominiums on these upper stories would return a residential element to lower Canal, missing for a century and a half.

Canal Street

circa 1905 Canal Street from the Bourbon intersection, looking up Carondelet Street

Looking into the Carondelet Street financial district from the corner of Bourbon and Canal. At right is the conspicuous Pickwick Club building, designed by N. C. Hinsdale and Oliver Marble and built in 1882; at center in the distance is the Hennen (Maritime) Building, an early steel-frame high-rise designed by Thomas Sully and built in 1893-95. James Gallier Sr., New Orleans' most influential architect, operated his offices near the Common Street corner to the right of the Hennen Building. *Detroit Publishing Company, Library of Congress, no. LC-D4-16321 DLC*

1997 Same site

A modernized set of structures now faces Canal Street, most notably the streamlined Gus Mayer Company (Lane Bryant) building that replaced the Pickwick Club edifice after its 1948 demolition. Dominating the background are the 1920s-era American Bank and Hibernia Bank buildings, with their two distinctive lantern cupolas. The St. Charles streetcar is an integral part of the crowded and bustling initial blocks of Carondelet. Though Gallier's office is gone, two of his structures may be seen to the left of the Gus Mayer building.

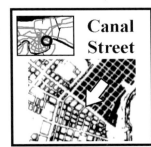

Canal Street

circa 1890 Looking up Canal Street from the Royal intersection

The Henry Clay Monument overlooked this prominent intersection from 1860 to 1901. The statue was a political jab of the uptown Anglos at their downtown Creole rivals: Clay, a prominent Whig, was a hero to moneyed Anglos; Andrew Jackson, a Democrat, represented the views of many Creoles and was recently memorialized by them at Jackson Square. During its four decades at this location, the Clay Monument occasionally served as a rendezvous for mobs, once for the Battle of Liberty Place in 1874 and again for the lynching of the Sicilians in 1891 (p. 150). On the extreme left is the Crescent Billiard Hall, built in a much simpler design in 1826 for Cornelius Paulding and converted to the Merchants Hotel by Cora Slocomb, 1858-65. Col. A. W. Merriam transformed the hotel into a billiard hall in 1865, and nine years later it was heavily remodeled with the Italian Renaissance and Greek Revival features seen here. Note the Pickwick Club behind the monument, and the Chess, Checkers, and Whist Club (white cupola in the distance) to its right. *Photograph by William Henry Jackson, Detroit Publishing Company, Library of Congress, no. LC-D418-8102 DLC*

1996 Same site

Almost the entire block of Canal Street from St. Charles to Carondelet maintains its turn-of-the-century architecture. The Clay Monument became a traffic obstacle (note the horse-drawn streetcar making its way around it in the *circa* 1890 photograph) and was retired to the more placid location of Lafayette Square in 1901, where it now stands among oak trees and pigeons (pp. 272 and 276). It is appropriate that the Clay Monument and its Whig origins came home to the Anglos' Lafayette Square just as the Jackson statue and its Democratic roots found home in the Creoles' Jackson Square. For years the galleries on the Canal and St. Charles sides of the Crescent Billiard Hall were prime viewing stands for Mardi Gras parades, and in 1948 the spectacular building became the headquarters, and later the property, of the Pickwick Club, founders of the Mistick Krewe of Comus in 1857. In his 1902 *New Orleans Guide*, James Zacharie identified this intersection as the "centre of [the] city," a description that holds true today.

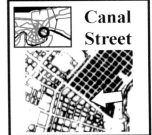

Canal Street

circa 1880 **Touro Row, Canal Street between Royal and Bourbon**

Historic Canal Street: Christ Church (1847) appears at left, Touro Row (designed by Thomas Murray and built for Judah Touro in the 1850s) connects Bourbon with Royal, and the Granite Building (1833) marks the corner at right. Note the Clay statue at the Canal/Royal intersection. In 1855 Canal Street was renamed Touro Avenue in honor of Judah Touro (1775-1854), a poor orphan of Sephardic Jewish ancestry who emigrated to Spanish colonial New Orleans from Rhode Island in 1801 to become one of the city's greatest citizens. Although Touro did more for Canal Street than the canal ever did (it was never dug), the new name never stuck. Judah Touro lived for a while in the former Second Christ Church's rectory, a three-story house tucked in Touro Row until it was demolished and the row was finally completed in the late 1850s. The site of his residence is the unit marked by a sunshade hanging from the second-floor gallery. *Photograph by George François Mugnier, The Historic New Orleans Collection, accession no. 1980.137.25*

196

1997 Same site

Maison Blanche (1909) marks the site of the old Christ Church, far left. The Bourbon Street end of Touro Row was redeveloped in the 1880s and burned in 1892 (p. 187); three remaining units at the Royal Street end are visible at center right (by the "Tax Free" sign), and four other adjoining units are disguised by modernized façades. Five of the surviving seven units retain their original hip roofs, but all traces of the splendid double galleries are gone. Had its contiguity and adornment survived intact, Touro Row would probably be a famous landmark in the city today, on par with the Pontalba Apartments or the French Market. (A better-preserved row of similar structures, built for Judah Touro in 1851 and also called Touro Row, survives at 301-311 St. Charles; see p. 212.) The indestructible Granite Building appears on the right, covered by billboards but still recognizable. The Clay statue was relocated to Lafayette Square in 1901 (p. 272) and remains there today.

Canal Street

1935 and 1947 218 to 232 Canal Street, corner of South Peters

Top scene, 1935: Blocks of parallelogram-shaped commercial buildings like this one lined the upriver side of lower Canal Street, along Water, Front, Fulton, and South Peters (see aerial photo on p. 224). Note the fire hydrant. **Bottom scene, 1947:** A change in occupants but little else. The old liquor distributor's painted advertisement is still visible on the wall. A 1922 photograph of the opposite side of this building appears on p. 220. *Charles Franck Collection, The Historic New Orleans Collection, accession nos. 1979.325.593 and 1979.325.540*

1996 Same site

Lower Canal's upriver side has been so drastically overhauled for the convention and tourism trade that entire blocks from the old port-warehouse days are in some places difficult to discern. This site was home to the free-form Rivergate Convention Center (1968; see p. 225 for aerial view) until its 1995 demolition for this Harrah's casino, shown here under construction. Behind the startling failure of casinos in downtown New Orleans is the fact that the typical tourist, often criticized for patronizing the ersatz, is more interested in the city's unique offerings than in gambling. Nevertheless, "gaming" has left its mark on lower Canal. The defense of the Rivergate as an architecturally significant structure worthy of reuse marked the last chapter in the six-decade career of New Orleans' greatest architectural historian, Samuel Wilson Jr. (1911-93). One element remains on this corner from a half-century ago: the fire hydrant, hidden by the safety fence but well marked.

Canal Street

circa 1905 **Canal Street at the Chartres intersection, looking up Camp Street**

Looking into lower Camp Street from the edge of the French Quarter. The seven-story Morris Building, designed by Thomas Sully and Albert Toledano in 1889, was the first high-rise on Canal Street, boasting steel girders, iron-reinforced columns, and a steam elevator to access the professional offices on its upper floors. The "fireproof" structure burned in 1900 but was promptly refurbished, with new bay windows and the cornice seen here. The ornate Romanesque edifice with the steep roof, one block up Camp, is the New Orleans National Bank, another Sully design and one of a series of prominent banks erected in the Central Business District in the late 1800s. Camp Street was once known as Newspaper Row for its concentration of local newspaper offices. *Detroit Publishing Company, Library of Congress, no. LC-D4-16322 DLC*

1996 Same site

Note the removal of the cornice and veranda and the addition of fire escapes on the Morris Building, three common alterations to downtown buildings over the years.

Canal Street

circa 1858 **Canal Street from the St. Charles intersection, looking toward the Chartres intersection**

The U.S. Custom House (1848-81) at right was under construction when this photograph was taken. At its base is the 1821 storehouse (p. 188) built by Pinson and Piseta and shown here in its original design. Note the diversity of retailers, the various advertisements, and the use of sunshades along the galleries, which must have created a marketplace atmosphere. At the time of this photograph, Canal Street had recently overtaken Chartres and Royal as the city's premier commercial street. Slow economic development on Canal in prior decades led to plans to construct a five-block market on the neutral ground from New Levee (now North Peters) to Bourbon, roughly the area in view here. Like the canal that was never dug, the market was never built on Canal Street (although James Dakin sketched its Greek Revival design), due in part to the 1837 financial crisis. See pp. 178-79 for views of Canal from the opposite direction. *Photograph by Jay Dearborn Edwards, The Historic New Orleans Collection, accession no. 1982.32.2*

1998 Same site

The U.S. Custom House (between the skyscrapers at right) is still utilized by the federal government. To its immediate left is the Pinson-Piseta store, remodeled in 1899 and now a Wendy's restaurant; inside are components of the oldest remaining structure on Canal Street. The only other surviving antebellum edifice in this view is the four-story building with the dangling top hat in the *circa* 1858 scene, visible here at center. See p. 184 for a *circa* 1945 scene of this area. Canal Street's distinctive street lights, designed in 1929-30 by the New Orleans Public Service Inc. (NOPSI), commemorate the city's political history on their bases: French Domination (1718-69), Spanish Domination (1769-1803), Confederate Domination (1861-65) and American Domination (1803-61, 1865 to present). (Some of those dates may need asterisks!) Although New Orleanians do not patronize Canal Street shops as they did before the age of automobiles and strip malls, the great boulevard is still vibrant and bustling.

Canal Street

circa 1903, 1921, and 1924 Chess, Checkers, and Whist Club, Canal Street at the Baronne intersection

Top-left scene, *circa* 1903: The Chess, Checkers, and Whist Club was a gentlemen's social and literary fraternity dedicated to "promote the knowledge and encourage the developement (*sic*) of the scientific games of Chess, Checkers and Whist," according to its 1903 yearbook. The club's *circa* 1880s building on Canal and Baronne replaced the Perry House (pp. 186-87), built after the 1850 demolition of the Louisiana State House that was originally Charity Hospital (1815). To the left is Grunewald Hall, an opera house that once bordered the University of Louisiana campus. Note the web of utility wires and streetcar cables overhead. **Top-right scene, 1921:** The corner cupola is gone, a fire escape has been added, and the Tulane & Crescent Theatres have moved into the former chess club; meanwhile, the ornate new Hotel Grunewald (1908; upper right) rises over University Place, on the site of the Mechanics Institute (p. 218) that last served as the campus library. **Bottom scene, 1924:** The finials have been removed from the parapet, the theaters are closed, and the upper floors are for rent. *Detroit Publishing Company, Library of Congress, no. LC-D4-16324 DLC and Charles Franck Collection, The Historic New Orleans Collection, accession nos. 1979.325.437 and 1979.325.436*

1936, 1996, mid-1997, and late 1997 Same site

Top-left scene, 1936: Grunewald Hall has been replaced by a high-rise annex (left) to the 1908 Hotel Grunewald and renamed the Roosevelt, while Chess, Checkers, and Whist has lost its gallery and its other cupola. **Top-right scene, 1996:** The entire Roosevelt Hotel complex, now the elegant Fairmont, is intact and prospering, while Chess, Checkers, and Whist has given way to a drugstore (1938) with a streamline-modern style that is now considered fashionably "retro." Its neighbors to the right, once the Newcomb movie house, have been remodeled with new faces, new floors, and a new occupant, the Cine Royal porno theater. **Bottom scenes, 1997:** In 1997 the theater was razed, while Walgreen's was gutted, rebuilt, and expanded into the empty lot, now marked by twin brick façades. An intriguing alley running from Baronne to University Place, well over a century old, still separates the rears of these Canal Street structures from the high-rise hotel behind them. *Charles Franck Collection, The Historic New Orleans Collection, accession no. 1979.325.438*

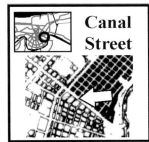

Canal Street

circa 1910 **Terminal Station, looking down Basin Street at the Canal Street intersection**

For two centuries Basin Street has guided visitors into downtown New Orleans via water, rail, and wheel. The street was named for the Carondelet Canal turning basin (1795; p. 156), five blocks down, which brought watercraft from the lake to the back door of the old city. Spanish Fort Railroad Station operated at this intersection in the late 1800s, and in 1908 this station, designed by Daniel Burnham (architect of Union Station in Washington), opened as the New Orleans Terminal Company Railroad Depot, later the Southern Railway Terminal

Station. Tracks to the station followed the bed of Carondelet Canal and appear in the aerial photos on pp. 146 and 381. Terminal Station was located near the brothels of Storyville (distant left) and the seediness of the French Quarter (distant right). The cast-iron cones on Canal Street were designed to demarcate turns and prevent corner cutting. *Detroit Publishing Company, Library of Congress, no. LC-D4-71104 DLC*

1996 Same site

Terminal Station was demolished in 1956, and its trackbeds were replaced by a grassy neutral ground with a series of statues commemorating Latin American liberators. Interstate 10's exit ramps now route vehicles onto Orleans Avenue, renamed Basin Street, which curves to merge with the original Basin Street that passes through this intersection—continuing its role as a pathway into and out of downtown New Orleans. The Krauss Building, home of the famous department store from 1903 to 1997, appears on the extreme left, and the Saenger Theatre (1927) is on the right.

Canal Street

207

1927 The Saenger Theatre, 1111 Canal Street between Basin and Rampart

The Saenger Theatre, nearing completion in 1927, was designed by Emile Weil for the Shreveport-based Saenger Amusement Company, an early cinema chain that would later operate hundreds of theaters throughout the South. The thirty-four-hundred-seat Saenger Theatre's lavish Italian Renaissance interior, surrounded by statuary and a twinkling evening-blue ceiling, enthralled moviegoers and complemented the epic silent films and orchestras. The Hotel La Salle operated in the upper floors of the Canal Street side of the structure, while the theater occupied the rear. *Charles Franck Collection, The Historic New Orleans Collection, accession no. 1979.89.7474*

208

1996 Same site

No more parking on the neutral ground. Together with the nearby Orpheum Theater, State Palace (formerly Loews), and Joy Theatre, the Saenger (now the Saenger Performing Arts Center) marks New Orleans' "theater district," the only economic district to have spanned the entire twentieth century. Other districts from the early 1900s that have since dispersed or disappeared include the cotton district at Carondelet and Gravier, the sugar and rice district at North Peters and Iberville, and the shipping district at the foot of Canal Street. The Hotel La Salle remains in operation next to the Saenger, behind the tree.

Canal Street

1952 The Central Business District

At upper right is the French Quarter and Canal Street, at lower left is Central City, and Lee Circle appears at the bottom. The triangular island at lower center (to the right of the terminus of the railroad tracks) was the New Basin Canal turning basin, dug by Irish immigrants in 1832-38 to connect the American Sector with Lake Pontchartrain. The heart of the Central Business District, formerly known as the American Sector and originally as Faubourg Ste. Marie (1788), is at center right. See pp. 268, 298, and the appendix for other aerial perspectives of this area. *U.S. Geological Survey*

1994 Same area

In a city of large and enduring historic districts, the Central Business District has witnessed sweeping changes over the past five decades. The four greatest areas of change are (1) the Pontchartrain Expressway corridor and Interstate 10, (2) the Poydras Street skyscraper district and its connection with Loyola Avenue, (3) the lower Canal and riverfront hotel/convention complexes, and (4) the Superdome and its adjacent facilities. Nevertheless, the Central Business District still has an extensive collection of historical blocks, including something the French Quarter lacks: an occasional street paved with cobblestone or brick. The Warehouse District (lower right) is an excellent example of a nineteenth-century industrial cityscape. *U.S. Geological Survey*

Central Business District

circa 1847 and *circa* 1858 First and Second St. Charles Hotels, St. Charles Avenue between Common and Gravier, in the Central Business District

Left scene, *circa* 1847: The original St. Charles Exchange Hotel, one of the most splendid structures in the nation and a landmark of the New Orleans skyline, was designed by James Gallier Sr. and probably Charles Dakin and was completed in 1837. Under its 185-foot dome and cupola were elegant accommodations and financial services (hence the term "Exchange Hotel") catering to a mostly American clientele. The Gothic chapel at the left is the First Presbyterian (1819), later known as Reverend Clapp's "Strangers' Church," and the six-story structure at left is Dakin and Dakin's Verandah Hotel (1838). This rare daguerreotype by Thomas Easterly, owned by the Missouri Historical Society, is the only known image of the first St. Charles. **Right scene, *circa***

1858: A terrible blaze consumed the St. Charles, Strangers' Church, and a dozen other buildings in January 1851. Two years later, a second St. Charles arose, similar to the original but without the costly dome. Like its predecessor, the hotel served as a focal point for Anglo businessmen in Faubourg St. Mary. Creole rivals hobnobbed at the St. Louis Hotel in the Vieux Carré. The second St. Charles Hotel also burned (1894), in a fire so severe that only the massive columns and pediment remained. The Verandah burned in 1855. *Circa 1847 daguerreotype by Thomas M. Easterly, Missouri Historical Society, St. Louis; circa 1858 photograph by Jay Dearborn Edwards, The Historic New Orleans Collection, accession no. 1982.32.10*

circa **1900 and 1998 Same site**

Left scene, *circa* 1900: This Italian Renaissance structure, the third and last of the three hotels named St. Charles, was designed by Thomas Sully and completed in 1896 on the site of its two Greek Revival predecessors. To the left of the hotel we see Judah Touro's "other" Touro Row, built in 1851 on the site of the Strangers' Church and similar in style to the block on Canal known by the same name (p. 196). The spire at the extreme left rises above the Masonic Temple (p. 252). The third St. Charles Hotel, which last operated as the Sheraton-St. Charles, was demolished in 1974. **Right scene, 1998:** In 1985 the postmodern Place St. Charles (First NBC Center) was erected on the lot that once hosted the grand hotels. The impressive fifty-three-story skyscraper, designed by Mathes, Bergman and Associates, casts an oblique glance down St. Charles Avenue and into the French Quarter, communicating a bend in the river to strollers on Royal Street. On the extreme left is the Courtyard Marriott Hotel, built in 1994 on the site of five 1850s buildings on the corner of St. Charles and Common, which were demolished in 1993. The hotel is notable because it was designed as the old Verandah Hotel, which occupied this corner from 1838 to 1855. In the background, top to bottom, are One Shell Square (1972), Masonic Lodge (1926), and United Fruit Company Building (1920). To experience the architectural impact of the long-lost first St. Charles Hotel, visit the similar Barton Academy (also designed by Gallier and Dakin and built in 1836) on Government Street in Mobile, Alabama. *Circa 1900 photograph: Detroit Publishing Company, Library of Congress, no. LC-D4-4893 DLC*

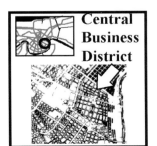

circa 1890 and *circa* 1900 Lower St. Charles Avenue, looking upriver from Canal Street, in the Central Business District

Top scene, *circa* 1890: This scene captures the second St. Charles Hotel (1853) standing grandly at the Common Street bend of St. Charles Avenue. See p. 212 for a *circa* 1847 view of the spectacular first St. Charles Hotel, which burned in 1851. Note the horse-drawn streetcars. **Bottom scene, *circa* 1900:** The third St. Charles Hotel (1896), designed by Thomas Sully, was erected two years after the second one burned. Note the contiguous galleries on both sides of St. Charles Avenue and also the electric streetcar. Circa *1890 photograph by William Henry Jackson, Detroit Publishing Company, Library of Congress, no. LC-D418-8103 DLC; circa 1900 photograph: Detroit Publishing Company, Library of Congress, no. LC-D4-4898 DLC*

214

circa 1910 and 1996 Same site

Top scene, *circa* 1910: The third St. Charles Hotel appears in the distance. Some of the iron-lace galleries on lower St. Charles have come down, perhaps as a result of initiatives in the early 1900s to remove all galleries from New Orleans streets. **Bottom scene, 1996:** Place St. Charles (First NBC Center) replaced the last St. Charles eleven years after its 1974 demolition. The new Courtyard Marriott (1994, behind the Meyer the Hatter sign) has replaced the antebellum buildings that occupied the St. Charles/Common corner in the other three photographs. The old buildings were demolished in 1993 for this reasonable replication of the Verandah Hotel (p. 212) that stood here from 1838 to 1855. Thanks in part to the remaining galleries on the first block of St. Charles, the modern scene still hearkens back to its former appearances. Kolb's, a famous German restaurant founded in 1899 by a Bavarian orphan named Conrad Kolb, operated until 1994. Circa *1910 photograph: Detroit Publishing Company, Library of Congress, no. LC-D4-71829 DLC*

Central Business District

215

No. 544. The City Hotel, Camp Str.

circa 1890 City (Bishop's) Hotel, Camp Street at the Common intersection, looking toward Canal, in the Central Business District

The Bishop's Hotel was built by Charles Zimpel in 1831 and remodeled to this appearance in 1873 as the City Hotel. Like the St. Charles Hotel, it hosted travelers and part-time residents doing business in the American part of town. In his 1834 travelogue of New Orleans, Joseph Holt Ingraham commented that the recently constructed Bishop's Hotel "is one of the largest in the Union. . . . Its barroom is more than one-hundred feet in length, and universally allowed to be the most splendid in America." In the dining room, "two-hundred to three-hundred people dine daily, of which not twenty of them are French." Ingraham also noted that a "peculiarity in this hotel is the exclusion of ladies from among the numbers of boarders. It is, properly, a bachelor establishment." *Photograph by George François Mugnier, The Historic New Orleans Collection, accession no. 1986.185*

1996 Same site

The Sheraton Hotel skyscraper now occupies the site. The only remaining structure in the scene is the building, now sans gallery, on the corner of Canal and Chartres, straight down Camp. This is the establishment that appears in J. D. Edwards's *circa* 1858 photograph on p. 202 with a large top hat dangling above its pediment.

Central Business District

circa 1890 **Mechanics Institute, Dryades Street (now University Place) between Canal and Common, in the Central Business District**

This stereogram depicts James Gallier Jr.'s Greek Revival-style Mechanics Institute (1856), headquarters for the New Orleans Mechanics Society, a local chapter of a nationwide artisans union. The building briefly served as the state capitol during the city's occupation and Reconstruction eras. On this site in 1866, a violent riot broke out between Radical Republicans and Democrats as the former group convened to revise the state constitution to enfranchise blacks. Dozen of people died in the street battle. After the state legislature moved to the old St. Louis Hotel, the former Mechanics Institute was purchased by Paul Tulane and used to house academic departments and the Fisk Free Library of the University of Louisiana, for which University Place was later named. The school evolved into Tulane University and moved uptown in 1894. The Mechanics Institute bore a resemblance to Gallier's French Opera House on Bourbon Street (p. 64). Canal Street appears in the distance. *The Historic New Orleans Collection, accession no. 1988.134.19*

1996 Same site

The Mechanics Institute was demolished in the early 1900s and replaced by the elegant Hotel Grunewald (1908). Later renamed the Roosevelt, it is now the Fairmont Hotel, which transverses the entire block from University Place to Baronne Street. See pp. 204-05 for a time sequence of the development of this historic hotel complex.

Central Business District

1922 101 to 107 Fulton Street at the Common intersection, looking toward Canal, in the Central Business District

This is the first tier of irregularly shaped blocks in the shipping district above lower Canal Street (right). Structures here conform to the parallelogram-shaped blocks laid out in the batture; this particular building's walls form angles measuring 120, 60, 130, and 50 degrees. See p. 198 for views of its Canal Street side. Note the U.S. Custom House in the distance (behind the pickup truck), the railroad car at left, and the interesting patterns of Belgian blocks in the foreground streets. The city engineering office listed forty types of paving in the streets of New Orleans in 1927, among them granite block, wood plank, asphalt, concrete, shell, sand, and gravel with cypress foundation. Much of old New Orleans' supply of granite for paving and construction arrived as ballast in ships. *Charles Franck Collection, The Historic New Orleans Collection, accession no. 1979.325.694*

1996 Same site

The block was replaced by the Rivergate Convention Center (1968), which was in turn demolished for this unfinished structure, the sprawling Harrah's casino, whose architecture appears to have been inspired by a Greek temple, a steamboat, and an aquarium. The startling failure of other casinos in New Orleans in the mid-1990s caused financial problems for this project, leading to construction delays and a scaling back of original grandiose plans. Note the antebellum U.S. Custom House, the sole vestige from the 1922 scene, peering through the framework. The block of mid-nineteenth-century stores to the right of the Custom House in the 1922 photograph survived until the 1970s oil and construction boom, when the Canal Place complex replaced it. This area—where Water, Delta, Front, and Fulton intersect Common, Gravier, and Poydras—is unrecognizable from photos as recent as the early 1960s.

Central Business District

1929 and 1945 100 to 110 Magazine Street at the Canal intersection, in the Central Business District

Top scene, 1929: This series of fine 1840s-era Greek Revival structures marked the point at which the lower Canal Street corridor of the early twentieth century transitioned from a wholesale shipping district to a retail commercial district. **Bottom scene, 1945:** Forlorn and empty on a winter morning. Occupants of this Canal Street row in 1940 included this rubber company, a dry-goods wholesaler, a wholesale florist, a casket factory, and a glassware warehouse and wholesaler. *Charles Franck Collection, The Historic New Orleans Collection, accession nos. 1979.325.745 and 1979.325.746*

1996 Same site

The wholesalers have been replaced by souvenir shops and retailers at street level and a variety of organizations at the upper levels. These antebellum structures, known collectively as the Sanlin Building, were masked by this once-fashionable metal façade in the 1960s, further marring a portion of lower Canal that already had been stripped of much of its historical character. Then in the 1970s, a block of similar structures across the street (p. 220) was leveled for the construction of the Canal Place complex. Still standing behind the Sanlin grille is one of the best intact examples of early Greek Revival architecture in New Orleans. Nevertheless, in 1996 a bold proposal to demolish these buildings and seven nearby historical edifices surfaced and started making its way through the permitting process. The plan, which entailed the construction of a four-hundred-room, twenty-six-story hotel, was defeated through community protest against an uncompromising developer.

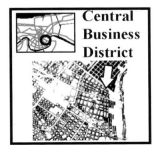

Central Business District

1952 The Warehouse District, between the Central Business District and the Mississippi River

This batture—alluvial deposition between the natural levee and the river—was formed by the shifting Mississippi in the early 1800s and exploited as a warehouse district by the 1840s. Note the many parallelogram-shaped structures between the river at bottom and Tchoupitoulas Street, the curved artery that roughly marks the natural levee. The parallelogram shapes are an impact of geography on architecture, resulting from the extension of old streets and the surveying of new streets in such a manner that angular blocks were formed in the narrow riverside batture. When these blocks were subdivided into lots,

the lots took on this parallelogram shape and compelled architects to design buildings that conformed to the odd configurations. In his classic *Frenchmen, Desire, Good Children,* J. C. Chase observed that the American-era batture streets tend to have functional geographical names (Water, Delta, Front) compared with the historically rich and fanciful names of the colonial-era inland streets (Tchoupitoulas, Carondelet, Dryades). The foot of Canal Street appears at lower right, and the prominent Annunciation/Tchoupitoulas fork is at left center. *U.S. Geological Survey*

1989 Same area

The Warehouse District was heavily affected by the demolition and construction boom of the 1970s and 1980s, with more than 50 percent of its structures and landcover altered. Some of the new facilities along the river, namely the Ernest N. Morial Convention Center (lower left), were developed for the 1984 Louisiana World Exposition and remain in service today as exhibit halls and meeting rooms for the city's millions of conventioneers. The large, square Rivergate Convention Center (1968) at the foot of Canal Street at lower right was demolished in 1995 for a Harrah's casino. The cruciform building casting a shadow upon the Rivergate is the International Trade Mart (1966, now the World Trade Center), the forerunner of a fleet of skyscrapers that were to be built in downtown New Orleans over the succeeding twenty-five years. *Army Corps of Engineers, New Orleans District*

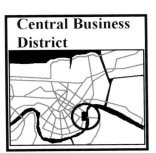

Central Business District

1944 Baronne Street near the Union intersection, looking downriver, in the Central Business District

A busy street scene in the heart of the Central Business District. At this time, Baronne Street was part of the St. Charles streetcar route, as it had been since the line began as the New Orleans & Carrollton Railroad in 1835. Heading down Baronne toward Canal Street, we see the Baronne Building (1902) with its prominent cornice, the Sears-Roebuck building (1931; see p. 229) at the Common Street intersection, and the Roosevelt Hotel, formerly the Grunewald (1908; see pp. 204-05). The structure with the fire escape (left) housed Philip Werlein's Southern Music House in 1870; it and its neighbors were adorned with balconies and galleries at the time. A *circa* 1911 perspective of Baronne Street taken from the roof of the Grunewald appears on p. 256. *Charles Franck Collection, The Historic New Orleans Collection, accession no. 1979.325.4854*

1996 Same site

The interesting heterogeneity of many mid-twentieth-century New Orleans streetscapes has been reduced in recent decades by the disappearance of protruding shop signs, an impact of the relocation of retailers and their customers to suburban areas. The scene today, though structurally similar, lacks the punc-tuated commotion of the old vista, and the eye is more likely to dismiss even handsome and historical buildings as unnoteworthy. The route of the St. Charles streetcar was switched to Carondelet Street in 1950.

227

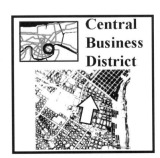

Central Business District

1920 and 1925 201 Baronne Street at the Common intersection, in the Central Business District

Top scene, 1920: This French Renaissance-style edifice, built in the 1870s, was home to the New Orleans Gas Company and later the New Orleans Public Service Inc. (NOPSI). The corner's obtuse angle reflects the interface between the street pattern of Faubourg Ste. Marie (to the left) and the commons (to the right) that separated the faubourg from the Vieux Carré during the early American years. Because these two communities abutted a curving river, the commons between them was shaped like a wedge. The downriver flank of the wedge became Canal Street, and the upriver flank became angular Common Street (seen here at right), which formed a series of nonorthogonal intersections like this one. **Bottom scene, 1925:** NOPSI added a new sign and minimized heat by shielding the building's eastern exposure to the morning sun with awnings. *Charles Franck Collection, The Historic New Orleans Collection, accession nos. 1979.325.447 and 1979.325.448*

1927 and 1998 Same site

Top scene, 1927: Vacant two years later. **Bottom scene, 1998:** An Art Deco-style retail building (1931), originally known as Feibleman's, conforms to the geometry of the obtuse intersection. This building, which housed Sears-Roebuck from the 1930s to 1982, was one of the first projects of famed New Orleans architect Samuel Wilson Jr. as a recent Tulane graduate working for Moise Goldstein. A 1937 WPA technical manual describes the soils beneath this building as a "sticky gumbo" laced with large cypress stumps, into which 1,800 60-foot pine pilings were driven for stabilization. Behind Sears is the twenty-eight-story skyscraper at 225 Baronne (1961), briefly the city's tallest structure. The former Sears building was renovated in 1997 as a Travelodge Hotel. *1927 photograph: Charles Franck Collection, The Historic New Orleans Collection, accession no. 1979.325.450*

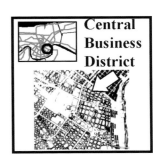

Central Business District

229

1951 300 to 400 block of Camp Street, looking toward Canal, in the Central Business District

The eight-story Gravier Building (1888, center) was built for the I. L. Lyons Wholesale Drug House and was among the city's earliest high-rises (though not supported by steel). To its right is Newspaper Row, district of the local press in the nineteenth century. The *Daily Picayune* office (1850) was located in the building above the words "Metal" and "Stencils" on the protruding sign at cen-

ter. On the left, starting from the Glass & Bern sign and coming this way, is a series of 1850s-era commercial structures, with one (407 Camp, far left) built in the 1830s. It recently lost a neighbor to a parking lot (extreme lower left). *Charles Franck Collection, The Historic New Orleans Collection, accession no. 1979.325.4900*

1996 Same site

The entire row of historical structures on the left was demolished in 1975, just prior to the demolition moratorium declared after the Central Business District lost 20 percent of its older structures in five years, leaving 40 percent of its acreage vacant. Across the street, Newspaper Row endures in good condition; the words "The Picayune" are still vaguely distinguishable on the old *Daily* *Picayune* building at 326 Camp, where Ed. Smith's Stencil Works operates to this day. Camp Street maintains a fairly intact collection of historical buildings, especially near St. Patrick's Church, a few blocks uptown.

Central Business District

1948 100 block of South Rampart Street, looking toward Canal, in the Central Business District

With the steeple of the Old Mortuary Chapel visible in the distance, North Rampart gives way to a multistory commercial district as it crosses Canal Street and becomes South Rampart. The first block of South Rampart marked the upper limit of the commons that separated the Vieux Carré from Faubourg Ste. Marie in the late Spanish and early American years. The commons extended as an elongated right triangle from here down to the river, ten blocks to the right; the base of the triangle was the first block of South Rampart (shown here), the leg became Canal Street, and Common Street formed the hypotenuse. See p. 383 for a 1927 oblique perspective of the former commons. Loew's State Theater (center right, with its marquee on Canal) opened in April 1926 to headlines in *The New Orleans Item* that read: "Elaborate New Structure Marks Important Page in New Orleans' Drama History; Is Artistic Triumph." *Charles Franck Collection, The Historic New Orleans Collection, accession no. 1979.325.5496*

1996 Same site

Loews closed in 1989 but reopened the next year as the State Palace Theater, on the corner of Canal and South Rampart. Both lanes of traffic on Rampart now curve into the interior of the Central Business District.

1946 100 block of South Rampart Street, in the Central Business District

North Rampart becomes South Rampart as it crosses Canal Street and heads uptown. Cardinal directions serve only to confuse in the older section of New Orleans; most people refer to lakeside/riverside as a local version of north and south, and uptown/downtown (or upriver/downriver) as adaptations of west and east. The Haverty Furniture Company advertisement is painted on the side of the Pickwick Club (1896), at 1030 Canal; the elaborate structure in the background is the Hotel Grunewald (1908, see pp. 205 and 219). *Charles Franck Collection, The Historic New Orleans Collection, accession no. 1979.325.5489*

1996 Same site

Fifty years of subtropical climate have faded but not erased the Haverty Furniture Company's advertisement. Old ads painted on brick walls (palimpsests) have become appreciated in recent years as nostalgic reminders of downtown bustle, long gone from many American cities but alive and well in New Orleans.

Central Business District

1945 300 block of South Rampart Street at the Perdido intersection, looking downriver, in the Central Business District

Heading up South Rampart, the multistory structures give way to pedestrian-scale shops and cottages that, in this photograph, form a curious montage. The dormered cottages at center, reminiscent of a Tremé or Marigny street scene, are remnants of a cluster of a dozen similar structures, six on this block and six behind. The Knights of Pythias Hall (1906, background), at seven stories plus a rooftop ballroom, was once among the largest black-owned buildings in America. Shops on South Rampart served patrons of all races during the segregationist era, unlike department stores on Canal. This neighborhood, extending a few blocks toward the lake (left) on Perdido and Gravier, constituted the black "Uptown District" of Storyville, operating in a quasi-legal state in the early twentieth century. *Charles Franck Collection, The Historic New Orleans Collection, accession no. 1979.325.5498*

1998 Same site

The Knights of Pythias Hall (now 234 Loyola), hidden behind the hotel at center, was expanded in the 1950s and masked by the striped façade visible at upper right. In the foreground block, only the fire hydrant remains; the former retail district was swept away by the socioeconomic changes of the 1960s. Hydrants have a notable "staying power" in New Orleans street scenes; more than five thousand were installed in 1919 as part of a citywide water system, and although the units have been replaced over the decades, the sites generally remain. The clarinet mural on the Holiday Inn, the sole clue that this scene is in New Orleans, commemorates the nearby area as one of the birthplaces of jazz.

Central Business District

1952 200 to 210 South Rampart Street at the Common intersection, in the Central Business District

The Fertel Building on South Rampart, with the Hibernia Bank Building in the distant left. South Rampart was a bustling retail district serving black and white New Orleanians in the days before integration, when African-Americans were not welcome at Canal Street department stores. This inter-section marked the lakeside/downriver corner of Faubourg Ste. Marie, New Orleans' first suburb, from its surveying in 1788 until the development of Canal Street about twenty years later. *Charles Franck Collection, The Historic New Orleans Collection, accession no. 1979.325.659*

1997 Same site

The intersection has been widened, obliterating all evidence of the old scene; above looms the Renaissance Center (Bank of New Orleans Building, 1971). Socioeconomic changes in the 1960s—integration and suburbanization—depleted the South Rampart business district of its clientele, and by the 1970s the street was characterized by skyscrapers and parking lots. From a preservationist perspective, the loss of the intimate street scene on the corner of Common and South Rampart is regrettable. From a geographical perspective, the drive to replace it with a skyscraper indicates that an economic magnetism still exists in downtown New Orleans, a force that has departed many other American downtowns for edge cities and industrial parks. The continued economic importance of old Faubourg Ste. Marie, transferred from building to building over the centuries, has a historical dimension of its own. A street scene similar to that of old South Rampart survives today in the 2000 block of Magazine Street.

Central Business District

1917 912 to 942 Gravier Street at the Dryades (now O'Keefe) intersection, in the Central Business District

This block is identified in the 1885 and 1908 Sanborn fire-insurance maps as the United Cotton Buildings, offices of cotton factors, with the ten-story Perrin Building (1902, later called the Baronne Building) anchoring the Baronne end of the block. One might imagine that the activity portrayed by Edgar Degas in his 1873 masterpiece *The Cotton Market in New Orleans*, which depicts a scene in Factors' Row on Perdido Street, went on in this building.

The tracks on Dryades (lower right) were part of the streetcar line that passed under the Poydras Market a few blocks uptown. See p. 256 for a *circa* 1911 view of a portion of this block, taken from the Hotel Grunewald. *Charles Franck Collection, The Historic New Orleans Collection, accession no. 1979.325.715*

1996 Same site

In the 1920s the massive structures were replaced by a series of commercial row buildings (mid-block on left) and on the corner by this edifice, originally known as Clark's Strand Garage. The garage, built early in the automobile age (1925), was designed by the noted architectural firm of Favrot and Livaudais and is stabilized upon 642 untreated yellow-pine pilings, a standard practice in late-nineteeth and early-twentieth-century New Orleans construction. The only trace of the old cotton buildings is the palimpsest on the wall of the neighboring Baronne Building (left), directly below the Hibernia Bank cupola.

Central Business District

1949 and 1954 300 to 310 Carondelet Street at the Gravier intersection, in the Central Business District

Top scene, 1949: Antebellum buildings with Italianate and Greek Revival styles line the corner of Gravier and Carondelet. To the left of the corner Paletou office is the New Orleans Stock Exchange (1906), noted for its beautiful pediment sculpture of allegorical figures. **Bottom scene, 1954:** Note the new Wait/Walk sign on the traffic post at left and the electric bus and streetcar on the right. Electric buses were first introduced to the city in 1929, and several lines operated into the 1970s. Carondelet Street replaced Baronne as part of the St. Charles streetcar route in 1950; Baronne had hosted the line since it began in 1835 as the New Orleans & Carrollton Railroad. *Charles Franck Collection, The Historic New Orleans Collection, accession nos. 1979.325.605 and 1979.325.606*

1997 Same site

Most of the buildings were demolished in 1971. Walls of the old Stock Exchange still stand, but its façade is completely removed and a diner now occupies the site. Attractive balconies grace the renovated corner structure, which now stands alone among parking lots. The currently unoccupied building recently housed the Hibernia Homestead & Savings Association and once was the site of the Spencer Business College, the Cassidy Hotel, and the Sazerac Bar. One Shell Square, the city's tallest building at 697 feet, stakes out the corner of St. Charles and Poydras. The St. Charles streetcar still travels these tracks.

Central Business District

1921 325 to 341 Carondelet Street at the Union intersection, in the Central Business District

This row of eight four-story granite-block commercial structures, reminiscent of a New York or Philadelphia street scene, was designed by George Purves and built in 1849 by Thomas Murray. The gallery on the corner building, added a few years after construction, puts a New Orleans touch in this otherwise Americanized block. Offices for cotton factors (agents) and other cotton-industry professionals occupied these buildings in the 1800s. The 1885 Sanborn fire-insurance map labeled some of these structures and many nearby buildings with the words "Cotton Samples," indicating a higher fire risk from the perspective of an underwriter. By 1921 a wide variety of businesses operated here. *Charles Franck Collection, The Historic New Orleans Collection, accession no. 1979.325.608*

244

1997 Same site

The label-style lintels on both the square and arched windows are distinctive in this well-preserved scene. One outstanding element of the American Sector and Canal Street was the integral row: matching structures spanning an entire block, harmonious in design, scale, setback, and use. Examples included Touro Row on Canal, Banks' Arcade on Magazine, and the Thirteen Sisters on Julia. Naturally, over the decades, adornment and utilization of the rows' components diversified, often creating complex and energized streetscapes. During the 1970s building boom, many integral rows were leveled to make room for a single skyscraper. This block on Carondelet (six of the original eight units survive) is a fine example of an antebellum American Sector row, restored by Lyons & Hudson for Citizens Homestead Association in 1981. Note the fire hydrant in both scenes.

Central Business District

circa 1924 Liverpool & London & Globe Insurance Building, 204 Carondelet Street at the Common intersection, in the Central Business District

The Liverpool & London & Globe Insurance Company Building, designed by Thomas Sully, guarded this busy intersection from 1895 to 1927. The early steel-frame building rested upon 359 50-foot pine pilings. On the corner to the left is the third and last St. Charles Hotel (1896), another Sully design; to the right is the Hibernia Building (1903), designed by Daniel H. Burnham and once the city's tallest structure at fourteen stories. *Charles Franck Collection, The Historic New Orleans Collection, accession no. 1979.325.598*

246

1996 Same site

The American Bank Building (now Bank One Centre), a twenty-three-story Art Deco structure with a six-story tower and lantern, was built by George J. Glover, Inc., on the site of the insurance building in 1928-29. The fireproof steel-frame building, designed by Moise Goldstein and Nathaniel Courtland Curtis, rests upon 1,653 untreated yellow pine pilings driven into the alluvial silt. During site preparation, engineers extracted the 359 pine pilings from the Liverpool & London & Globe Building and filled the holes with sand; attempts were made to rehammer the old pilings, but they quickly deteriorated with exposure. The American Bank Building's modernistic spire complements the classical Hibernia Bank cupola across the street, both of which are dramatically illuminated and conspicuous to the revelers on Bourbon Street. The First NBC Center (Place St. Charles, 1985, left) marks the site of the third St. Charles Hotel, destroyed in 1974; the former Hibernia Building (1903; far right) is now the Hampton Inn and University of New Orleans Conference Center.

Central Business District

circa 1910 Scottish Rite Temple (McGehee Church), 619 Carondelet Street between Girod and Lafayette, in the Central Business District

The original Methodist Episcopal Church (1837), located on Poydras and Carondelet, burned in 1851 and was replaced by this structure, the Edward McGehee Church of the Methodist Episcopal Church ("McGehee Church"). In the original design, the stained-glass window at center was the entrance, and a tall cupola rose from the roof. Its architect is unknown; a cornerstone plaque identifies the Stone Bros. as architect and A. Leibe as builder, but this probably refers to alterations made in the early 1900s. In Mills Lane's 1997 publication, *Architecture of the Old South: Louisiana*, the author speculates that James Dakin may have played a role in the design of this structure because its cupola, based on the classical Choragic Monument of Lysicrates, resembled a tower that Dakin planned for a New Orleans fire station. A rare photograph of the McGehee Church with its cupola appears in Lane's excellent book. The church was purchased in 1906 by the Grand Consistory of Louisiana, a Masonic organization, and renamed the Scottish Rite Temple. The "Glad U Kum" sign may have been intended to welcome Masons to a convention in April 1910. *Detroit Publishing Company, Library of Congress, no. LC-D4-71821 DLC*

1998 Same site

The Scottish Rite Temple with new doors, staircases, iron gates, and lamppost. The cupola is long gone, but the steep hip roof remains, contrasting with the building's Greek-temple design. The St. Charles streetcar passes in front of this conspicuous business-district landmark as it returns from its route from downtown to Carrollton.

Central Business District

circa 1858 700 block of Girod Street, between St. Charles and Carondelet, in the Central Business District

At right is the American Fire Company building (note the ladders on the carts and the emblem above the entrance), built in 1837 and used as a firehouse until 1960. The double façade at center is the Washington Artillery Hall, an armory designed by William A. Freret and recently completed in this view; to its left is an inset pair of Greek Revival townhouses (1838) and an adjoining house built around 1850. On the corner is a gabled townhouse (1832), one in a row of five, with a servants' quarters in its courtyard. The pole at center may be a lookout tower, located away from the firehouse to allow the carts to maneuver into the street. A similar apparatus appears in the *circa* 1858 firehouse photograph on p. 342. This scene is typical of the American Sector in the antebellum era. *Photograph by Jay Dearborn Edwards, The Historic New Orleans Collection, accession no. 1982.167.12*

1997 Same site

Despite its location in the Central Business District, this block of Girod Street maintains its antebellum scale and appearance. Every other structure remains: the firehouse (note the hydrant) was remodeled in the 1960s and is now an office; the twin Greek Revival houses were rescued from slumhood and restored in the late 1970s, and the corner cottage now operates as a tavern. The twin houses, built for Bank of New Orleans President Andrew Hodge, are noteworthy for their raised basements and carriageways, rarities in the American Sector. The Washington Artillery Hall was captured by Union troops in 1862,

sold, and burned within the year. The surviving façade was fitted with a new structure, identified as a soda-water factory in the 1885 Sanborn insurance map, and finally dismantled in the 1930s. Maj. Gen. Allison Owen salvaged the façade of the old armory and installed it at the Washington Artillery Park, near the Decatur/St. Peter intersection across from Jackson Square, where it stood from 1938 to 1972.

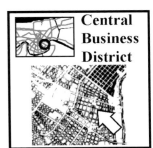

Central Business District

circa 1910 **Masonic Temple, 333 St. Charles Avenue at the Perdido intersection, in the Central Business District**

The imposing Masonic Temple, built in 1891 from designs by James Freret, resembled a medieval castle crossed with a Gothic cathedral. A statue of Solomon stood upon the spire (p. 212) of the massive structure, which rested upon square-hewn cypress pilings. This temple was the most impressive of a series of Masonic buildings dating back to the Spanish colonial era, when emigrating Americans established a lodge at Camp and Gravier in the new Faubourg Ste. Marie, away from the disapproving Spanish administrators and Catholic bishops in the Vieux Carré. See p. 384 for a *circa* 1924 oblique photograph of this area. *Detroit Publishing Company, Library of Congress, no. LC-D4-39618 DLC*

1996 Same site

The current Masonic Lodge Building, designed by the Stone Bros. and built by James Stewart & Co. in a modernized Gothic style, replaced the old temple in 1926. The square-hewn cypress pilings from 1891 were extracted and found to be in good condition, but after decades of submersion in water and silt, a fungus deteriorated them in a matter of months. The new lodge rests on 1,850 yellow-pine pilings of various lengths, driven through two layers of ancient cypress stumps, silt, and, in some places, a sturdy old sandbar. The eighteen-story high-rise served as the state Masonic headquarters until its sale in 1982; it now operates as an office building, though the Masonic emblems and the frieze ("Erected by the Grand Lodge of Louisiana") remain. To its right is the United Fruit Company Building (1920), known for its extravagant cornucopia sculpture above the entrance.

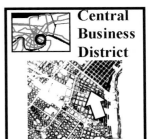

Central Business District

1950 Temple Sinai, 1032 Carondelet Street at the Calliope intersection, in the Central Business District

A towering landmark for decades, Temple Sinai (1872) served as the first home of New Orleans' oldest Reform Jewish congregation until it moved uptown in the 1920s. In 1929 the building was sold and fitted with the ungainly but harmonious appendage in front, covering the cast-iron doorway and marble steps as it geared up for commercial use. From then on, the former holy place was used for offices, storage, as a theater, and as an advertising studio (seen here).

The temple's original striped two-tone coloring (p. 308) had been painted over by the time of this photograph. The pipe cleaner on the top of the pilaster (left) *may* be a Christmas tree (the photo was taken on December 2), but all bets are off. The dome of the old New Orleans Public Library (p. 304) is visible at right. *Charles Franck Collection, The Historic New Orleans Collection, accession no. 1979.325.623*

1997 Same site

The former Temple Sinai survived modernization of the Central Business District and was narrowly missed by the expressway to the Greater New Orleans Bridge (p. 296), but eventually fell for a parking lot in 1977. Preservationists noticed the roof being dismantled one day in July of that year and began a frantic last-minute effort to save the 115-foot-high landmark, but by late July the city approved the demolition permit. The building's last owner was associated with K&B Drugstores, which occupied the office building (visible through the trees at right) that replaced the old library in 1961. The obelisk at Lee Circle is now visible at center. See pp. 302, 308, 391, and 393 for various perspectives of this lost landmark. The new Temple Sinai is located at 6227 St. Charles Avenue, next to Loyola University.

Central Business District

circa 1911 View up Baronne Street from the Hotel Grunewald, looking uptown into the Central Business District and Central City

At center right are the ten-story Baronne (Perrin) Building and the adjoining cotton buildings on Gravier Street that appear on p. 240. The large smokestack at right marks the powerhouse of the New Orleans Railway and Light Company, later the New Orleans Public Service Inc. (NOPSI), which had its office (p. 228) on the Baronne/Common corner in the immediate foreground.

Note the Hotel De Soto (1906), originally known as the Denechaud Hotel, on the corner of Baronne and Perdido (beneath the smoking chimney). In the distant upper right is St. John the Baptist Church on Dryades Street at Clio. *Detroit Publishing Company, Library of Congress, no. LC-D401-15657 R DLC*

1996 Same view

The two high-rises on the left are the modern Gothic-style Pere Marquette Building (1925) and the Canal Bank Building (1927, now First National Bank of Commerce). The De Soto is now Le Pavillon Hotel, visible in front of the BellSouth building on Poydras. The site of the NOPSI office, now occupied by a Travelodge Hotel (formerly Sears, 1931, p. 229), appears above the tennis courts.

Central Business District

circa 1906 **Elk Place, looking upriver from Canal Street, in the Central Business District**

The Orleans Parish Criminal Courts Building (left) was built in 1893 and served as the city's police headquarters, corrections facility, and court until the 1930s. The three-story Elks Club appears on the right, and the club's statue stands in the middle of the neutral ground. This block is part of the historic Basin Street corridor, which originally ran from the basin of the Carondelet Canal in Faubourg Tremé to Central City but has been renamed a number of times over the decades, in parts as Saratoga Street, Loyola Avenue, and for this particular block, Elk Place. *Detroit Publishing Company, Library of Congress, no. LC-D4-19305 DLC*

1996 Same site

The Criminal Courts Building was a city landmark until its demolition in 1949; the New Orleans Public Library (1959) now occupies the site. The neutral ground of Elk Place (which becomes Loyola Avenue at the next intersection) is one of the few in downtown to retain its width and natural landscape over the years. During and after World War II, a Veterans Service Center operated in a temporary structure in the immediate foreground; note the "Molly Marine" monument on the extreme right. Visible through the foliage at center is the Eye, Ear, Nose, and Throat Hospital, being prepared for demolition (p. 262). Within a few days it would join the Criminal Courts Building as a memory.

Central Business District

1925 Criminal Courts Building, Saratoga Street (formerly Basin and now Loyola) at Tulane, in the Central Business District

A closer look at the Orleans Parish Criminal Courts Building (1893). Despite its fortresslike appearance, the edifice was plagued with structural problems. After police operations and correctional functions moved into a new facility (still in use at Tulane and Broad) in 1931, the old courthouse served as a municipal court and as an office for the Works Progress Administration. The strategically located tower commanded views of the Central Business District, Mid-City, Central City, the Basin Street corridor, Faubourg Tremé, and the French Quarter. See pp. 382-83 for oblique perspectives of the courthouse and its environs. *The Historic New Orleans Collection, accession no. 1974.25.3.234*

1998 Same site

The Old Criminal Courts Building, its tower removed in its latter years, was demolished in 1949, when Saratoga Street was widened and renamed Loyola Avenue. The footprint of the old landmark is now occupied by the asphalt of the avenue and the International-style New Orleans Public Library (right), which came to this site when its domed predecessor at Lee Circle (p. 304) was demolished in 1959. In addition to its general stacks, the library houses genealogical records, Sanborn insurance maps, city newspapers on microfilm, and a wealth of other historical data on New Orleans. To the right on Tulane Avenue is New Orleans' "hospital district," home of a number of major medical facilities and teaching hospitals; to the left on Loyola Avenue is the seat of city government.

Central Business District

1996 Eye, Ear, Nose, and Throat Hospital, Elk Place at the Tulane intersection, in the Central Business District

Top-left scene: The Eye, Ear, Nose, and Throat (John Dibert Memorial) Hospital survived as one of the few veteran buildings in the modernistic Loyola Avenue corridor. The institution, established by Dr. A. W. DeRoaldes in 1889 to serve the poor, originally operated on South Rampart and later on North Rampart near the French Quarter. Funds were raised in the early 1900s to purchase this property, site of the Silver Dollar Saloon; a clinic was built in 1907, followed by this structure in 1921. The operation moved to Napoleon Avenue in 1988 and was purchased by a healthcare corporation in 1996, thus ending New Orleans' last stand-alone specialty hospital. In 1995 the City Council rejected the planning commission's stance to save the structure from a demolition proposal, and on April 20, 1996, a wrecking ball quickened the pace of time on this downtown corner. **Top-right scene:** One week later. **Bottom-left scene:** Rear of the structure, viewed from Tulane Avenue, April 20. **Bottom-right scene:** Same view, one week later.

1996 Same site

New Basin Canal's turning basin was filled during the 1930s, and the remainder of the waterway was eliminated by the 1950s to provide a corridor for Interstate 10 (Pontchartrain Expressway). Commuters use the 165-year-old path cleared by the Irishmen as they drive from the Interstate 10/610 split to the Superdome. The turning basin itself lies under parking lots and Loyola Avenue asphalt in this thoroughly modernized government district. Note St. Patrick's, the sole trace of the 1929 scene.

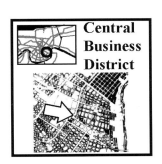

Central Business District

1950 1205 to 1215 Julia Street at the Saratoga (formerly Basin and now Loyola) intersection, in the Central Business District

These ramshackle buildings, some of which appear on the left side of the previous photograph (p. 264), once faced the turning basin of the New Basin Canal. *Charles Franck Collection, The Historic New Orleans Collection, accession no. 1979.325.729*

1996 Same site

This portion of Julia Street no longer exists, replaced by the vast infrastructural developments that include the creation of Loyola Avenue and its accompanying office buildings and parking lots, the Superdome and its appendages, and a snarl of expressways, on-ramps, and off-ramps. The New Basin Canal turning basin is now a series of streets and lots, and Joe Stamps's shanty at 1215 Julia is history.

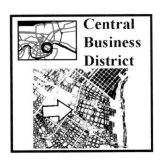

Central Business District

1952 Railroad yards and industrial area between South Rampart and Claiborne, near the Central Business District

The perforated triangle at upper left marks the site of the turning basin of the New Basin Canal (p. 264), dug by Irish immigrants in the 1830s to improve transportation between the American Sector and Lake Pontchartrain. It was filled in about twenty years before this photograph was taken. The perforated rectangle at center marks the Girod Street Cemetery (1822), a Protestant bur- ial ground that served the American population in Faubourg St. Mary. By the 1950s the cemetery, which had above-ground tombs, was overgrown and neglected. Poydras Street, once the route of the Gravier Canal (1805), runs along the bottom, and Claiborne Avenue appears on the right. *U.S. Geological Survey*

1989 Same area

The turning basin is lost amidst Loyola Avenue asphalt. Girod Street Cemetery was deconsecrated in 1957, relieved of its human remains, and obliterated. The site now lies under Macy's department store and the ancillary facilities near the Superdome. Largest unsupported indoor space in the world, the Superdome was completed in 1975 and has since become a signature of the city. The domed stadium overlays nineteenth-century cotton presses, coal yards, an old jail yard (1896), and the city stables (1908), testimony to the incredible transformations of the built environment in the twentieth century. The Superdome contributes greatly to the continued economic importance and cultural relevance of downtown. It is especially astounding in its nighttime illumination. *Army Corps of Engineers, New Orleans District*

Central Business District

circa 1858 City Hall (formerly Municipal Hall, now Gallier Hall), St. Charles Avenue at Lafayette Square, in the Central Business District

Photographed about five years after its dedication, James Gallier Sr.'s Municipal Hall served as City Hall when power swayed away from the Creoles in the Vieux Carré and toward the Americans in Faubourg St. Mary (the American Sector) after the 1852 consolidation of the city. It is often cited as Gallier's greatest work and the best example of Greek Revival architecture in New Orleans. Note the earlier Second Municipal Hall on the left and the fence around Lafayette Square. *Jay Dearborn Edwards, The Historic New Orleans Collection, accession no. 1982.167.7*

1910 and 1998 Same site

Top scene, 1910: Soulé Commercial College and Literary Institute moved into the gable-roofed former Second Municipal Hall in the 1870s and remodeled it for its needs, eventually replacing it with the corniced brick building (1902) at extreme left. Also gone is the fence surrounding the square. Visible between City Hall and the palm tree is the monument to John McDonogh, benefactor of the city's public schools. **Bottom scene, 1998:** Although city government moved out in 1957 and modern skyscrapers arose nearby, Gallier Hall still maintains a commanding presence over Lafayette Square, and it endures as the premier monument to New Orleans' most influential architect. Soulé College moved to the Buckner House on Jackson Avenue (p. 344) in 1923; its former home here on Lafayette Square is now the Louisiana Bar Center. The relocation of City Hall to the landscaped civic center on Loyola Avenue represents the city's postwar push to modernize, to depart from the crowded confines of old down-town, and to concentrate scattered government offices into a single locale. But Gallier Hall remains the symbolic seat of city government, as evidenced in part by this film crew preparing a scene for a movie. *1910 photograph: Detroit Publishing Company, Library of Congress, no. LC-D4-39621 DLC*

Central Business District

271

circa 1910 **Lafayette Square, viewed from the corner of Camp and North (now North Maestri), in the Central Business District**

Lafayette Square was the Americans' equivalent to the Creoles' Place d'Armes (Jackson Square). The Americans worshipped at the Gothic-style First Presbyterian Church (left, 1856), correlative to the St. Louis Cathedral, and governed from James Gallier's Greek Revival Municipal Hall (right, 1850), counterpart to the Cabildo. The First Presbyterian Church seen here replaced an earlier Greek Revival church, built in 1835 and burned in 1854. In *Architecture of the Old South: Louisiana*, Mills Lane comments: "The erection of the steeple of the Presbyterian Church was a spectacular event. The steeple was prefabricated within the walls of the tower, then raised into place with ropes and pulleys." At the extreme left appears the galleried Penn House (1856), a reminder that Lafayette Square also had a residential component. Note the Henry Clay monument at center, removed to this site in 1901 from its original location at Canal and Royal (p. 194). *Detroit Publishing Company, Library of Congress, no. LC-D4-71836 DLC*

272

1996 Same site

The steeple of the First Presbyterian Church was destroyed by the 1915 hurricane; the structure itself, plus the Penn House and its antebellum neighbors, was razed in 1938 for the construction of the federal building (1939-40) visible above the trees at left. In the following decades, modern high-rises and a forest of oak trees grew to envelop Lafayette Square. Gallier Hall still guards the lakeside flank of the shady plaza, overlooking the clanking streetcars and annual Mardi Gras parades on St. Charles Avenue. The Henry Clay statue, once the epicenter of the city, now stands among the oaks at the center of the park. Lafayette Square has become an unintended refuge for homeless people in recent years.

Central Business District

273

1934 Choctaw Club, 518 St. Charles Avenue at the North (now North Maestri) intersection, in the Central Business District

The Choctaw Club was a descendant of the city's Crescent Democratic Club, a political machine of the late nineteenth century. Its office on Lafayette Square was located in this American townhouse, known as the McDermott Building, built in 1841 from designs by James Gallier Sr. The corner townhouse, which anchored a block of identical structures that spanned from Poydras Street to North Street, was later adorned with these grand iron-lace balconies, similar to the galleries of the LaBranche House on Royal Street in the French Quarter (p. 52). *The Historic New Orleans Collection, accession no. 1979.325.356*

1996 Same site

The graceful Choctaw Club building and the entire block of antebellum Gallier townhouses were demolished in the 1970s and replaced with the hard lines and glaring façade of this International-style edifice, which was refurbished in 1997 and now operates as the Parc St. Charles Hotel. Only the lamppost remains. Of the scores of old buildings that were demolished in the Central Business District during the 1970s, many were razed not for a new edifice nor even for a parking lot, but simply to seize the opportunity to control the future of a parcel before restrictions could be imposed on the demolition of its historical structure.

Central Business District

1950 View from above Lafayette Square looking down St. Charles Avenue, into the Central Business District

Lafayette Square, lower right, was laid out by Carlos Laveau Trudeau (1788) when Faubourg Ste. Marie was subdivided out of the Gravier plantation as New Orleans' first suburb. The plaza was called Place Gravier until it was renamed for the Marquis de Lafayette to commemorate the Revolutionary War hero's 1825 visit to the city. Within a few decades this area became the hub of the American element and the seat of city government. In the foreground is Gallier's Municipal Hall (1850), which served as City Hall into the 1950s. At the corner of Lafayette Square is the Choctaw Club (p. 274) and its connecting townhouses (1841), also Gallier designs. At center background is the Hibernia Bank Building (1921), the city's high point at 355 feet; the spire to its right marks the American Bank Building (1929, p. 247); and the high-rise at right is the Masonic Lodge (1926, p. 253). Note the Hotel De Soto at extreme left. *Charles Franck Collection, The Historic New Orleans Collection, accession no.1979.325.6468*

1996 Same view

Poydras Street now dominates the scene, with 697-foot One Shell Square (1972, designed by Skidmore, Owings & Merrill) replacing the little hotel on the corner of Poydras and St. Charles. The endearing Choctaw Club and its neighbors have been replaced by an office building, and the modernistic Federal Reserve Bank (center, 1966) contrasts with the classical lines of neighboring City Hall (now called Gallier Hall and no longer used for city government). At upper right, the Poydras Center (1983) turns its back to the past importance of Lafayette Square, addressing instead the Texas-style success of Poydras Street. The Hotel De Soto is now Le Pavillon (p. 285), visible above the rear of Gallier Hall. Temporary stands on St. Charles Avenue, which appear in the 1950 perspective as well, mean Carnival season in New Orleans.

Central Business District

circa 1890 and *circa* 1925 Poydras Market, looking down (top) and up Dryades Street from the Poydras intersection, in the Central Business District

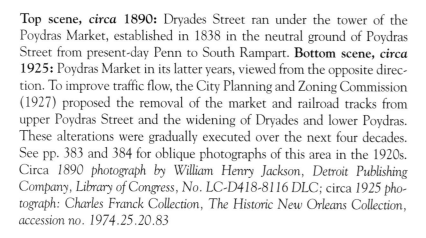

Top scene, *circa* 1890: Dryades Street ran under the tower of the Poydras Market, established in 1838 in the neutral ground of Poydras Street from present-day Penn to South Rampart. **Bottom scene, *circa* 1925:** Poydras Market in its latter years, viewed from the opposite direction. To improve traffic flow, the City Planning and Zoning Commission (1927) proposed the removal of the market and railroad tracks from upper Poydras Street and the widening of Dryades and lower Poydras. These alterations were gradually executed over the next four decades. See pp. 383 and 384 for oblique photographs of this area in the 1920s. *Circa 1890 photograph by William Henry Jackson, Detroit Publishing Company, Library of Congress, No. LC-D418-8116 DLC; circa 1925 photograph: Charles Franck Collection, The Historic New Orleans Collection, accession no. 1974.25.20.83*

1996 Same sites

Top scene: Poydras Market was demolished in 1932, and both Poydras and O'Keefe have been widened and modernized beyond recognition. (Dryades Street, originally called Philippa, is now called O'Keefe between Howard and Common.) Note the former home of Maylie's Restaurant on the left corner: this famous café was founded in 1876 by two market workers in a building to the right of the one visible here, which was removed when O'Keefe was widened in 1959. Maylie's operated for 110 years. **Bottom scene:** Looking up O'Keefe, with the Plaza Tower in the distance. There were nineteen public markets in New Orleans in 1935; now, except for the French Market in the Vieux Carré, no permanent outdoor marketplaces remain in the city. However, some market structures have been refitted as grocery or food stores, most notably the St. Roch Seafood Market on St. Claude Avenue in New Marigny and the Claiborne Circle Market on St. Bernard Avenue in Tremé.

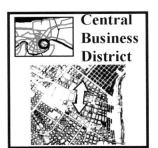

Central Business District

279

Insert shows 50 year old Wistaria vine, growing from inside of Restaurant. Below, shows same vine in bloom on front balcony. Maylie's Restaurant, New Orleans, La., Est. 1876

MAYLIE'S RESTAURAN
POYDRAS, CORNER
DRYADES

circa 1935 Maylie's Restaurant, 1009 Poydras Street at the Dryades (now O'Keefe) intersection, in the Central Business District

The coffee stall of Maylie and Esparbé in the old Poydras Market (which paralleled these buildings in the middle of Poydras Street) moved to this corner building in the 1880s and later expanded into the gabled building (1894) on the left. It gradually migrated upward in its cuisine and its reputation, becoming the stuff of postcards by the 1930s. The restaurant once had a "stag policy," serving men only. *The Historic New Orleans Collection, accession no. 1959.2.56*

1996 and 1998 Same site

Maylie's remained in operation and in the family for 110 years, even after the widening of Dryades Street in 1959 forced the restaurant to move into its gabled annex (1894), seen here. **Top scenes, 1996:** Maylie's finally closed on December 31, 1986, and stood empty and deteriorating for more than a decade in the shadows of modern skyscrapers across the street. The restaurant's last owner, Willie Maylie, grandson of the founder, said in a 1992 interview with Bill Grady of *The Times-Picayune,* "I dream every night of that damned restaurant. Last night I dreamed the old restaurant was full of people, and I was sitting at a table with two of my old customers, Judge Alexander Reynold and Paul Chazez, one of Huey Long's fair-haired boys. When I think of things like that, I start to cry a little bit. Fifty-three years I spent in there." A few scrawny branches of the famous wisteria cling to the balcony, though the foot-wide trunk disappeared from the enclosed alley that was part of the dining room. Plans to restore the building and reopen the restaurant surfaced a number of times over the years; then, in 1997, the acclaimed Manhattan steakhouse Smith & Wollensky bought the site to establish an elegant restaurant in the Burk furniture warehouse to the left of the former Maylie's and a grill in the old landmark itself. **Bottom scenes, 1998:** By late 1998, the $4 million restoration was complete and Smith & Wollensky's opened for business, breathing new street-level life into the Poydras skyscraper district. On this historic corner, the future looks as bright as the past.

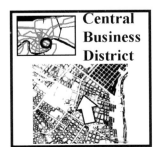

Central Business District

281

1941 921 to 935 Poydras Street, between Dryades (now O'Keefe) and Penn, in the Central Business District

Linearity and repetition in a Poydras streetscape. This row of three-story structures, designed by R. Seaton on property owned by John Gleises, was contracted in 1845 to be built on Poydras between Philippa (later Dryades and now O'Keefe) and Penn for the sum of $27,000. Nine and a half of the ten units in the row survived a century later. The old Poydras Market (p. 278), built on land donated by a railroad company to sell rail-transported produce in the American Sector, occupied the center of this street from 1838 to 1932. Franck (center) is an important name in New Orleans street photography; the company photographed countless commercial buildings and street scenes in the city from 1917 to 1955. *Charles Franck Collection, The Historic New Orleans Collection, accession no. 1979.325.821*

1997 Same site

Not even a lamppost remains. Only the three units near Penn Street remained by 1964, and the entire row was gone by 1967. Verticality, in the form of the thirty-seven-story Louisiana Land and Exploration (LL&E) Tower, erected in 1987 in a modernized Art Deco style, now defines the block. *David* and *The Lute Player* are 1988 sculptures of one of New Orleans' greatest artists, Enrique Alférez. Born in 1901 in central Mexico, Alférez served in Pancho Villa's revolutionary army and moved to Chicago in the 1920s to study art. His illustrious career in New Orleans began in 1929 and has spanned an incredible eight decades.

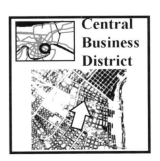

Central Business District

1924 Looking down Baronne Street from the Poydras intersection, in the Central Business District

Transportation in an era of change: pedestrians, a cyclist, a horse-drawn cart, two types of streetcars, and automobiles ply the streets beneath the elegant Hotel De Soto. The nine-story steel-frame structure (1906) was designed by Toledano and Wogan and built by Milliken Bros. as the Denechaud Hotel, with its primary orientation toward Baronne Street. The hotel occupies the former site of Werlein Hall (National Theater), corner of Baronne and Perdido. A century earlier, the terminus of the Gravier Canal (1805), a ditch excavated to drain the Poydras Street corridor, was located near this intersection. *Charles Franck Collection, The Historic New Orleans Collection, accession no. 1979.325.4857*

284

1996 Same site

Poydras Street (on which the horse was traveling) was widened in the mid-1960s and is now the city's principal office district, an impact of oil money and Texas style. As a result of the widening, the two-story structure abutting the Hotel De Soto in the 1924 scene was eliminated, and the hotel (now Le Pavillon) was expanded to fill a portion of the gap and reoriented to address the newfound importance of Poydras Street. The addition does not flatter the otherwise attractive structure. To visualize Le Pavillon's former appearance, see the Fairmont Hotel (1908, formerly the Grunewald and the Roosevelt; pp. 219 and 234) on University Place. It has similar bay windows and still retains its cornice.

Central Business District

1920 and 1942 Perdido Street (left) at the Dryades (now O'Keefe) intersection, in the Central Business District

Top scene, 1920: A solid commercial structure with simple but attractive brickwork. The Hotel De Soto (1906) appears at left. **Bottom scene, 1942:** Changes in infrastructure: the cobblestones of Dryades Street have been replaced with asphalt, and the overhead cables and corresponding streetcar rails have been removed. The manhole covers, however, keep their ground. Note the simplification of the hotel's cornice. *Charles Franck Collection, The Historic New Orleans Collection, accession nos. 1979.325.779 and 1979.325.780*

1997 Same site

Today, the scene is inverted: the corner building has been flattened into a parking lot as its neighbor, the Louisiana Land and Exploration Tower (p. 283), has risen into the sky. Hotel De Soto is now Le Pavillon; One Shell Square (1972) appears on the upper left.

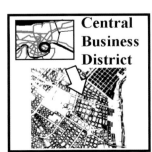

Central Business District

1949 423 to 437 Poydras Street between Magazine and Tchoupitoulas, in the Central Business District

A row of nineteenth-century stores with Italianate details, later utilized as warehouses, along lower Poydras Street near the Magazine intersection. The components on the left were the office of J. B. Vanhorn & Co. Commission Merchants in 1871; the plainer structures on the right were part of the Leon Israel Coffee Mill in the early 1900s, one of a number of coffee importers in this area. Wholesale grocers, liquor distributors, and other port-oriented businesses operated in the other units and in nearby blocks until the mid-twentieth century. *Charles Franck Collection, The Historic New Orleans Collection, accession no. 1979.325.812*

1996 Same site

A 1927 *Major Street Report* by the New Orleans City Planning and Zoning Commission proposed the widening of Poydras Street, plus a number of other arteries, to adapt the old river city to the new needs of the automobile age. The plan was finally executed nearly forty years later, when Poydras Street between Penn and the river was widened from six lanes (78 feet including sidewalks) to eight lanes plus a two-lane-wide neutral ground, spanning 132 feet. (The blocks above Penn were already wide on account of the Poydras Market, p. 278.) The expansion came at the expense of the downtown side of the street, so that today there are no old structures facing Poydras on its downriver flank below O'Keefe. The few historical structures still visible along the expansion area, seen on this page and on the next page, are parallel, not perpendicular, to Poydras, because they were designed to front the neighboring streets of Camp, Magazine, Tchoupitoulas, etc. The old warehouses of this block are now a volume of air through which thousands of motorists pass daily on modernized Poydras Street. See pp. 384 and 389 for Poydras scenes before and after the widening.

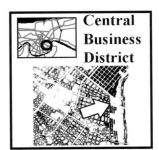

Central Business District

1996 Poydras Street between Camp and Magazine, in the Central Business District

This termite-infested rear appendage of an old brick structure at 414 Camp Street, parallel to modernized Poydras Street, gave way one stormy night in March 1996. For many decades home to the Levin's Auction Exchange and last used as the 1995 gubernatorial campaign office of politician Mary Landrieu (daughter of Moon Landrieu, New Orleans mayor from 1970 to 1978), the turn-of-the-century building was hidden from Poydras until the 1960s, when the street was widened and the structures fronting it were torn down. Deterioration and collapse are the inevitable downsides of New Orleans' poetic and much-celebrated embrace of subtropical decadence.

1996 Same site

A month later, cars park on the lot before the rubble is fully removed, revealing the dynamics of supply and demand for space in the Central Business District. On July 12, 1998, another scourge—fire, probably arson—visited the main structure (beyond view to the left), destroying the edifice and rendering the entire parcel a parking lot by the end of the summer.

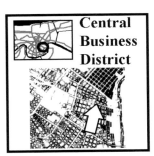

Central Business District

1945 510 to 524 South Peters Street between Poydras and Lafayette, in the Warehouse District/Central Business District

A typical block of shops and warehouses, dating from the 1850s to the early 1900s, in the rugged industrial section of the Central Business District. The J. Watts Kearney & Sons building is identified as a cement warehouse in the 1908 Sanborn map; its neighbors to the right housed the Columbia Coffee Mills and the New Orleans Coffee Company. These buildings are among the scores of parallelogram-shaped structures visible in the aerial photograph on p. 224. *Charles Franck Collection, The Historic New Orleans Collection, accession no. 1979.325.794*

1997 Same site

The trees and new windows indicate an adaptive reuse of old buildings in this area: since the 1984 Louisiana World Exposition, the Warehouse District has steadily developed into a "Southern SoHo," with art galleries, professional offices, and ensconced nightclubs sharing the streets with hulking nineteenth-century warehouses. In 1993, as the city swooned under the promises of the gambling industry, a proposal by Christopher Hemmeter and Caesars World called for the demolition of this block for an enormous casino parking garage.

The plan also proposed the closure of nearby streets for the construction of lagoons, waterfalls, and other such buffooneries. By 1996, legalized gambling in New Orleans was well on its way to becoming a disaster of legendary proportions; the garage was built on a much smaller scale, and today these old buildings on South Peters stand in good shape.

Central Business District

293

1921 and 1949 1148 South Peters Street at the Calliope intersection, in the Warehouse District/Central Business District

Top scene, 1921: The Fulton Bag and Cotton Mill (left, with tower) was designed by the Stone Bros. and built in 1909 on the site of an old cotton press at the Gaienne intersection of South Peters. The five-story, red-brick Crane Company warehouse, designed by Emile Weil, was annexed to it in 1920 and was near completion at the time of this photograph. Both buildings are representative of the many massive and attractively designed turn-of-the-century warehouses in this industrial district. **Bottom scene, 1949:** Maison Blanche was using the structure for storage at this time. *Charles Franck Collection, The Historic New Orleans Collection, accession nos. 1979.325.805 and 1979.325.807*

1996 Same site

The major change here is not the buildings but their environs: ramps for the Crescent City Connection, located directly above the photographer, launch traffic over the Mississippi River from Algiers, while the immense Ernest N. Morial Convention Center lies across the street toward the right. The Fulton Bag and Cotton Mill was until recently the Krauss warehouse, supplying the Canal Street department store that operated at the Basin Street intersection from 1903 to 1997. The warehouse's fine brick tower, now without its pyramidal roof, serves as a dramatic landmark dominating the first panoramic views of downtown New Orleans for motorists arriving from the West Bank.

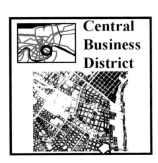

Central Business District

circa 1957 Looking into the Central Business District from above the corner of St. Charles and Clio

The construction of the Pontchartrain Expressway (foreground) and the Greater New Orleans Bridge in the late 1950s was the single greatest agent of change in historic New Orleans in this era. Note the Temple Sinai (1872, p. 254) at center and the domed New Orleans Public Library (1908, p. 304) at right, near Lee Circle. This photograph was taken from the roof of the building now known as the Saint Charles Regency Apartments. *Charles Franck Collection, The Historic New Orleans Collection, accession no. 1974.25.8.61*

1996 Same view

The library was demolished in 1959 and Temple Sinai followed in 1977. Four structures in this view held or hold the subtitle "tallest building in New Orleans": St. Patrick's Church (1840; 185 feet) at far right; Hibernia Bank (1921; 355 feet) at center; the 228 Baronne Building at left center, with overhanging top (1962, 362 feet); and One Shell Square (1972; 697 feet), the current leader. Until fairly recently, true skyscrapers were thought to be unbuildable on the deltaic muck below New Orleans. Construction engineers then began exploiting the compacted clays, silts, and sands in the Pleistocene strata by driving concrete pilings more than 70 feet into the earth to form a stable foundation for a modern skyscraper. A typical New Orleans highrise rests on hundreds of pilings penetrating 100 feet into the earth. One Shell Square's 500 18-inch-wide pilings are 210 feet long.

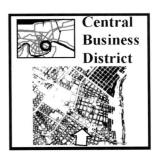

Central Business District

circa 1967 **The Central Business District and surrounding areas**

An oblique perspective of the Central Business District viewed from Central City looking toward Algiers (across the river). The city's two new skyscrapers, the International Trade Mart near the river and the Plaza Tower at right, were revolutionary not only for their heights but for their locations outside the core business district. The Trade Mart's site reflected an expectation of office-build-ing construction along newly widened Poydras Street, while the Plaza Tower foresaw the Loyola Avenue corridor as New Orleans' future "Sixth Avenue." The Superdome was in design phase at this time. *The Historic New Orleans Collection, accession no. 1974.25.8.74*

circa 1974 **Same view**

The Louisiana Superdome—"the largest 'people place' in the history of mankind . . . a monument to man's daring imagination, ingenuity and intelligence," according to a 1974 press release by the facility's public-relations group—was completed in 1975 at a cost of $163 million. It prompted a swath of office-building construction along Poydras Street during the OPEC oil boom that lasted until the mid-1980s, drawing these once-obscure railroad yards into the domain of the Central Business District. One of the first skyscrapers on Poydras is now the city's tallest structure, One Shell Square (1972; 697 feet),

at the corner of St. Charles Avenue. These developments made Poydras the city's new showcase for private-sector wealth, while Loyola Avenue hosted somber government buildings, open spaces, and the isolated Plaza Tower. The French Quarter and Faubourg Marigny appear at upper left, Algiers at upper right, and Central City in the foreground. *The Historic New Orleans Collection, accession no. 1974.25.8.76*

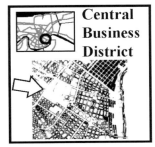

Central Business District

299

1931 and 1952 917 to 921 St. Charles Avenue at Lee Circle, in the upper Central Business District, near the Lower Garden District

Top scene, 1931: A Texaco station and garage occupy the ground floor of this flamboyant Moorish structure, built in 1926 and configured to the curves of Lee Circle. The doors on the second floor resemble those of a Mexican palace. **Bottom scene, 1952:** With the neighboring house at left removed and new signs installed, the corner starts to look more like a gas station. Note the prices. Refer to pp. 390-91 for oblique perspectives of Lee Circle. *Charles Franck Collection, The Historic New Orleans Collection, accession nos. 1979.325.891 and 1979.325.893.*

1996 Same site

It couldn't have lasted. The Texaco station occupies a more predictable structure now.

Central Business District

circa 1918 700 Howard Avenue at Lee Circle, in the upper Central Business District, near the Lower Garden District

This interesting montage incorporates a variety of architectural signatures of New Orleans' diverse cultural heritage: a Creole-style dormer and hip roof at left; a Tudor mansion at right (perhaps "imported" by a Northerner); a recently modernized commercial building at center; and in the background, the Temple Sinai, a "Roman-Byzantine" place of worship for the city's influential Reform Jewish community. The streetcar tracks in the foreground curve to the shape of Lee Circle. Note the early fire hydrant on the left and the newer model to its right. See p. 308 for a *circa* 1895 perspective of these buildings. *Charles Franck Collection, The Historic New Orleans Collection, accession no. 1979.325.426*

302

1996 Same site

Only the fire hydrant remains. The corner has been stripped of its geographical identity and replaced by an expedient service station. From the perspective of the station owner and customers, the change increases convenience and reduces costs. From the perspective of the city and the neighborhood, the alteration degrades the area and homogenizes what was once distinctive. Lee Circle, from which this photograph was taken, endures as an interface point between commercial and residential New Orleans. The streetcar tracks, too, keep the "New Orleans" in this once-interesting scene.

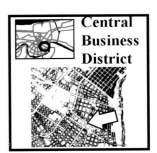

Central Business District

circa 1910 New Orleans Public Library, St. Charles Avenue at Lee Circle, in the upper Central Business District, near the Lower Garden District

Financed by Andrew Carnegie and the city, New Orleans Public Library (1908) was built on the site of the old Carrollton Railroad Depot, which was removed in 1866 and overlaid in 1871 by the foundation of what would have been an imposing Masonic temple. Infighting among the Masons led to the abandonment of the plan, and the foundation served as a platform for traveling circuses, theaters, and even a roller coaster. In 1890 this locale accommodated an ornate temporary hall for the German-American singing club, Saengerbund, to house the group's festival in New Orleans. The $50,000 hall was used for four days and cleared away by the Masons within the year. The Roman-temple design of this library was created by Diboll, Owen, and Goldstein and constructed upon concrete pilings instead of the yellow pine trunks traditionally used for foundations in turn-of-the-century New Orleans. For fifty years the towers of the Temple Sinai (distant right), combined with the copper dome of the library, made for an impressive sight in the Lee Circle area. *Detroit Publishing Company, Library of Congress, no. LC-D4-71105 DLC*

1996 Same site

The structure was torn down in 1959 after the library moved to a new facility (p. 261) on Loyola Avenue with four times the floor space. During demolition, workers encountered the wooden pilings from the foundation (1871) of the never-constructed Masonic temple as well as the concrete pilings (1908) of the old library. The former John Hancock Building (1961, designed by Skidmore, Owings & Merrill) now occupies the library site, an empty lot overlays the Temple Sinai, and the Pontchartrain Expressway whisks over St. Charles Avenue. Now known as K&B Plaza, this modernistic landmark is noted for its outdoor sculpture gallery. K&B Pharmacy was founded by Gustave Katz and Sydney Besthoff at 732 Canal Street in 1905 and grew into a regional chain of 180 stores until it was acquired in 1997 by the Rite Aid Corporation.

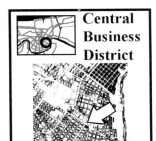

Central Business District

1906 Lee Circle, St. Charles Avenue and Howard Avenue, in the upper Central Business District, near the Lower Garden District

Once part of the Delord-Sarpy plantation, this land was sold in 1807 to a Creole planter, Armand Duplantier, who hired surveyor Barthelemy Lafon, designer of Faubourg Marigny, to lay out a community in this upriver frontier of the city. Lafon designed a grand and classical urban area in what is now the Lower Garden District, with canals, parade grounds, parks, marketplaces, civic structures, and a rich collection of mythological street names. Though the plan was only partially successful, one enduring element was Place du Tivoli, a rotary that coupled street patterns in adjacent areas and later would route the flow of traffic in four directions. Nearly three-quarters of a century later, when cultural sympathies of the city no longer lay with the European aspirations of the old Creole populace, a monument to Confederate Gen. Robert E. Lee was erected on Place du Tivoli, and the site was renamed Lee Circle. A photograph of the monument's 1884 unveiling shows a group of about six hundred children arranged to form the Confederate battle flag, another design of a local Creole, Gen. P. G. T Beauregard. *Detroit Publishing Company, Library of Congress, no. LC-D4-19310 DLC*

1996 Same site

The building with the mansard roof and dormer is the last house (now a restaurant) on Lee Circle, probably dating from the early 1880s but with some components possibly twenty years older. It appears as a three-story "French roof" structure in the 1885 Sanborn insurance map, not far from a bowling alley, a vapor bath house, a temporary roller coaster set up on the foundation of the never-built Masonic temple, and other odd establishments surrounding Lee Circle. The house's distinctive shape makes it ubiquitous in many old photographs and sketches of the area, like Louisiana artist George Rodrigue's Blue Dog. Lee Circle today serves as a node among three districts: the commercial Central Business District and the residential neighborhoods of both the Lower Garden District and Central City.

Central Business District

circa 1895 **Looking up Howard Avenue to Lee Circle, in the upper Central Business District, near the Lower Garden District**

Only in New Orleans would a prominent monument to the Confederacy (Lee Monument, 1884) and a major Jewish temple (Temple Sinai, 1872) share a vista. The visual association had a historical parallel: Judah P. Benjamin, the Confederate States of America's attorney general, secretary of war, and secretary of state, hailed from New Orleans' Jewish community. Temple Sinai is seen here in its original two-tone striped coloring; the onion-dome steeple of St. John the Baptist on Dryades Street is visible behind the base of the monument. See p. 302 for a view of the cluster of buildings behind Lee Circle. *Detroit Publishing Company, Library of Congress, no. LC-D4-5750 DLC*

308

1997 Same site

Temple Sinai was felled from the scene in 1977. The Romanesque curves in the foreground form the turret of the Howard Memorial Library, since 1888 a landmark to travelers winding around Lee Circle. Refer to pp. 390-91 for oblique perspectives of Lee Circle.

Central Business District

circa 1900 Howard Memorial Library, Howard Avenue at Lee Circle, in the upper Central Business District

The "Richardson Romanesque" style of Howard Memorial Library (1888) is a contribution of Louisiana-born architect Henry Hobson Richardson, who died two years before the Boston firm of Shepley, Rutan, and Coolidge finished its construction. Richardson was born on the Priestly plantation in St. James Parish in 1838, lived for a while on Julia Street, and studied in New Orleans before moving on to great notoriety in the Northeast. This design was originally submitted but not selected for the Hoyt Library in Saginaw, Michigan; after Richardson's untimely death, it was commissioned by the influential Howard family for a library at Lee Circle. Howard Memorial Library was not a public book-lending institution but a privately funded reference library, established by Annie Howard Parrott in honor of her father, Charles T. Howard. The collection, which specialized in Louisiana history, grew from 30,000 items in 1897 to 107,000 items in 1938, when it merged with Tulane's Tilton Library. The collection moved uptown to the new Howard-Tilton Memorial Library on the Tulane campus in 1941 and again in 1968 to the current building. *Detroit Publishing Company, Library of Congress, no. LC-D4-4889 DLC*

1996 Same site

After the departure of the library, the brooding sandstone fortress served as a British War Relief warehouse during World War II and suffered a fire, possibly by saboteurs, that damaged the interior and roof. A radio station, a private company, and a law firm occupied the structure at various times over the past five decades as its interior was continuously remodeled and its exterior became cloaked in ivy. The former Howard Memorial Library, one of two remaining nineteenth-century buildings on Lee Circle, will soon be occupied by the University of New Orleans Ogden Museum of Southern Art. The Richardson Romanesque style is reflected in New Orleans today by a number of mansions on St. Charles Avenue and many older structures on the campus of Tulane University. A dramatic carving on the arch at the library's entrance (center) depicts *Ignora* as a snarling beast, with chains around its neck symbolizing the enlightening function of the library.

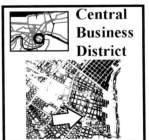

Central Business District

circa 1910 **Memorial Hall (Confederate Museum), 929 Camp Street, in the upper Central Business District**

One block riverside of Lee Circle stands Memorial Hall (1891), envisioned by philanthropist Frank T. Howard and designed by Thomas Sully and Albert Toledano expressly as a meeting place for Confederate veterans and an archive for their relics. Its Romanesque style matches the neighboring Howard Memorial Library (1888, left); the tower and portico were added in 1908. The eight-inch Columbaid cannon in front was cast in Selma, Alabama, and used by the Washington Artillery of New Orleans to defend Spanish Fort in Mobile Bay until its capture in the last week of the war. It was found in 1891 and placed here in 1899 by the company's survivors. Across the street from this site stood the Delord-Sarpy House, a French Creole mansion (*circa* 1815) that survived until the 1950s as the oldest house in the area. *Detroit Publishing Company, Library of Congress, no. LC-D4-16325 DLC*

1996 Same site

Memorial Hall, now connected to the former library, serves the same purpose a century later and is the oldest museum in the state of Louisiana. It is owned and operated by a private group, the Louisiana Historical Association. The museum inside retains its traditional open layout in a beautiful polished-wood cathedral-ceiling hall, a refreshing change from the compartmentalized multi-media cubicles of so many modernized history museums. Note the depiction on the wall of Lee and Jackson's last meeting at Chancellorsville and also the Columbaid cannon below the painting (moved to this site to accommodate parking). The angle of the high-rise in the background indicates the curvature of Lee Circle, an appropriate neighbor to the Confederate Museum. Behind the photographer to the left is the expressway off-ramp that replaced the Delord-Sarpy House in 1957.

Central Business District

1920s and 1957 Delord-Sarpy House, 534 Howard Avenue near the Camp intersection, in the upper Central Business District

Top scene, 1920s: The Delord-Sarpy House, a first-generation structure in Lafon's layout of Faubourg Duplantier, survived to become the oldest building above Canal Street. Built a few years after the colonial era (*circa* 1815), this French Creole country house stood its ground for 140 years as its Old World countryside evolved into a sweaty port-city warehouse district. As one of the first houses in the area, it was oriented to face the river, not the street; hence we are looking at the side of the house here, with the front galleries appearing on the left. The Delord-Sarpy House was stylistically similar to the Girod House, its contemporary on Chartres Street (p. 78), and both were probably designed by Jean Hyacinthe Laclotte. **Bottom scene, 1957:** The river gave it life and the river took it away: by a matter of feet, the Delord-Sarpy House interfered with the ramps planned for the Greater New Orleans Bridge. This is the opposite end of the front gallery, during demolition. Note the square columns, staircase, and the impressive line of servants' quarters across Howard Avenue. *Charles Franck Collection, The Historic New Orleans Collection, accession nos. 1985.120.35 and 1981.3243.1018*

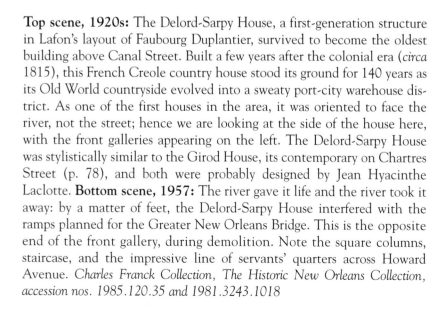

314

1996 Same site (corresponds to 1920s perspective)

In 1955 Samuel Wilson Jr. and the Louisiana Landmarks Society proposed a slightly altered plan for the exit ramp that would have spared the old house, but New Orleans authorities (and the public, for that matter) in the 1950s prioritized for the least-cost path to economic development, and the proposal fell on deaf ears. Drivers arriving from the West Bank and exiting onto Howard and Camp now pass right through the space of the lost mansion. See pp. 320-21 and 390-91 for aerial perspectives of this area in the last years before the expressway.

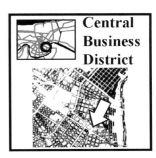

Central Business District

FEB. 10, 1933

1933 Looking down Howard Avenue from the Dryades (now O'Keefe) intersection, in the upper Central Business District

Howard Avenue formed a border between the Central Business District to the left and residential Central City to the right. This corridor was formerly the Duplantier plantation, a typical French long lot accessing the river at one end (straight ahead) and disappearing into the backswamp at the other, a distance of about 40 arpents (about 1.5 miles). The street was originally called *Cours des Tritons* (Tritons Walk), after the mythological sea god, and was fused with Delord Street when both were renamed Howard Avenue in honor of the benefactors of Howard Memorial Library. This photograph was taken from what was New Orleans' backswamp frontier in about 1820. Note the mixed commercial and residential use and the presence of pedestrians. Lee Circle is at center. *Charles Franck Collection, The Historic New Orleans Collection, accession no. 1979.325.4815*

1996 and 1998 Same site

Top scene, 1996: Howard Avenue is now entirely commercial, and pedestrians are uncommon. The avenue's role as a border between the Central Business District and Central City has been eclipsed by the Pontchartrain Expressway, which runs to the right of this perspective. The wedge-shaped Howard Building (1926, left center) is an architectural product of New Orleans geography, its shape reflecting the interior of the Mississippi River crescent. A local television station, WDSU Channel 6, breathed new life into this area when it constructed its studios here in 1995 (domed tower on right). The chimneyed shotgun house at far right, the Kate Casey House (1884), was the last structure of its type on increasingly modernized Howard Avenue. **Bottom scene, 1998:** Encircled by concrete, construction, and traffic, the Kate Casey House finally burned down in 1997, depriving Howard Avenue of its last residential element.

Central Business District

1950 The Southern (Howard) Building, 829 to 841 Howard Avenue at the St. Joseph intersection, in the upper Central Business District

A closer look at the wedge-shaped Williams Company building ("The Southern"), New Orleans' answer to New York City's famous Flatiron Building. It was designed by W. E. Spink and built by W. Horace Williams Co. Engineers in 1926. The seven-story steel-frame structure rests on 137 peeled yellow-pine pilings, each about fifty feet long. Like an old French long lot, the structure and its block open up toward the Mississippi, a mile in the distance. Note the web of streetcar cables. *Charles Franck Collection, The Historic New Orleans Collection, accession no. 1979.325.721*

1996 Same site

Instead of advertising to motorists and pedestrians on Howard Avenue, as the W. Horace Williams sign did in 1950, a billboard atop the same building (renamed "The Howard") now addresses the traffic on the Pontchartrain Expressway, a few hundred feet to the right. Note the Maginnis Cotton Mill water tower still standing beyond Lee Circle in the distant right. Other wedge-shaped intersections, components of a street network derived from the French arpent land-division system, appear on pp. 104, 132, 324, 332, and 356.

Central Business District

319

1952 The Lower Garden District

The area named the "Lower Garden District" by architectural historian Samuel Wilson Jr. in 1962 comprises six late-eighteenth-century long-lot plantations—Duplantier, Solet (Saulet), La Course, L'Annunciation, des Religieuses (Ursuline Nuns), and Panis—that developed into three nineteenth-century neighborhoods: Coliseum Square, Annunciation Square, and portions of the Irish Channel. These lands originally pertained to Bienville and later to the Jesuits until their expulsion after the French and Indian War in 1763. The plantations were subdivided in 1806-10 by Barthelemy Lafon and reached full development by the 1840s. The Lower Garden District today is notable for its absorbing variety of mid-nineteenth century residences and for its unforgettable street names, celebrating the Greek muses and reflecting Lafon's classical aspirations. Heading from Lee Circle upriver (upper left toward lower left), the streets are Calliope, Clio, Erato, Thalia, Melpomene, Terpsichore, Euterpe, Polymnia, and Urania. *U.S. Geological Survey*

1994 Same area

The Greater New Orleans Bridge and its expressways cut a swath through the areas now known as the Warehouse District and Lower Garden District in the late 1950s, eliminating scores of old structures and punctuating the formerly gradual transition between commercial and residential New Orleans. A second span was opened in 1988. Until 1958, commuters in downtown New Orleans rode ferries to reach the West Bank. One of the landmarks lost to the bridge construction was the Delord-Sarpy House (*circa* 1815, p. 314), which appears in the 1952 aerial photo about 1.3 blocks to the right of Lee Circle, on Howard near the corner of Camp. Its site is now occupied by the off-ramp visible at the top of this 1994 photo. The ramp on the opposite side of the expressway was removed soon after this photograph was captured. *U.S. Geological Survey*

Lower Garden District/ Warehouse District

UP CAMP AT POEYFARRE
11-19-47

1947 Looking up Camp Street at the Poeyfarre intersection, into the Lower Garden District

Along this portion of Camp Street, businesses and warehouses petered out and Barthelemy Lafon's nineteenth-century residential neighborhood emerged. The three churches in the background are St. Paul's Episcopal Church (1893), Coliseum Place Baptist Church (1855), and St. Theresa of Avila Roman Catholic Church (1849), at Margaret Place and Coliseum Square. See pp. 390-91 for oblique views of this area. *Charles Franck Collection, The Historic New Orleans Collection, accession no. 1979.325.4907*

1996 Same site

Practically the entire street scene was wiped off the map in the late 1950s by ramps for the Greater New Orleans Bridge. Of the three churches, less than two remain: St. Theresa's still stands at center right behind the Margaret Monument, and the Coliseum Place Baptist Church (center in the extreme distance) still faces Coliseum Square, but without its steeple, which Hurricane Betsy knocked off in 1965. St. Paul's was demolished in 1958, after it was prac-tically entwined in expressways and ramps. The ramp that doomed St. Paul's was in turn removed in 1994. The hard-fought "liberation" of that portion of Camp Street (Melpomene to Clio) from the congestion and darkness of the ramp was a significant victory for residents of the Margaret Place and Coliseum Square neighborhoods.

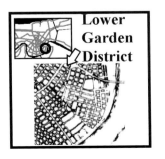

Lower Garden District

circa 1910 Margaret Place, intersection of Camp Street and Prytania Street, in the Lower Garden District

The Crescent City is filled with wedge-shaped intersections that open up to the river perpendicularly; this one, formed by Camp and Prytania, parallels the river. It was part of the vast Bienville land grant (1719) that was sold to the Jesuits in 1726; after their exile in 1763, the Solet (Saulet) family purchased the plantation (see p. 328) and owned this site until 1856, when it was sold to the New Orleans Female Orphan Asylum (building at center, 1840). The city donated additional land to the asylum in 1866, eventually forming this park.

The monument at center (1884), sculpted by Alexander Doyle and labeled simply "Margaret," is the city's loving memorial to Margaret Haughery, an Irish immigrant who devoted her life to helping New Orleans' orphans and others in need. It is among the first statues in the United States to honor a woman. At left is St. Theresa of Avila Church (1849). *Detroit Publishing Company, Library of Congress, no. LC-D4-39627 DLC*

324

1996 Same site

Today the bridge expressways overrun the vertex of Margaret Place, now shaded by oaks instead of palms. The Margaret statue shows the effects of 114 years of subtropical humidity on the white marble of Carrara, Italy, from which it was sculpted. The name for this general area, Lower Garden District, coined by Samuel Wilson Jr. in 1962, stuck because it makes sense: it is geographically lower (closer to Canal and downriver) and economically lower than the opulent Garden District, yet akin to it in the style of residential living. Other examples of acute-angle, wedge-shaped intersections appear on pp. 104, 132, 318, 332, and 356.

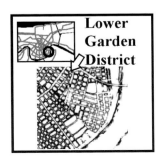

Lower Garden District

circa 1900 **St. Paul's Episcopal Church, Camp Street at the Gaiennie intersection, in the Lower Garden District**

Riverside of the Margaret Monument (left) stood St. Paul's Episcopal Church (1893), serving the Protestant populace of the area. It replaced a similar structure with the same name, built in 1853 and burned in 1891. *Detroit Publishing Company, Library of Congress, no. LC-D4-4895 DLC*

1998 Same site

Margaret still watches over the triangular park at Prytania and Camp, but St. Paul stood too close to the Camp Street on-ramp for the Greater New Orleans Bridge and was demolished in 1958, after the infrastructure was already in place. The Camp Street ramp was removed in 1994.

Lower Garden District

1906 St. Simeon's Select School, Annunciation Street between Melpomene and Thalia, in the Lower Garden District

St. Simeon's Select School occupied this remodeled antebellum mansion, the Saulet House, built in the 1830s. The Saulet (Solet) plantation, carved out of the Jesuits' land after their 1763 exile, comprised a long lot perpendicular to the river that roughly corresponds to the downriver flank of today's Lower Garden District National Historic District. This mansion was the second to be built on the Saulet property, replacing a 1760s structure from the plantation era. The Sisters of Charity bought the Saulet House in 1860 and operated St. Simeon's Select School until 1912. Note the schoolchildren clinging to the fence. *Detroit Publishing Company, Library of Congress, no. LC-D4-19316 DLC*

1996 Same site

Last occupied by a hospital, the Saulet House, its appendages, and the property were sold in 1959 and cleared for this supermarket, itself something of a relic now.

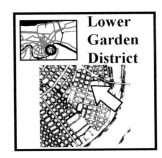

Lower Garden District

1932 Hastings Row, 1809 to 1837 Magazine Street between St. Mary and Felicity, in the Lower Garden District

A caricature of New Orleans architecture on one of the city's most interesting streets. These structures, identified as Hastings Row in the 1883 *Robinson Atlas of the City of New Orleans*, were designed by Thomas Gillam for commercial/residential use (store at street level, residence above, kitchen extending from the rear) and were built in 1860 for owner Samuel Hastings. The galleried portion of the block was built about ten years after the units on the far end, which lack rear appendages. *Charles Franck Collection, The Historic New Orleans Collection, accession no. 1979.325.759*

1997 Same site

Sixty-five years later, twelve of the twenty-two dormers and a small section of the galleries remain. Hastings Row is very much a vibrant and functioning component of the Magazine Street scene, but it lacks the outrageous charm of its former appearance. Dormers are often removed from older structures to minimize maintenance costs, but from an inspection of aerial photographs, it appears that some of the current dormers on this row are actually recent additions. The airborne photographs also reveal a complete set of eight larger dormers on the backslope of the roof, above eight separate kitchen appendages.

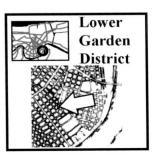

Lower Garden District

circa 1858 **Intersection of Polymnia Street and Felicity Street from the Dryades intersection, in Central City**

The angle formed by these muddy streets reflects the convergence of long lots that occurred when the arpent system for land division was applied to the interior of a river meander. The river runs about a mile ahead in this perspective, and the backswamp occurs about a mile behind. Note the raised sidewalks supported in places by wooden curbs, bringing to mind the early Vieux Carré sidewalks that were described as *banquettes* (little benches). *Photograph by Jay Dearborn Edwards, The Historic New Orleans Collection, accession no. 1982.32.14*

1996 Same site

Only the cars, utilities, and pavement indicate that 140 years have passed at this sleepy intersection. Although these buildings all postdate the Civil War, the structures from the *circa* 1858 street scene are all familiar and common styles throughout present-day Central City and Lower Garden District. The wisteria-covered brick building at left, probably once a school, was constructed in the 1880s; other buildings in the scene date from the early twentieth century. Until the 1960s, this area was loosely known as the Dryades Street neighborhood, an integrated working-class community served by a business district on Dryades Street and noted for its Jewish populace and synagogues. Though just a few blocks from prosperous St. Charles Avenue and the Garden District, much of this historic area, now known as Central City (bordered by South Claiborne, Pontchartrain Expressway, St. Charles, and Louisiana), is decaying. The remnant business district on Dryades (now Oretha Castle Haley Boulevard) is in shambles.

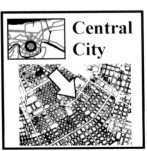

Central City

circa 1922 **View of Central City from the corner of St. Charles Avenue and St. Mary Street**

This photograph captures the crowded, multifaceted residential district of Central City (once informally known as the Dryades Street neighborhood) and its relationship with the Central Business District. The angled street in the foreground is Felicity Street, upper limit of the city of New Orleans until the annexation of Lafayette in 1852. The Baroque church at far left is St. John the Baptist (1872); to its right in the extreme distance is the turreted Criminal Courts Building (1893). The new Hibernia Bank Building (1921) is the high point at center; the twin Byzantine towers (one obscures the other) mark the profile of the Temple Sinai (1872); the crenelated tower to its right is St. Patrick's (1840); and the obelisk just to its right is the Lee Monument (1884) at Lee Circle. *Charles Franck Collection, The Historic New Orleans Collection, accession no. 1979.325.6470*

1997 Same view

This photograph was taken from the Pontchartrain Hotel, a perch two blocks upriver and a few stories higher than that of the *circa* 1922 perspective. The Central City neighborhood in the foreground, whose inventory of old buildings has been reduced by half in seventy-five years, has been the site of an urban-planning controversy that has pitted suburban-style development against historic preservation. In the background, the gentle downtown skyline is now boxy and irregular, though many old elements still stand and others are simply obscured. Note the Pontchartrain Expressway crossing the scene, dividing the commercial and residential districts even in this oblique perspective.

Central City

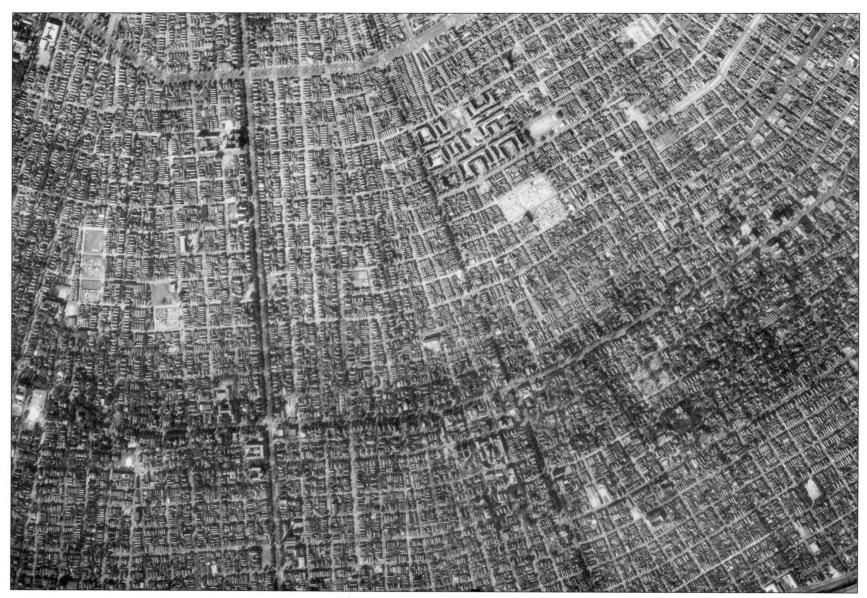

1952 Uptown, Central City, and the Garden District

Shady St. Charles Avenue, spinal column of the city, curves across this aerial perspective of Central City and Uptown. St. Charles parallels the curving Mississippi halfway between the riverbank and the former backswamps beyond Claiborne Avenue at top center, a distance originally measured as 40 arpents. An arpent equals approximately 192 feet; 40 arpents (about 1.5 miles) was a standard length for a French plantation grant in the eighteenth century. The foliated area at right center marks the opulent Garden District, bordered by Jackson, Magazine, Louisiana, and St. Charles. In contrast, note the mosaic of treeless blocks in Central City (upper center and right), packed to capacity with shotgun houses, abodes of the working class and the poor. In much of New Orleans, a neighborhood's quantity of tree coverage is correlated with its prosperity. *U.S. Geological Survey*

1994 Same area

Quick glances between the 1952 and 1994 photographs reveal the extent and distribution of landscape change in uptown New Orleans. Most of the areas shown here are now designated as National Historic Districts: Uptown (left half of photo), Central City (upper right), Garden District (lower center right), and Irish Channel (extreme lower right). *U.S. Geological Survey*

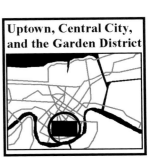

Uptown, Central City, and the Garden District

1925 and 1933 2130 St. Charles Avenue at the Jackson intersection, near the Garden District

Top scene, 1925: This prominent structure, built in 1896, once served as home of the Harmony Club, a local Jewish organization, and housed the first New Orleans office of Standard Oil (now Exxon) at the time of these photographs. Note the recently planted trees about fifteen feet to the left and right of the fire hydrant. **Bottom scene, 1933:** An Art Deco office building replaces the neighboring frame house, and a new traffic light guards the corner. Note the growth of the palms and the young oak trees. *Charles Franck Collection, The Historic New Orleans Collection, accession nos. 1979.325.910 and 1979.325.911*

1948 and 1996 Same site

Top scene, 1948: The sturdy buildings are gradually engulfed by the vegetation, with one surviving palm nearly exceeding the height of the structure. Bottom scene, 1996: The Standard Oil building, like many other structures on this portion of St. Charles, did not survive the 1950s, though the curbside details persist. The two live oaks, saplings in 1925, are gracefully gnarled at the tender old age of about seventy-five years. *1948 photograph: Charles Franck Collection, The Historic New Orleans Collection, accession no. 1979.325.912*

Garden District

circa 1858 Adams House, 2624 to 2634 Prytania Street at the Fourth intersection, in the Garden District

The present-day Garden District and adjacent areas were subdivided from a series of plantations in the 1820s to become the city of Lafayette in 1833. Lafayette's riverside section was a rough port district known as the Irish Channel, while its inland section evolved into a garden suburb popular with professional-class Anglo-Saxon Americans, many of whom were recent arrivals from the North. By the time Lafayette was absorbed into New Orleans in 1852, distinctly American styles of residential living defined the Garden District: houses set back from the streets; ample space between neighbors, gardens and trees surrounding the house; and nonindigenous architectural styles influencing design. This mansion, owned by Thomas A. Adams, a Bostonian who founded New Orleans' insurance industry, is somewhat unusual architecturally but is typical of the Garden District—of *America*—in terms of spacious residential layout. Contrast this scene with any French Quarter vista to appreciate the gulf between Americans and Creoles in the nineteenth century and the impact of that difference on the urban geography of the city. *Photograph by Jay Dearborn Edwards, The Historic New Orleans Collection, accession no. 1982.32.8*

1996 Same site

The Adams House is long gone, though its landscaping seems to live on. Note the transformation of features in the scene: gas light replaced by electric, wooden fences replaced by iron, muddy streets now paved with asphalt, corduroy crosswalks replaced by painted lines, wooden street signs changed for metal ones, brick *banquettes* now concrete, and a spacious home and foliated property still at center. Only the utility wires are "new." The unusual "cornstalk" fence surrounding Colonel Short's Villa, completed a few years after the historical photograph was taken, appears on the right.

Garden District

circa 1858 Washington Avenue at the Magazine intersection, looking toward Lake Pontchartrain, in the Garden District

This spacious intersection in the former city of Lafayette was photographed about six years after it was annexed into New Orleans. By the mid-nineteenth century, the grand sweep of the crescent above Felicity Street was striped with plantations and the cities of Lafayette, Jefferson, and Carrollton; wedge by wedge, these lands were enveloped into the city limits, creating the scallop-shell topology of the Crescent City's street network. The platform at right is the Chalmette Fire Tower, and the hip-roofed building to its left is the Washington Avenue Firehouse (1851). This station, later known as Chalmette #23, used horse-drawn vehicles until the early 1920s. The store at left was apparently a pharmacy. See p. 394 for a scene taken from the Chalmette Fire Tower *circa* 1858. *Photograph by Jay Dearborn Edwards, The Historic New Orleans Collection, accession no. 1982.32.4*

1996 Same site

As in the *circa* 1858 photo, a small business district at the Washington/Magazine intersection serves the surrounding neighborhood. The most outstanding change in the scene is the foliage, some of which obscures the old firehouse, restored in 1949 and now serving as the New Orleans Fire Department Museum and Education Center. Curator Robert B. Whitman and Superintendent Emeritus William J. McCrossen of the New Orleans Fire Department are encyclopedias on the history of fire fighting in a city where fire has been a major agent of landscape change.

Garden District

circa 1858 Buckner House, 1410 Jackson Avenue at the Coliseum intersection, in the Garden District

This Greek Revival mansion on affluent Jackson Avenue was home to the wealthy Kentuckian cotton investor Henry Sullivan Buckner, an important figure in New Orleans and especially the Garden District during and after the antebellum era. The Buckner House (1856) was designed by Lewis E. Reynolds, architect, of Factors' Row on Perdido Street and Stanton Hall in Natchez, Mississippi, one of the most palatial antebellum buildings in the South. The path in the middle of Jackson Avenue is the trackbed for a horse-drawn streetcar, a connecting route of the New Orleans & Carrollton Railroad. *Photograph by Jay Dearborn Edwards, The Historic New Orleans Collection, accession no. 1982.32.5*

1996 Same site

The Buckner mansion (minus its belvedere) is just as splendid today, after having served for sixty years as the Soulé Business College. The school came to this site in 1923 after nearly fifty years on Lafayette Square. A mosaic on the sidewalk in front of the entrance reads: "From Education, As The Leading Cause, The Public Character Its Color Draws." The Jackson Avenue route of the New Orleans & Carrollton Railroad (now the St. Charles streetcar line) served this intersection from 1835 to 1947.

Garden District

circa 1858 Perkins House, 1411 Jackson Avenue at the Coliseum intersection, in the Garden District

Across from the Buckner House is this asymmetrical and vertical Greek Revival mansion, also designed by Lewis E. Reynolds and built for William Martin Perkins in 1851. At the time, Jackson Avenue was emerging as one of the most prestigious addresses in Lafayette and neighboring New Orleans. Note the deep drainage ditches visible in the foreground. *Photograph by Jay Dearborn Edwards, The Historic New Orleans Collection, accession no. 1982.32.3*

1996 Same site

The year after the Perkins House was constructed, Lafayette was annexed into New Orleans, and the uptown Anglos became the dominant group in the newly consolidated city. The mansion is now Canon Turner Hall, serving as a preschool for the Trinity Episcopal Church (built in 1853 for a congregation formed in 1847), located across Coliseum Street to the right. Thick hedges and a single live oak, possibly one from the *circa* 1858 view, hide the L-shaped masonry mansion from passersby on Jackson Avenue.

Garden District

circa 1906 **Robb House, Washington Avenue between Camp and Chestnut, in the Garden District**

James Robb, an eccentric, globe-trotting Pennsylvanian who made millions in banking, utilities, and railroads during the golden age of the 1840s and 1850s, had this Italian palazzo-style mansion built in the heart of the Garden District in the mid-1850s. Long considered the most splendid home in the city, the mansion was surrounded by gardens and statuary that covered an entire city block. The original square-shaped structure, designed in part by James Gallier Jr., comprised the lower story of the building on the left, to which an ornate balustrade was added in the late 1850s. The second floor and annexes date after the 1880s and 1890s, when the structure housed Sophie Newcomb College. *Detroit Publishing Company, Library of Congress, no. LC-D4-19358 DLC*

1996 Same site

Family tragedy, financial crisis, and civil war reversed Robb's fortunes and prevented him from ever enjoying his mansion; he eventually returned to the North and never regained the aristocratic lifestyle he had earned in New Orleans. After Newcomb College moved to the campus of Tulane University in 1918, a Baptist seminary operated in the greatly expanded complex for the next few decades. The Robb mansion was demolished in 1954, a century after construction, and replaced by these homes. The redevelopment of this block is one of the few large-scale changes in the Garden District, one of historic New Orleans' most economically and physically stable neighborhoods.

Garden District

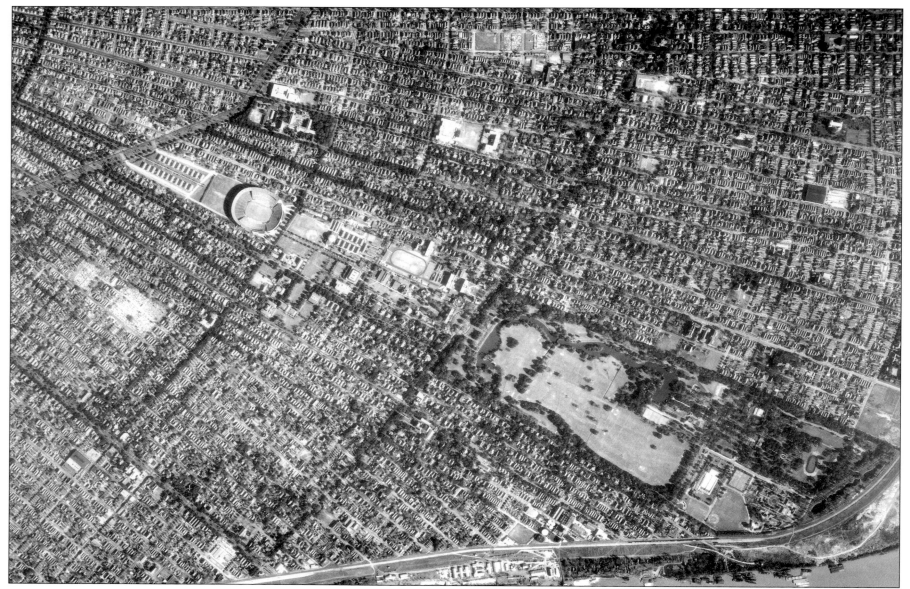

1952 Uptown and University

Uptown New Orleans: St. Charles Avenue divides the scene diagonally from upper right to lower left; the campuses of Tulane and Loyola are at center, and the Riverbend neighborhood of Carrollton appears at the ninety-degree junction of St. Charles and Carrollton Avenue at lower left. The 1884 World's Industrial and Cotton Centennial Exposition took place on the old Foucher long-lot plantation, which from 1896 to the 1910s was landscaped by the famed Olmstead and Brothers firm to become Audubon Park (lower right). Tulane Stadium (upper left), home of the Sugar Bowl from 1935 to 1974, was built in 1926 and enlarged to a capacity of 81,000 by 1950. The Mississippi flows across the bottom of this perspective. *U.S. Geological Survey*

1994 Same area

Compared with Central City, Uptown has been fairly well preserved throughout the late 1900s; most alteration here has been concentrated on the Tulane and Loyola campuses. One great improvement was the renovation of the old zoo into the world-class Audubon Zoological Gardens, located at the tip (lower right) of machete-shaped Audubon Park. The rectangular portion of the golf course near the zoo roughly outlines the footprint of the Main Building of the 1884 exposition, then the world's largest exhibition space. After Tulane Stadium was demolished in late 1979, the Sugar Bowl has been played at the Superdome, where it is a national New Year's Day tradition. *U.S. Geological Survey*

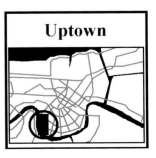

circa 1906 Tulane University, St. Charles Avenue, in Uptown/University

Tulane University, founded in 1834 as the Medical College of Louisiana and renamed in 1884 for benefactor Paul Tulane, moved uptown in the early 1890s when its Common Street campus proved inadequate. Shown here are Tilton Memorial Hall (left, 1902), original home of Tulane Law School, and Gibson Hall (1894), administrative and symbolic heart of the institution. Most of the oldest buildings on campus exhibit the Romanesque styles of native Louisianian architect Henry Hobson Richardson. *Detroit Publishing Company, Library of Congress, nos. LC-D4-10990 L DLC and LC-D4-10990 R DLC*

1997 Same site

Tulane University is now an internationally acclaimed institution, with nine colleges at the uptown campus and two medical schools downtown. In 1918 Tulane was joined by Newcomb College, a women's higher-learning institution previously located in the old Robb mansion in the Garden District (p. 348), to form the first coordinate college system, predating the better-known association of Harvard and Radcliffe. Tulane's beautiful 110-acre campus, growing by about one new building per year, still generally conforms to the configuration of the old Foucher long-lot plantation on which it was laid out (see aerial photos on previous pages). Coupled with neighboring Loyola University, the Tulane campus marks the heart of uptown New Orleans. Many of the oaks that appear as saplings in the *circa* 1906 scene have grown to maturity.

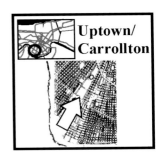

Uptown/
Carrollton

circa 1906 Audubon Place, St. Charles Avenue, in Uptown/University

Uptown New Orleans boomed in the late 1800s and early 1900s as Audubon Park, Tulane University, Loyola University, and new upscale residential neighborhoods assured the importance of the area. This private boulevard, Audubon Place, was established adjacent to the Tulane campus in 1894; its first residences are visible here between the Romanesque-style gatehouses, designed by Thomas Sully. Audubon Place was one of a series of residential "park" communities in uptown New Orleans, a trend apparent in other American cities but a world away from the crowded European cityscape of downtown New Orleans. *Detroit Publishing Company, Library of Congress, no. LC-D4-19299 DLC*

1996 Same site

The owner of this Castellon Pharmacy raised the ire of Riverbend residents by demolishing adjacent cottages on Dante Street, using the lots for unpermitted parking, and proposing to build a larger suburban-style retail operation on the block. Neighbors picketed the business in 1997 with placards that read "Castellon Rapes the Riverbend & Goes Home to Metairie," and in March 1998 the City Planning Commission denied Castellon permission to expand. The neighbors have something to cherish in Oak Street: bristling with poles, wires, and protruding shop signs, the little business district feels like a small-town Main Street in the 1950s. The appearance and economy of this quaint street are remarkable remnants of the way commercial New Orleans looked and operated before the middle-class exodus, expressway construction, and homogenization of recent decades.

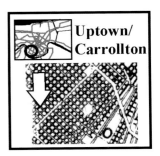

Uptown/ Carrollton

1899 Carrollton Streetcar Barn, Dublin Street between Willow and Jeanette, in the Riverbend section of Carrollton

New Ford, Bacon & Davis streetcars are readied for dispatch inside the Carrollton Station (Carrollton Streetcar Barn), built by the Berlin Iron Bridge Company in 1893 and noted for its steel trusses and spacious interior. First put into service in 1893, electrified streetcars replaced nearly all animal-traction lines by the end of the century. *The Historic New Orleans Collection, accession no. 1984.218.34*

1996 Same site

The barn today is the main terminal for the city's 1920s-era Perley Thomas cars, an unofficial museum for retired models, and an engineering shop for new cars. Here, the nation's premier streetcar craftsmen maintain and reconstruct these world-famous rolling landmarks. Visitors are not permitted, but a quick walk-through is usually forgiven. Streetcar lines throughout the city were gradually retired as automobiles came to dominate the streets, and all remaining routes except for the St. Charles line were terminated by May 30, 1964, a milestone in the city's postwar era of modernization. Since then, the cherished icons have gradually made a comeback: the Riverfront line was installed in 1988 to connect the French Quarter with the Warehouse District and may be expanded to link Bywater with Audubon Zoo. On Canal Street, new tracks were installed in 1997 as part of a line from the river to City Park Avenue, with the firm of Gannet-Fleming, Inc., designing the project. There is even talk of reinstalling the legendary Desire line. The return of streetcars to downtown New Orleans is one of the most exciting prospects in the restoration of the old city's bustle and charm.

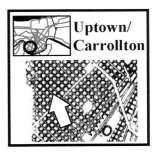

Uptown/ Carrollton

1952 Mid-City

This scene captures the former beds of the Americans' New Basin Canal (1838; wide diagonal swath with bend at Pelican Stadium) and the Creoles' Carondelet Canal (1795; upper right, touching the tip of Bayou St. John). At center is the chaotic street convergence produced when the French arpent system of land division, which demarcated long-lot plantations between the river and the backswamp, was applied to the interior of a river meander and maintained throughout the city's development. The highway running from upper left to lower right is Huey Long's Airline Highway, part of famous Highway 61 and the primary corridor between Louisiana's largest city and its capital before Interstate 10. Airline Highway (renamed "Drive" in Orleans and Jefferson parishes) becomes Tulane Avenue as it approaches downtown, merging with Common Street as it reaches the Mississippi River. *U.S. Geological Survey*

1994 Same area

Interstate 10 (Pontchartrain Expressway) utilizes the old bed of the New Basin Canal from the I-610 fork to the Superdome (extreme lower right). Between the former canal beds is the Mid-City National Historic District, and adjacent to former Carondelet Canal (upper right) are the Parkview and Esplanade Ridge National Historic Districts, covering parts of Faubourg St. John. Pelican Stadium, the home of New Orleans' minor-league baseball team from 1915 to 1957, was demolished in 1958. *U.S. Geological Survey*

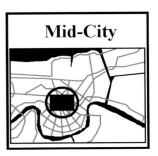

Mid-City

circa 1910 **Entrance to Metairie Cemetery, intersection of Metairie Road and the New Basin Shell Road (now Interstate 10)**

Metairie Cemetery was laid out in the 1870s on the old Metairie Race Course, a famous pre-Civil War horse track abutting historic Metairie Road on the well-drained natural levee of extinct Bayou Metairie. The cemetery is the first major landscaped burial place in the city, complete with lakes, trees, and street networks (in a racetrack pattern), in contrast to the tiny crowded cemeteries in the older part of town. A few hundred feet to the right ran the New Basin Canal and its famous shell road. Shown here is the cemetery's entrance gate (1883); the sixty-foot obelisk at left is the Moriarty Tomb (locally identified as the tallest privately owned monument in the country), and the mound at right is the Army of the Tennessee Tomb, guarded by a stirring statue of Gen. Albert Sidney Johnston. Johnston, who was killed at Shiloh, and Gen. P. G. T. Beauregard, native son and a major figure in Civil War and New Orleans history, are buried inside. The Johnston statue (1887) was sculpted by Alexander Doyle, creator of the Robert E. Lee figure at Lee Circle. *Detroit Publishing Company, Library of Congress, no. LC-D4-13523 DLC*

1997 Same site

The entrance gate was removed in 1953, when the Pontchartrain Expressway was in planning phase. Now the expressway shadows the former New Basin Canal through the cemeteries of Metairie, Greenwood, St. Patrick's, Odd Fellows Rest, and Gates of Prayer, offering motorists on the interstate glimpses of some of the nation's most unusual burial places. The "hilly" terrain (by local standards) visible in this scene is a product of landscaping built upon the alluvial uplands of Metairie Ridge and the depression excavated in the 1830s for the creation of the New Basin Canal.

Metairie/ City Park

circa 1906 City Park, near the intersection of Anseman Avenue and City Park Avenue

Located at the junction of extinct Bayou Metairie and Bayou St. John, the former Allard plantation passed into the hands of wealthy and renowned eccentric John McDonogh in 1845. Upon his death in 1850, McDonogh, long considered a miser, willed his estate to the children of New Orleans and his hometown of Baltimore. A portion of the donation went to launch New Orleans' public schools, while in 1854 the city set aside the lower part of the old Allard plantation as a park. City Park was landscaped in the 1890s under the leadership of Victor Anseman and expanded by nine hundred acres to its current size in 1927. *Detroit Publishing Company, Library of Congress, no. LC-D4-19319 DLC*

1996 Same site

Though not as manicured as it was ninety years ago, the gentle curves of the old scene endure in beautiful City Park today. The older section of City Park has a more intimate and local atmosphere than Audubon Park, with pedal boats for rent on the lagoons, red beans and rice on the menu at the "Casino" cafeteria, and families with children outnumbering roller-blading college students. It has the festive atmosphere of a city park in a Latin American capital. To the right beyond view is the spectacular oak grove made famous as a dueling grounds in the nineteenth century. Note the elbow in the tree branch on the left, recognizable from the *circa* 1906 view.

Metairie/ City Park

circa 1910 The Peristyle, on present-day Dreyfous Avenue, in City Park

The Peristyle was designed by Paul Andry and built in 1907 to shelter concerts and dancers during the heyday of elegant outings at City Park. The pavilion, which was improved by the Works Progress Administration in 1935-36 and renovated in 1989, comprises thirty-six Ionic columns plus four corner pillars supporting a massive wooden ceiling and a roof lined with a detailed parapet, visible here. The parapet caused puddling on the roof and was later removed.

The Peristyle originally marked the center of the landscaped portion of the park, which has since grown to become the fifth-largest urban park in the nation, with 1,500 acres, millions of visitors, and 250 live oaks listed on the national registry. City Park is about three times the size of the French Quarter. *Detroit Publishing Company, Library of Congress, no. LC-D4-71841 DLC*

1997 Same site

Still framed by the twisted oak, the Peristyle, adorned with garlands for the annual "Celebration in the Oaks" Christmas lights display, is tucked behind vegetation across the last remnant of Bayou Metairie. This bayou, a distributary of the Mississippi that broke off from the river centuries before settlement, built up enough sediment during its working days to form a natural levee (Metairie Ridge, about three feet above sea level) that is visible in today's maps as Metairie Road, a half-mile to the left of this scene. Unlike rugged places where moving water carves *down*, hydrology in this flat deltaic region builds *up* surrounding lands through the accumulation of flood-deposited sand and silt over thousands of years. For this reason, the lower Mississippi River has *distributaries*, not tributaries: although it drains more than a million square miles of the North American interior, it actually sheds local rainfall.

Metairie/City Park

1891 Duverjé House, Morgan Street between Seguin and Bermuda, in Algiers Point (on the Mississippi's western bank)

Barthelemy Duverjé acquired property across the river from the Vieux Carré in 1805 and built this French Creole-style plantation house in 1812. Note the mansion's stylistic similarities to its contemporary across the river, the Delord-Sarpy House (p. 314). Algiers was subdivided in 1842 and in 1870 was annexed into the city as the Fifth District; at the time of this photograph, the Duverjé House was in service as a courthouse. *The Historic New Orleans Collection, accession no. 1977.79.17*

1996 Same site

The great fire of 1895 leveled the Duverjé House and converted ten square blocks of old Algiers into a forest of chimneys. One year later, this Moorish-style structure, with crenelated, asymmetrical towers, was built by John NcNally as the new Algiers Courthouse from designs by city engineers Linus Brown and Alonzo Bell. The landmark was threatened with demolition in the mid-1970s but was saved by community action and renovated by the city in 1979-84. Its sound condition and useful role in the community of Algiers Point are due in large part to local citizens groups such as the Friends of the Algiers Courthouse. Perched on the tip of the point bar formed by the river's eastward bend, the Algiers Courthouse is a familiar landmark to people in downtown New Orleans.

Algiers
West Bank

circa 1858 **Harvey Canal, near present-day Destrehan Avenue, in Harvey, Jefferson Parish (on the Mississippi's western bank)**

This West Bank canal was dug in the early 1840s as the Destrehan Canal, connecting the Mississippi River with Bayou Barataria and Barataria Bay. The scene was captured from the levee looking south, with the Mississippi River passing behind the photographer from right to left. Note the absence of a lock at the head of the canal (lower left); instead, boats were transported on a "submarine railway" from the river, over the levee, and into the canal. The Gothic Revival "Harvey Castle" (which had a locally inspired double gallery) was built in 1844 as the home of the owners of the canal, Joseph Hale Harvey and his wealthy Creole wife, Marie Louisa Destrehan. Note the pirogues in the canal at extreme left and the tollgate at right. *Photograph by Jay Dearborn Edwards, The Historic New Orleans Collection, accession no. 1982.32.11*

1996 Same site

After serving as a courthouse for Jefferson Parish from 1874 to 1884, Harvey Castle deteriorated and was eventually cleared away in 1924 by the federal government to allow for the widening of the canal. Locks completed in 1907 anti-quated the old submarine railway, and in 1924, the Harvey Canal (left) became a component of the Gulf Intra-coastal Waterway. A roadside park overlooks the site.

Harvey
West Bank

circa 1930 Seven Oaks Plantation House, intersection of Louisiana 18 and River Road, in Westwego, Jefferson Parish (on the Mississippi's western bank)

Seven Oaks was a storybook plantation mansion located across the river in Westwego, Jefferson Parish, directly west of present-day Audubon Zoo. Built *circa* 1840 by the Zeringue family (a Gallicized version of the Bavarian *Zehringer*) on a land grant from French colonial days, the hip-roofed Greek Revival mansion had eighteen rooms, a peristyle of twenty-six columns, and a belvedere commanding a view of the river and distant New Orleans. After its sugar and cotton days had passed, it was used as the Columbia Gardens resort in the 1890s and ended up in the hands of the Missouri Railroad Company in 1912, indicative of the shift in the West Bank's economy from agriculture to industry and transportation. After the last occupants departed in 1954, the mansion fell into a ruin hastened by Hurricane Betsy in 1965, vandals, and years of exposure to the subtropical climate. *Photograph by Richard Koch, The Historic New Orleans Collection, accession no. 1985.120.277*

1996 Same site

By the 1970s, Seven Oaks was the epitome of ruin: dormers and belvedere sunken into the attic, roof collapsing, wisteria-covered columns standing free of the house. A civic battle ensued among preservationists, local governments, and the Texas Pacific-Missouri Pacific Railroad Company, each claiming to be acting in the public interest. An aerial photograph by Betsy Swanson in 1977 shows the ruins falling in dignity among storage tanks and leafless trees on a winter morning of its last year. Seven Oaks was finally razed in August 1977 by the railroad company, depriving greater New Orleans of an important landmark and Westwego of its premier point of historical interest. Oak Alley, fifty miles upriver in the town of Vacherie, is the nearest surviving antebellum mansion comparable to Seven Oaks in size, style, and grandeur.

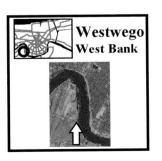

Westwego
West Bank

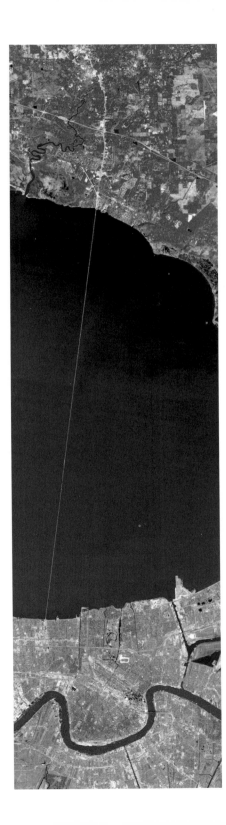

A Bird's-Eye Appendix to New Orleans

New Orleans from the perspective of Lake Pontchartrain and the Florida Parishes.
Landsat Thematic Mapper satellite imagery courtesy Louisiana State University
Department of Geography and Anthropology

French Quarter

1922 Jackson Square and the French Quarter, looking up Decatur and Chartres into the Central Business District, two hundred years after the original city was laid out. See pp. 30-39, 92, and 102 for other distant perspectives of the French Quarter. *The Historic New Orleans Collection, accession no. 1979.325.6419*

1922 The French Quarter (left), Esplanade Avenue, and Faubourg Marigny (right), looking toward City Park and the lake. Note the buildings bordering Gallatin Street, removed by the WPA during the Depression, in front of the U.S. Mint at lower left. On the right, overlooking Washington Square, appears the Third Presbyterian Church (1858, demolished in the late 1960s), and on Elysian Fields at lower right, the Pontchartrain Railroad (New Orleans' first, 1831-1932) is visible. This scene covers some of the city's most densely populated neighborhoods, with as many as four hundred people per block acre in the early 1900s—still village scale compared with the cities of the Northeast. See pp. 134-35 for other aerial perspectives of this area. *The Historic New Orleans Collection, accession no. 1979.325.6418*

Esplanade Avenue

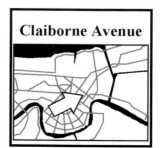

Claiborne Avenue

1922 Claiborne Avenue (shady, crooked street, top to bottom) at the Esplanade Avenue (across center, left to right) intersection, looking downriver, with the St. Bernard Circle appearing at the elbow of Claiborne at top center. The diagonal road across the lower center is Bayou Road/Governor Nicholls Street, following a stretch of uplands that served as an old Indian portage and colonial-era road between the Mississippi River and Bayou St. John. Bayou Road's properties and houses are oriented to face the old portage, while post-subdivision houses are oriented perpendicular to the larger grid pattern. Note the intricate roofscape formed by countless chimneys and dormers. See pp. 146-47 and 152-53 for aerial perspectives of this area. *The Historic New Orleans Collection, accession no. 1979.325.6428*

1922 Lower Tremé and adjacent areas, including Storyville, the famous legalized red-light district (1897-1917), appear among the above-ground St. Louis cemeteries at left center; Carondelet Canal divides the scene; Congo Square appears to the right of the canal's turning basin; and the Tremé Market is located two blocks above Congo Square in the middle of Orleans Street. In its heyday, every structure in Storyville except a firehouse and a church was devoted to prostitution. Note the railroad tracks following Carondelet Canal and Basin Street to Terminal Station (p. 206). At one time, St. Louis Cemetery No. 1

(1789, lower center) spanned to the rear of the Old Mortuary Chapel (1826, to the right of the base of the smokestack). Traffic to and from the Carondelet Canal turning basin led to the development of Basin Street, for which the lower portion of the cemetery was removed. See pp. 146 and 152 for other aerial views of this area. *The Historic New Orleans Collection, accession no. 1979.325.6423*

Faubourg Tremé

Tulane Avenue

1922 Tulane Avenue and Canal Street (wide streets running top to bottom) at Rampart and Basin (two angled streets along the bottom), looking toward the lake. Tulane Avenue is the terminus of the legendary Highway 61, which starts near the headwaters of the Mississippi in Minneapolis and follows the river past St. Louis, Memphis, the Delta, Vicksburg, Natchez, Baton Rouge, and finally New Orleans. While Highway 61 is synonymous with the blues musical tradition, its terminus in the Tulane-Rampart area (lower center) marks an important neighborhood in jazz history. Note the Charity Hospital complex (1832) at center, the turreted Criminal Courts Building three blocks below it on Tulane Avenue, and Terminal Station at Basin and Canal (lower right). *The Historic New Orleans Collection, accession no. 1979.325.6424*

1927 Looking down Common Street into the Central Business District, with Saratoga (Basin) Street in the foreground and the Mississippi River in the background. The triangle (left third of photograph) formed by Canal, Rampart, and Common was an undeveloped commons separating the Vieux Carré (upper left) and Faubourg Ste. Marie from 1788 until the 1810s, when it was subdivided and developed. Note the Criminal Courts Building at the extreme lower center and Lafayette Square at right. See p. 210 for an aerial perspective of the Central Business District. *The Historic New Orleans Collection, accession no. 1979.325.6444*

Central Business District

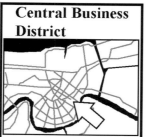

Central Business District

Circa 1924 The Central Business District, with Poydras Street on the left and Canal Street on the right. Note the castlelike Masonic Temple in its last years on St. Charles and Perdido (left center; see p. 252), the Poydras Market in the middle of Poydras (upper left; see p. 278), and the new Hibernia Bank Building at upper center, the tallest building in town at the time. *The Historic New Orleans Collection, accession no. 1979.325.6421*

Circa 1911 The Central Business District from the Hotel Grunewald, looking toward the river. This photograph is a closeup of the Common Street corridor covered in the 1927 view on p. 383. The dome in the foreground belongs to the original Jesuit Church (Church of the Immaculate Conception), built *circa* 1850, demolished in 1928 because of structural problems, and rebuilt two years later. Under construction at upper right is the Whitney National Bank, on Gravier between St. Charles and Camp. The smokestacks at upper left mark the sugar refineries of the French Quarter batture. *Detroit Publishing Company, Library of Congress, no. LC D401-15657 C DLC*

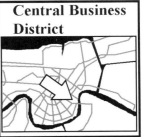

Central Business District

Central Business District

Circa 1911   Adjacent view of the Central Business District from the Hotel Grunewald. The Hennen Building (1895) appears at left center; behind it is the Hibernia Building (1903); and to its lower left, in the shadows of the Carondelet/Common intersection, is the Liverpool & London & Globe Insurance Company Building (1895). In the distance are St. Patrick's Church (1840, with crenelated tower), serving the Irish community, and the First Presbyterian Church (1856, with spire), serving the area's Protestants. *Detroit Publishing Company, Library of Congress, no. LC D401-15657 RC DLC*

1936 The Central Business District and French Quarter viewed from a point above Algiers. Jackson Square appears at the lower right, the riverbend near Carrollton is visible in the distant upper left, and Lake Pontchartrain appears in the distant upper right. *The Historic New Orleans Collection, accession no. 1979.325.6441*

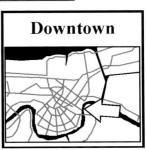

Downtown

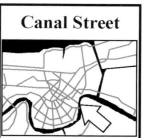

Canal Street

Circa 1950 Looking up Canal Street from the Mississippi River to Lake Pontchartrain, with the Central Business District on the left, the French Quarter at right, and City Park in the upper right. This perspective of Canal Street dramatizes the role of the 171-foot-wide corridor as the cultural and geographical axis of New Orleans. The covered wharves lining the riverfront were installed during the port improvements of the early twentieth century (see p. 34 for a partial view of the formerly open riverfront); now these too are past, and the downtown riverfront is open once again, now for tourism and recreation. See p. 224 for an aerial photograph of the batture at lower left. *The Historic New Orleans Collection, accession no. 1984.166.2.4*

Circa **1967** Looking up recently widened Poydras Street into the Central Business District. New Orleans' first modern skyscrapers break the 1920s-era skyline: the Plaza Tower at far left and International Trade Mart (World Trade Center) in the foreground. Their distance from the traditional business-district core near the Carondelet/Gravier intersection (center right) reflected an expectation of modern high-rise construction to occur either on Loyola Avenue or on Poydras Street. Over the next two decades, most of the expected growth would occur on Poydras. Note the Rivergate Convention Center under construction behind the Trade Mart. *The Historic New Orleans Collection, accession no. 1974.25.8.63*

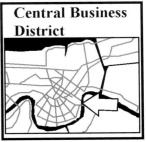

Central Business District

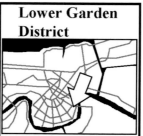

Lower Garden District

1955 The Lost Neighborhood: Lee Circle and the Lower Garden District, looking upriver along Magazine, Camp-Prytania, and St. Charles, a few years before the construction of the Greater New Orleans Bridge. The oldest structure in the scene is the Delord-Sarpy House (*circa* 1815; see p. 314), located above the row of ser-vants' quarters (near the parking lot) at lower left center. By 1958, a swath was cut across this area for the Pontchartrain Expressway; the Delord-Sarpy House was among the many historical structures lost. Refer to pp. 320-21 for an aeri-al sequence of the old neighborhood and the new expressway. *The Historic New Orleans Collection, accession no. 1984.166.2.10*

1955 Opposite view of the Lower Garden District (foreground), looking down Camp Street toward the Central Business District. Nearly everything to the left and right of St. Paul's Episcopal Church (center) was demolished for the Greater New Orleans Bridge expressway (see pp. 320-21). The Maginnis Cotton Mill (1884) and its distinctive water tower are visible at the extreme right center, and Temple Sinai (1872) appears two blocks left of Lee Circle. *The Historic New Orleans Collection, accession no. 1984.166.2.11*

Lower Garden District

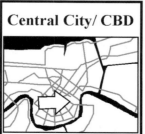

1955 Intersection of Howard Avenue (crossing the scene left to right) with Loyola, South Rampart, and Dryades, looking toward the Central Business District. A traffic circle was once planned (1927) to route vehicles at this busy intersection, as Lee Circle does a few blocks down on Howard; instead, the curved street at lower left was built, connecting present-day Loyola and Simon Bolivar Avenues. St. John the Baptist Church (1872) fronts Dryades Street at lower center. The new Union Passenger Terminal (left, accessed by the loop drive) consolidated a number of old train stations throughout the city when it opened in 1954. *The Historic New Orleans Collection, accession no. 1984.166.2.12*

1955 Looking down Calliope Street, the planned corridor for the Pontchartrain Expressway and the Greater New Orleans Bridge, completed in 1958. In the lower left are railroad tracks leading to the Union Passenger Terminal. Note the twin towers of Temple Sinai to the right of Lee Circle (upper left), the rear of St. John the Baptist Church at center, and residential Central City to the right. *The Historic New Orleans Collection, accession no. 1984.166.2.2*

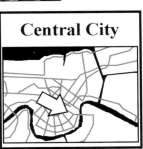

Central City

Garden District

Circa 1858 View from the Chalmette Fire Tower (p. 342) into the Garden District, looking down Camp Street at the Fourth Street intersection. The Chalmette Fire Tower served the Washington Avenue Firehouse on Washington between Camp and Magazine. Note the Buckner House (1856) and its belvedere (second high point in from the left horizon, p. 344) and the twin spires of the Trinity Episcopal Church (1853). Both still stand on Jackson Avenue, though the Buckner House lacks the prominent belvedere and Trinity Church was remodeled with a new tower in 1873. The brick tower to the right of Trinity's twin spires resembles St. Mary's Assumption but is actually a church near Coliseum Square. St. Patrick's Church (1840) in Faubourg St. Mary appears in the distant left, and in the extreme distant center, ship masts are visible. Note the profusion and variety of fences in this early American suburb. *Photograph by Jay Dearborn Edwards, The Historic New Orleans Collection, accession no. 1982.32.9*

Circa **1950** Arabi (foreground, in St. Bernard Parish), Holy Cross, the Industrial Canal, and Algiers (on the point bar to the left of the river), looking upriver toward downtown New Orleans. Tucked among trees between the Chalmette Slip (lower left) and the American Sugar Refinery is Three Oaks, an 1831 plantation home demolished in 1965. The slip itself marks the site of the Macarty House, used by General Jackson during the Battle of New Orleans in 1815. It burned in 1896 and was cleared away in 1907 for the excavation of the slip. The Industrial Canal (1923, center right) was the fulfillment of a two-hundred-year-old dream to connect the Mississippi River with Lake Pontchartrain and other waterways. The sugar-processing industry moved from the French Quarter batture (pp. 30-33) to these rural outskirts in the early 1900s and still operates in the foreground complex (1906). Jackson Barracks (p. 170) is visible at center, where the foliated area abuts the river. *The Historic New Orleans Collection, accession no. 1984.166.2.55*

Chalmette

1940 Looking down Orleans Street toward the St. Louis Cathedral in the French Quarter, viewed from the Municipal Auditorium at Congo Square. *The Historic New Orleans Collection, accession no. 1979.325.6443*

Bibliography

New Orleans amid the spheres that formed it: the North American interior to the left, the open waters of the Gulf of Mexico to the right, and the Mississippi River linking the two. *Landsat Thematic Mapper satellite imagery courtesy Louisiana State University Department of Geography and Anthropology*

American Institute of Architects, New Orleans Chapter. *A Guide to New Orleans Architecture*. New Orleans, La.: American Institute of Architects, 1974.

Baker, Liva. *The Second Battle of New Orleans: The Hundred-Year Struggle to Integrate the Schools*. New York, N.Y.: Harper Collins Publishers, 1996.

Baumbach, Richard O., Jr., and William E. Borah. *The Second Battle of New Orleans: A History of the Vieux Carré Riverfront-Expressway Controversy*. Tuscaloosa, Ala.: The University of Alabama Press, 1981.

Blassingame, John W. *Black New Orleans, 1860-1880*. Chicago, Ill.: The University of Chicago Press, 1973.

Brand, Steward. *How Buildings Learn: What Happens After They're Built*. New York, N.Y.: Penguin Books, 1994.

Bridaham, Lester Burbank. *New Orleans and the Bayou Country: Photographs (1880-1910) by George François Mugnier*. Barre, Mass.: Barre Publishers, 1972.

Bureau of Governmental Research. *Plan and Program for the Preservation of the Vieux Carre*. New Orleans, La.: City of New Orleans, 1968.

Bureau of Governmental Research. *Vieux Carre Historic District Demonstration Study*, 6 vols. New Orleans, La.: The Bureau, 1968.

Cable, George Washington. "The Dance in Place Congo." Reproduced from *The Century Magazine* (February and April 1886). New Orleans, La.: Faruk von Turk, 1976.

Cable, Mary. *Lost New Orleans*. Boston, Mass.: Houghton Mifflin Co., 1980.

Chase, John Churchill. *Frenchman, Desire, Good Children and Other Streets of New Orleans*. New York, N.Y.: Collier Macmillan Publishers, 1979.

Chase, John Churchill et al. *Citoyens, Progrès et Politique de la Nouvelle Orléans 1889-1964*. New Orleans, La.: E. S. Upton Printing Co., 1964.

Cristovich, Mary Louise et al. *The American Sector*. New Orleans Architecture, vol. 2. Gretna, La.: Pelican Publishing Co., 1972.

Cristovich, Mary Louise, Sally Kittredge Evans, and Roulhac Toledano. *The Esplanade Ridge*. New Orleans Architecture, vol. 5. Gretna, La.: Pelican Publishing Co., 1977.

Deléry, Simone de la Souchère. *Napoleon's Soldiers in America*. Gretna, La.: Pelican Publishing Co., 1972.

Detroit Publishing Co. photographic archives, Library of Congress, Washington, D.C., 1996-98.

Domínguez, Virginia R. *White by Definition: Social Classification in Creole Louisiana*. New Brunswick, N.J.: Rutgers University Press, 1986.

Evans, Oliver. *New Orleans*. New York, N.Y.: Macmillan Co., 1959.

Farnsworth, Jean M., and Ann M. Masson, ed. *The Architecture of Colonial Louisiana: Collected Essays of Samuel Wilson, Jr., F.A.I.A.* Lafayette, La.: The Center for Louisiana Studies, University of Southwestern Louisiana, 1987.

Friends of the Cabildo. *The University Section*. New Orleans Architecture, vol. 8. Gretna, La.: Pelican Publishing Co., 1997.

Forman, L. Ronald et al. *Audubon Park: An Urban Eden*. New Orleans, La.: Friends of the Zoo, 1985.

Fortier, Alcée. *A History of Louisiana*. Paris, France: Goupil & Co., 1904.

Fortier, Alcée. *Louisiana: Comprising Sketches of Parishes, Town, Events, Institutions, and Persons, Arranged in Cyclopedic Form*. N.p.: Century Historical Association, 1914.

Fossier, Albert E. *New Orleans: The Glamour Period, 1800-1840*. New Orleans, La.: Pelican Publishing Co., 1957.

Gallier, James. *Autobiography of James Gallier, Architect*. New York, N.Y.: Da Capo Press, 1973.

Garvey, Joan B., and Mary Lou Widmer. *Beautiful Crescent: A History of New Orleans*. New Orleans, La.: Garmer Press, 1994.

Gill, James. *Lords of Misrule: Mardi Gras and the Politics of Race in New Orleans*. Jackson, Miss.: University Press of Mississippi, 1997.

Gleason, David King. *Over New Orleans*. Baton Rouge, La.: Louisiana State University Press, 1983.

Gorin, Abbye Alexander. *Conversations with Samuel Wilson, Jr., Dean of Architectural Preservation in New Orleans*. New Orleans, La.: The Samuel Wilson, Jr. Publications Fund of the Louisiana Landmarks Society, 1991.

Gorin, Abbye Alexander. *Samuel Wilson, Jr.: A Contribution to the Preservation of Architecture in New Orleans and the Gulf South*. Ph.D. diss., Virginia Polytechnic Institute and State University, 1989.

Guilbeau, James. *The Saint Charles Streetcar, or the History of the New Orleans and Carrollton Railroad*. New Orleans, La.: Louisiana Landmarks Society, 1977.

Hall, A. Oakey. *The Manhattaner in New Orleans; or, Phases of "Crescent City" Life*. Clinton Hall, N.Y.: J. S. Redfield, Clinton Hall; New Orleans, La.: J. C. Morgan, 1851.

Haring, L. Lloyd, John F. Lounsbury, and John W. Frazier. *Introduction to Scientific Geographical Research*. Dubuque, Iowa: Wm. C. Brown Publishers, 1992.

Heard, Malcolm. *French Quarter Manual: An Architectural Guide to New Orleans' Vieux Carré*. New Orleans, La.: Tulane School of Architecture, 1997.

Hesse-Wartegg, Ernst von. *Travels on the Lower Mississippi, 1879-1880: A Memoir by Ernst von Hesse-Wartegg*. Edited and translated by Frederic Trautmann. Columbia, Mo.: The University of Missouri Press, 1990.

Historic New Orleans Collection: photograph, manuscript, and microfilm collections, plus staff consultation, New Orleans, La., 1996-98.

Holditch, W. Kenneth, ed. *In Old New Orleans*. Jackson, Miss.: University Press of Mississippi, 1983.

Holmes, Jack D. L., ed. *A Guide to Spanish Louisiana, 1762-1806*. Louisiana Collection Series. New Orleans, La.: A. F. Laborde & Sons, 1970.

Huber, Leonard V. *Creole Collage: Reflections on the Customs of Latter-Day New Orleans Creoles*. Lafayette, La.: Center for Louisiana Studies, University of Southwestern Louisiana, 1980.

Huber, Leonard V. *Landmarks of New Orleans*. New Orleans, La.: Louisiana Landmarks Society and Orleans Parish Landmark Commission, 1984.

Huber, Leonard V. *New Orleans: A Pictorial History*. Gretna, La.: Pelican Publishing Co., 1971.

Huber, Leonard V., Peggy McDowell, and Mary Louise Cristovich. *The Cemeteries*. New Orleans Architecture, vol. 3. Gretna, La.: Pelican Publishing Co., 1974.

Huber, Leonard V., and Samuel Wilson Jr. *The Basilica on Jackson Square: The History of the St. Louis Cathedral and its Predecessors, 1727-1965*. New Orleans, La.: A. F. Laborde and Sons, 1972.

Ingraham, Joseph Holt. "The South-west by a Yankee." Condensed from the original 1835 travelogue and reprinted in *New Orleans Is My Name*, by James Register, Shreveport, La.: Mid-South Press, 1971.

Janssen, James S. *Building New Orleans: The Engineer's Role*. New Orleans, La.: Waldemar S. Nelson and Co., 1987.

Jewell, Edwin L., ed. *Jewell's Crescent City, Illustrated*. New Orleans, La., 1873.

Kaslow, Andrew J. *Neighbors: Soul of the City*. New Orleans, La.: Arts Council of New Orleans, 1985.

Kemp, John R. *New Orleans: An Illustrated History*. Woodland Hills, Calif.: Windsor Publications, 1981.

King, Grace. *New Orleans: The Place and the People*. New York, N.Y.: Macmillan, 1895.

Kirk, Susan Lauxman, Helen Michel Smith, and Thomas G. Krentel. *The Architecture of St. Charles Avenue*. Gretna, La.: Pelican Publishing Co., 1977.

Kniffen, Fred B., and Sam Bowers Hilliard. *Louisiana: Its Land and People*. Baton Rouge, La.: Louisiana State University Press, 1988.

Lane, Mills. *Architecture of the Old South: Louisiana*. Savannah, Ga.: Beehive Press, 1997.

Laughlin, Clarence John. *Ghosts Along the Mississippi: An Essay in the Poetic Interpretation of Louisiana's Plantation Architecture*. New York, N.Y.: American Legacy Press, 1948.

Leavitt, Mel. *A Short History of New Orleans*. San Francisco: Lexikos, 1982.

Leavitt, Mel, and David H. Jones. *New Orleans: America's International City*. Chatsworth, Calif.: Windsor Publications, 1990.

Lemann, Bernard. *The Vieux Carré—A General Statement*. New Orleans, La.: School of Architecture, Tulane University, 1966.

Lewis, Peirce F. *New Orleans: The Making of an Urban Landscape*. Cambridge, Mass.: Ballinger Publishing Co., 1976.

Louisiana Travel Promotion Association. *Louisiana Tour Guide*. Baton Rouge, La.: Louisiana Travel Promotion Association, 1997.

Martinez, Raymond J., and Jack D. L. Holmes. *New Orleans: Facts and Legends*. New Orleans, La.: Hope Publications, 1970.

McAlester, Virginia, and Lee McAlester. *A Field Guide to American Houses*. New York, N.Y.: Alfred A. Knopf, 1984.

Medley, Keith Weldon. "The Sad Story of How 'Separate But Equal' Was Born." *Smithsonian*, February 1994.

Miller, Marc H., ed. *Louis Armstrong: A Cultural Legacy*. Queens, N.Y.: Queens Museum of Art; Seattle, Wash.: University of Washington Press, 1994.

Mitchell, William R., Jr., and James R. Lockhart. *Classic New Orleans*. New Orleans, La., and Savannah, Ga.: Martin-St. Martin Publishing Co., 1993.

New Orleans Chess, Checkers and Whist Club. *New Orleans Chess, Checkers and Whist Club Yearbook*. New Orleans, La.: The Club, 1903.

New Orleans City Planning and Zoning Commission. *Major Street Report*. New Orleans, La.: City Planning and Zoning Commission, 1927.

New Orleans Public Library: Louisiana Division, New Orleans, La., 1997.

Newton, Milton B., Jr. *Louisiana: A Geographical Portrait*. Baton Rouge, La.: Geoforensics, 1987.

Norman, Benjamin Moore. *Norman's New Orleans and Environs*. Edited by Matthew J. Schott. Baton Rouge, La.: Louisiana State University Press for the Louisiana American Revolution Bicentennial Commission, 1976.

Notarial Archives, City of New Orleans. Various contracts, legal documents, plans, and surveys. New Orleans, La., 1998

Orleans Parish School Board. *The New Orleans Book*. New Orleans, La.: Orleans Parish School Board, 1919.

Perez, August & Associates, Architects. *The Last Line: A Streetcar Named St. Charles*. Gretna, La.: Pelican Publishing Co., 1973.

Planer, Edward. "The Riverfront Wrangle." *New Orleans Magazine* October 1966.

Port of New Orleans. *Annual Directory 1997-1998*, New Orleans, La., 1997.

Preservation Resource Center of New Orleans: numerous articles in *Preservation in Print*, 1995-98.

Preservation Resource Center of New Orleans. *Historic Neighborhoods of New Orleans* (map). New Orleans, La.: Preservation Resource Center of New Orleans, 1995.

Reeves, Sally K. Evans et al. *Historic City Park, New Orleans*. New Orleans, La.: Friends of City Park, 1982.

Reps, John W. *Cities of the Mississippi: Nineteenth-Century Images of Urban Development*. Columbia, Mo.: The University of Missouri Press, 1994.

Robinson, Elisha. *Atlas of the City of New Orleans, Louisiana*. New York, N.Y.: Elisha Robinson, 1883.

Rose, Al, and Edmond Souchon. *New Orleans Jazz: A Family Album*. Baton Rouge, La.: Louisiana State University Press, 1984.

Sanborn Map and Publishing Co. *Sanborn Fire Insurance Map of New Orleans, Louisiana*. Sanborn Map and Publishing Co., New York, N.Y., 1885, 1895, 1896, 1908, 1937, 1940.

Schlesinger, Dorothy G., Robert J. Cangelosi Jr., and Sally Kittredge Reeves. *Jefferson City*. New Orleans Architecture, vol. 7. Gretna, La.: Pelican Publishing Co., 1989.

Scully, Arthur, Jr. *James Dakin, Architect: His Career in New York and the South*. Baton Rouge, La.: Louisiana State University Press, 1973.

Searight, Sarah. *New Orleans*. New York, N.Y.: Stein and Day, 1973.

Seymour, William H. *The Story of Algiers, 1718-1896*. Gretna, La.: Pelican Publishing Co., 1971.

Sexton, Richard, and Randolph Delehanty. *New Orleans: Elegance and Decadence*. San Francisco: Chronicle Books, 1993.

Siegel, Martin, and Howard B. Furer. *New Orleans: A Chronological and Documentary History*. Dobbs Ferry, N.Y.: Oceana Publications, 1975.

Smith, Margaret Denton, and Mary Louise Tucker. *Photography in New Orleans: The Early Years, 1840-1865*. Baton Rouge, La.: Louisiana State University Press, 1982.

Soulé, Leon Cyprian. *The Know Nothing Party in New Orleans*. Baton Rouge, La.: Louisiana Historical Association, 1961.

Starr, S. Frederick. *New Orleans Unmasqued*. New Orleans, La.: Édition Dedeaux, 1985.

Starr, S. Frederick. *Southern Comfort: The Garden District of New Orleans, 1800-1900*. Cambridge, Mass.: MIT Press, 1989.

Swanson, Betsy. *Historic Jefferson Parish: From Shore to Shore*. Gretna, La.: Pelican Publishing Co., 1975.

The Times-Picayune, The States-Item, The Times-Democrat, The Picayune, The New Orleans States, The Orleans Item, and other city newspapers, New Orleans, La., 1800s-1998.

Tinker, Edward Larocque. *Creole City: Its Past and Its People*. New York, N.Y.: Longmans, Green & Co., 1953.

Toledano, Roulhac, Sally Kittredge Evans, and Mary Louise Cristovich. *The Creole Faubourgs*. New Orleans Architecture, vol. 4. Gretna, La.: Pelican Publishing Co., 1974.

Tulane University School of Architecture. *The New Orleans Guide*. London: International Architect Publishing Limited, 1984.

Tulane University School of Architecture. *New Orleans and the River*. New Orleans, La.: Tulane University, 1974.

Tulane University School of Architecture. *Study of the Vieux Carré Waterfront in the City of New Orleans*. New Orleans, La.: Tulane University, 1969.

Tulane University School of Architecture. *The Vieux Carré Survey: A Pictorial Record and a Study of the Land and Buildings in the Vieux Carré*. New Orleans, La.: Tulane University, 1960.

U.S. Army Corps of Engineers. *Water Resources Development in Louisiana 1995*. Vicksburg, Miss.: Dept. of the Army, Lower Mississippi Valley Division, 1995.

U.S. Department of Transportation. Eighth Coast Guard District, New Orleans, La. *Draft Environmental Impact Statement: Greater New Orleans Mississippi River Bridge No. 2, Orleans Parish-Jefferson Parish, Louisiana*. 4 vols. New Orleans, La.: Eighth Coast Guard District, 1976.

Vogt, Lloyd. *New Orleans Houses: A House-Watcher's Guide*. Gretna, La.: Pelican Publishing Co., 1987.

Waldo, J. Curits. *Illustrated Visitors' Guide to New Orleans*. New Orleans, La.: L. Graham, 1880.

Ward, Geoffrey C, Ric Burns, and Ken Burns. *The Civil War: An Illustrated History*. New York, N.Y.: Alfred A. Knopf, 1990.

Widmer, Mary Lou. *New Orleans in the Fifties*. Gretna, La.: Pelican Publishing Co., 1991.

Wilson, Samuel, Jr. *The Battle of New Orleans: Plantation Houses on the Battlefield of New Orleans*. New Orleans, La.: Louisiana Landmarks Society, 1989.

Wilson, Samuel, Jr. *A Guide to Architecture of New Orleans, 1699-1959*. New York, N.Y.: Reinhold Publishing, 1959.

Wilson, Samuel, Jr. *The Vieux Carre, New Orleans: Its Plan, Its Growth, Its Architecture. Historic District Demonstration Study*. New Orleans, La.: City of New Orleans, 1968.

Wilson, Samuel, Jr., and Leonard V. Huber. *The Cabildo on Jackson Square*. New Orleans, La.: The Friends of the Cabildo, 1970.

Wilson, Samuel, Jr., and Bernard Lemann. *The Lower Garden District*. New Orleans Architecture, vol. 1. Gretna, La.: Pelican Publishing Co., 1971.

Works Progress Administration. *Some Data in Regard to Foundations in New Orleans and Vicinity*. New Orleans, La.: Works Progress Administration of Louisiana and Board of State Engineers of Louisiana, 1937.

Works Progress Administration. *The WPA Guide to New Orleans*. Boston, Mass.: Houghton Mifflin, 1938.

Zacharie, James S. *New Orleans Guide*. New Orleans, La.: F. F. Hansell & Bros., 1902.